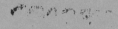

& WILD BEASTS
& IDLE HUMOURS

& WILD BEASTS
& IDLE HUMOURS

THE INSANITY DEFENSE FROM
ANTIQUITY TO THE PRESENT

DANIEL N. ROBINSON

HARVARD UNIVERSITY PRESS

Cambridge, Massachusetts, and London, England   1996

Library of Congress Cataloging-in-Publication Data
Robinson, Daniel N., 1937–
Wild beasts and idle humours : the insanity defense
from antiquity to the present / Daniel N. Robinson.
p. cm.
Includes index.
ISBN 0-674-95289-8 (alk. paper)
1. Insanity—Jurisprudence—History. I. Title.
K5077.R63 1996
345'.04—dc20
[342.54] 96-5644

Acknowledgments

Much of the research for this book was completed during Michaelmas term in 1991 and again during Trinity terms in 1993 and 1994 at the University of Oxford. A course of lectures I offered with Rom Harré sharpened a number of questions with which these chapters are concerned. I was properly tested on one or another proposition by his gentle probing as well as by questions raised by a shifting cadre then in attendance; especially by Charles Taliaferro, Jil Evans, Francine Robinson, Jens Brockmeier, and Fred Vollmer. Occasional conversations on various points of law with Robert George, John Finnis, and Tony Honoré were predictably illuminating. The staff of the University of Oxford Law Library was most helpful and resourceful. Needless to say, access to the Bodleian collection greatly eased the burdens of scholarship.

A more diffusely distributed debt is owed to many different persons and places at Oxford; to Linacre College, by now our home away from home; to Tim del Nevo for University housing—and more; to Carol Bateman and staff at the University Computing Centre; to Jane Hardie who keeps everything (and everyone!) in working order at 10 Merton Street.

During early phases of the research I gave invited lectures on aspects of the work at the University of Edinburgh and at the University of Tübingen. Professor Peter Jones at Edinburgh and Dr.

Professor Eberhart Zrenner at Tübingen were gracious hosts who provided an atmosphere at once congenial and intellectually challenging.

A redaction of some of the main points developed in this book was prepared for the Royal Institute of Philosophy's Lecture Series in 1993–94. I wish to thank the Institute for providing an occasion for me to clarify my thoughts further and for the subvention to give the public lecture in London.

On the homefront, Georgetown University helped measurably by tacking an additional term on to my sabbatical in 1991, thus affording a full year's leave of absence. A special thanks to Renée Boland and the staff of my Department for their continuous support across the Atlantic. I note here, too, my colleague Norman Finkel, who offered good words and encouragement, and Dean Judith Areen, for arranging to include me on the Law School's LEXIS roster, thus saving many hours of labor and travel. My editor at Harvard University Press, Angela von der Lippe, offered needed guidance and encouragement. Anita Safran's thoughtful manuscript editing improved the text in ways large and small.

Finally, it is not possible to record briefly the number of ways my best friend and spouse of more than a quarter of a century has contributed to this volume—to all the volumes. Expressions of gratitude here must be reduced to tokens. It is to Francine, then, that this book is dedicated.

Contents

So fearfully and wonderfully are we made, so infinitely subtle is the spiritual part of our being, so difficult is it to trace with accuracy the effect to all who hear me, whether there are any causes more difficult, or which, indeed, so often confound the learning of the judges themselves, as when insanity, or the effects and consequences of insanity, become the subjects of legal consideration and judgement.

Thomas Erskine,
address to the jury in the *Hadfield* case

WILD BEASTS
& IDLE HUMOURS

INTRODUCTION

I became interested in the subject of this book some twenty years ago, when I was writing the first edition of *An Intellectual History of Psychology* (1976). I thought then that I would include summaries of scholarly research on the subject of legal insanity, but was surprised to discover that little historical material was available for periods before the eighteenth century. Scattered reports of one sort or another did exist, but nothing of a systematic inquiry into the subject; at least nothing that might be reliably passed on in a general history of psychology. Nor had matters changed enough for the second edition (1982) or, for that matter, for the first paperback edition (1987). By then I had more or less committed myself to the project, but suspected that it would be frustrating and ultimately incomplete. This suspicion was grounded in both personal and objective considerations, a few words on each being in order here.

Law has always been a special subject. Its form and content over the epochs have not been transparent to the uninitiated, even if its final public expression has been crafted to be generally accessible. Accordingly, the history of law is something of a duchy unto itself, and one not very hospitable to mere visitors. Within that duchy, the issues of insanity and of mental competence occupy one of the more remote territories. Indeed, as the first complete transcript of a criminal trial featuring the insanity defense does not appear until the eighteenth century, part of the territory is more than remote; it is altogether invisible. The project, then, which would tax the powers of the nonspecialist in any case, was made still more difficult by the paucity of evidence; put another way, by the wealth of indirect evidence calling for more than the usual degree of integration and interpretation.

That the completed project would be nonetheless incomplete was ordained by the very nature of the subject and the limitations of the author. Entire non-Western legal traditions have been all but ignored. Within the legal traditions considered, only the criminal law covering serious crimes against persons and property, and only the civil law pertaining to testamentary capacity have been examined in any detail. The larger social history within which major developments take place is treated in fairly general terms and, again, chiefly within the Anglo-European context. Someone, no doubt, will write the fully warranted thousand-page treatise. I have not; my objective was different.

Several connected approaches are available to those who would resurrect the psychological understandings of earlier times. The one most frequently adopted is intellectual history, with its focus on major philosophers. Its chief limitation is that leading philosophers seldom reflect the general perspectives of their age and often treat their subjects in ways too abstract to illuminate the thinking of their time. But it is precisely here that the history of law, especially as it pertains to concepts of insanity and responsibility, provides so useful and important a supplement. The law in every epoch must dispose of concrete cases and solve actual problems in ways and words intelligible to disputants and defendants, judges and juries alike. Even when grounded in abstract philosophical principles, it lays down procedures and yields outcomes that record the broader assumptions and convictions of an age; at least those shared by the most influential members of society, if not society at large.

In light of this, the aims of the present work are easily summarized, for it is restrained in its ambitions. I have tried to trace the major terms of an ongoing dialogue between legal and extralegal conceptions of human nature; legal and extralegal conceptions of persons, powers, capacities, duties, motives, rights. The dialogue, in periods of juridical reflection and development, tends to be disciplined and formal, even philosophical. These periods also tend to be times of scientific and psychological reflection, generative of significant theories regarding the determinants of human conduct and the sources of moral and political life. The law's obligation to clarity and fairness seldom fits comfortably with that unavoidably open-textured conception of human nature that is at once the gift and the problem of all the social sciences. The chief aim of this book is to examine just how these disciplines have participated in the enduring dialogue, and how and whether the formal and structured character of law has been influenced by them.

The book begins with a review of ancient legal and customary understandings on which developed Roman law depended. These are taken to be grounded in what is referred to (often misleadingly) as "natural law theory," itself a theory of human nature. The examination of the laws pertaining to insanity in Homeric times and then in classical Greece and Rome reveals the willingness of jurists to consider the complexities of human motivation and the determinants of conduct while preserving the legally necessary presumption of agent-causation. Thus, even as Hellenic dramatists explored the darker sources of behavior and philosophers speculated on madness, ancient courts generally confined themselves to the weighing of the actions themselves.

The coherence between the juridical and the larger cultural dimensions of the ancient world is less evident during the early Middle Ages. The great cultural and political disruptions that would gradually replace classical institutions and classical forms of life become apparent in legal history as well. For, although grounded in the same core of assumptions about human fitness for the rule of law, the classical and the Christian perspectives diverged in a number of ways. The collapse of imperial Rome and the growing authority of the Christian Church produced sharp points of conflict between Roman law and the increasingly official religious precepts of a postclassical and Christian world. Chapter 2 identifies these points first within the context of Germanic customs (which also had to be reconciled with Roman law), and next within the canonical teachings of the Church. In striving to be true to the historical record, the text here must take on a somewhat episodic character, especially when perceived against the background of the more coherent classical world. The insanities so routinely accommodated within Roman law now come to take on altered meaning calling for different remedies. The revised theory of human nature generates new procedures, new penalties, new rationales.

The third chapter is devoted to the witch trials and panics that occupied the period from 1400 to 1700. Several aspects of this complex and macabre turn in European history warrant the attention given here. First, although legal provisions for dealing with witches and sorcerers appear as early as Rome's *Twelve Tables,* it was only in the Christian West that all forms of witchery were assimilated to the category of *heresy* and thus rendered felonious. This was inevitable on the dual assumption that persons cannot have their moral freedom stolen by the devil, and that events falling outside the natural order must be engineered by supernatural means or with supernatural assistance. With only marginal exceptions, the very nature of the theory of witchcraft effectively removed the plea of insanity as a defense in such cases, even though the defense was available and invoked in other contexts. Moreover, the special nature of the compact between witches and demons called for new and uncommon trial procedures and for discovery phases involving experts and specialists. It is with the witch trials that experts make if not their first then their portentous appearance in the adjudicative arena. They arrive armed with coherent and persuasive theories, promising to uncover those hidden forces by which minds are controlled and possessed. When finally these experts are recruited from medicine, the questions and issues facing them will arise from theoretical considerations far removed from medical science, even as it was understood at the time. The precedent will be set, however, for looking to the experts to illuminate the more obscure regions of human cognition.

In time, and in large measure a result of the very extremes to which this entire line of juridical and theological reasoning moved, consideration of mental life takes a decisive shift toward *naturalistic* and *scientific* explanations. As modern chemistry was forged in the busy kilns of alchemy, modern psychiatry and psychology found a nurturing climate in a world shocked by its own excesses. Nonetheless, even the scientists of the Renaissance had set upon a course somewhere between "natural magic" and natural science. Well into the seventeenth century theories of insanity and diminished responsibility were beholden to astrological and Hermetic theories. In Chapter 4 the slow march toward a more fully secular and scientific conception of insanity is charted, along with the mirrored steps taken by Coke, Hale, and other leading jurists of the period. The chapter then turns to the more or less settled position reached in the Enlightenment; a settled but not entirely sound position that would regard the mind as but another natural phenomenon, explicable in the same terms and through the same methods as those productively applied elsewhere.

The secularization of mental life inevitably connected insanity to biology and, more specifically, to neurology. In Chapter 5 the quickly developing field of medical jurisprudence in the nineteenth century is explored. Such celebrated cases as *Hadfield* and *McNaughtan* are examined against the background of scientific advances, social and political reforms, and the more general positivistic outlook that had been bequeathed by the Enlightenment. One consequence of the new perspective was the increased reliance of courts and legislators on scientific authority, the results again being mixed.

The final chapter explores the inevitable confusions and conflicts spawned by attempts to import scientific conceptions of human nature into jural contexts. Fragmented attempts to pin down a credible and defensible version of the "insanity defense" are reviewed, as are some of the lingering difficulties and their implications. Even after all the scientific progress and hopefulness of preceding centuries, today's dilemmas and habits of thought faithfully echo reasonings and assumptions fashioned centuries ago, when the law looked beyond its own resources to determine guilt and innocence.

This book is intended as a modest contribution to the histories of both psychology and law. I should add that the case law discussed in my later chapters, especially that of the eighteenth and nineteenth centuries, covers territory quite familiar to students of the insanity defense who have had the benefit of any number of excellent and recent treatments. The earlier chapters examine less familiar terrain though, again, I have attempted neither an exhaustive review nor even a representative sampling, if such is meaningful in the context. The record in some epochs is far too thin to sustain any hope of representativeness even on the part of those who would undertake a detailed study of statutes and cases. Thus, although I hope the work will add something to the robust scholarship in history of law, the more general aim points to intellectual history and the relationship between the culture of law and the wider culture.

If the principal objective in these pages is to examine what is a dialogue of sorts between legal and extralegal sources of authority, its task must be to shed light on how that dialogue may challenge and alter the very presuppositions in which such authority is grounded. Legal history, though never fully insulated from the larger culture, does have a culture of its own. One of the shadowy themes of the present work points to the manner in which momentous cultural events summon jurists to depart from the law's own culture, and how such departures can modify or extend or blunt what already are the formidable powers of law.

1

FURIOSI

Surely one of the earliest recorded insanity defenses is to be found in Book XIX of the *Iliad* when Achilles and Agamemnon are at last reconciled. For his part, Achilles has abandoned his righteous indignation in the face of momentous reality. "If we have been angry," he says, "necessity has schooled our anger. I put it from me." Next to speak is King Agamemnon and, far from explaining his offending actions, he disowns them: "It was not I that did it: Zeus and Fate, and Erinys that walks in darkness struck me mad when we were assembled on the day that I took from Achilles the prize that had been awarded to him. What could I do? All things are in the hand of heaven, and Folly, eldest of Zeus' daughters, shuts men's eyes to their destruction. She walks delicately, not on the solid earth, but over the heads of men to hurt them or to ensnare them" (*Iliad,* XIX, 86–134).[1]

Referring to Agamemnon's excuse as an "insanity defense" is to speak loosely, of course, for the ancient Greek world had no written law until one was elaborated under the archonship of Draco late in the seventh century B.C. Nor is there evidence suggesting that Draco's laws left much room for the sort of mitigating circumstances from which Agamemnon's appeal is drawn. (If Plutarch is to be believed, when Draco was asked why so many offenses resulted in the death penalty under his laws, he replied that minor offenses warranted death and thus no greater punishment was available for graver ones![2])

But there is no reason to think that Homer has given improbable lines to Agamemnon or expects his audience to think of this hero as dissimulating or unworthy of sympathy. The epics leave no doubt that even great offenses might be forgiven when it is shown or reasonably assumed that, in the circumstance, the actor was a pawn of the gods or otherwise beside himself. When in Book IV of Odyssey Helen makes her appearance and speaks of the recent war, she marks the time when she was prepared to abandon Troy for her homeland and laments "the madness that Aphrodite bestowed when she led me there" (260). Menelaos immediately replies that this account is entirely fair and in good order. (Whether he has accepted her explanation without reservation or is simply willing to let bygones be bygones is open to conjecture.)

Yet there is nothing exceptional here. Homer's characters routinely claim to be compelled, moved, distracted, or deceived by the gods. The world of the ancient Greeks, long before the classical period and before written law, recognized madness as exculpatory. The most ancient of the generic terms for the grossly distorted mind, *entheos,* refers to "a god within." The victim or vessel of *entheos* is thereby irresistibly enthralled.[3] The god might speak only to the chosen one, exciting wild and uncoordinated movements; or induce a frenzy as the sign of divine anger; or lead the victim to speak in tongues.[4] The usual treatment for such mind-robbing disorders is ritual purification, recorded as early as myth-bearing Hesiod and impatiently dismissed later, in the more scientific age of Hippocrates.[5]

How and whether the Homeric epics and Hesiodic fragments may be used to illuminate archaic legal conceptions of insanity must remain an open question, any plausible answer finally depending on the concept of law one has adopted. There is no doubt, however, that two of the central features of any legal system—that is, delineated procedures and the public dissemination of the regulative maxims or principles—are present in the eighth-century Greek world of Homer.[6] Even a version of *stare decisis* is evident, for these very procedures are defended in the language of precedents *(thesmia)*, as Aristotle would later observe in *The Constitution of Athens.*[7]

A reliance on precedent as well as on the general expectation that orderly procedures will be followed must suggest an essentially jural perspective within these ancient communities. To look to precedent is not merely to honor the past or be caught up in a habit. After all, any number of customary practices are jettisoned by every society, often in response to external influences but also as a result of internal developments. Allegiance to precedent in settling disputes, however, is grounded in something more fundamental than "customary practices." It is grounded in the belief and the judgment that what is arbitrary or capricious or *ad hoc* is incompatible with justice itself. Not surprisingly, then, Homer has formal complaints heard and settled in public places (typically in the *agora*) by kings or elders or an person chosen because of his widely recognized sound judgments.

Illustrations of this abound, but one will suit present purposes. In Book XVIII of *Iliad* the goddess Thetis is found doing all she can for her doomed and inconsolable son. She implores Hephaistos to make a shield, "renowned and radiant armor," for Achilles. Once completed by this "renowned smith of the strong arms," the extraordinary shield depicts earth and sky, the oceans and the tireless sun, marriage feasts and weary plowmen refreshed in their triple-plowed fields by a flagon of honeyed wine. Also carved thereon is an assembly in the *agora* where two disputants now argue over the proper amount of blood-money to be paid as compensation for a homicide. Failing to reach an agreeable sum, they then turn to judges seated in a circle on benches of polished stone. Between the contestants are placed two talents of gold, the prize to be paid to the judge who delivers "the straightest opinion." Two centuries later, when the mythic world bequeathed by Homer has merged into the historical world of the Greek people, the law-giver tracked down and appointed by the Athenians is Solon, a poet known for his ability to give judgments that are straight *(ithys)*.

How are the scenes depicted on the shield of Achilles to be understood in light of later developments in ancient law? The evolution or transition from reliance on "straight judgments" to the dispositive power of written statute is an especially difficult problem in classical scholarship. It is not enough to observe that in Homer and Hesiod the good judge, who offers "straight" rather than "crooked" rulings, is the one sought out by disputants. It is not enough simply to include this as an anthropological fact without inquiring further as to why the "straightness" of a judgment has come to be decisive. Or, again, the archaic accounts indicate that it is important for judges to be faithful to the customs and precedents *(thesmia)* of the community, for this fidelity is included in any estimation of the soundness of the judgments themselves. The ancient way is best *(archaios aristos)*, says Hesiod, to an audience not expected to doubt it.

It seems necessary to explore how this criterion of venerability is to be understood within an otherwise fast-changing world. Returning to the shield of Achilles, we find not only disputants and judges, but also heralds and a crowd of animated onlookers, cheering on their favorite contestant. The award for sound judgment is not made by the judges alone; their rulings are to be weighed by the assembly. Although this procedure has begun to replace or has at least attained parity with older means of settling differences, such as hand-to-hand combat, the triumph of right reason over might is never total or complete in the Homeric epics. Yet the very appearance of public hearings and of rewards for sound judgment establishes a self-consciously *jural* perspective; the recognition that consequential actions bear the burden of justification, and that principles of justification—because they are principles—will be coherent, intelligible, and persuasive to an assembly of rational beings.[8] To the authority of straight judgments and conventional practices are added the rhetorical elements of law, the discursive tools of persuasion.

As Hesiod taught, only that *polis* in which law *(dike)* prevails can enjoy general prosperity, in contrast to the city ruled by *hybris,* which breeds every form of misery and vice.[9] This is surely not an essentially empirical claim, for such facts of history as might have been generally known at the time would have been sufficient to defeat the theory. Rather, Hesiod records an insight, shared by all reasonable persons who give the matter thought, as to the necessary connection between law and a certain kind of general prosperity; a prosperity not enjoyed even by the most successful tribes of lawless pirates and highwaymen. What Hesiod asserts is that justice is nothing less than the command of Zeus to those who would seek a flourishing life. The just *polis* is the natural home for human beings who, unlike other animals, can resolve differences wisely and with straight judgments. In this Hesiod anticipates what was to become a fixture in the political theory of the Stoics.

Only through a general acceptance of this view of the prosperous *polis* could the later written law come to enjoy the people's allegiance; their willingness to abandon schemes of vendetta that had been in place since times out of memory; and their ungrudging movement toward legal rather than phratric grounds of social cohesion and organization. This acceptance, however, was shaped by a more fully developed respect for the individual person, the recognition that every human being has the power to act, and a more skeptical attitude toward older mythic alternatives. Indeed, once modes of adjudication include these rhetorical features, it is clear that the concept of justification is now inextricably bound up with individual judgments and personal criteria of validity. There is all the difference in the world between adjudication as the performance of fixed rituals, and adjudication as the marshaling of evidence for the purpose of convincing an audience that a crime has been committed.

The story here is again complex and elusive. Some progress may be made by appreciating the significance of epic poetry itself. As Eric Havelock observed, "Spoken language does not fossilize."[10] Amidst the development of language and the evolution of meanings within it, a preliterate society will have to have something more stable than daily discourse if, once established, norms and values are to be preserved intact. The appearance of the epic marks the period in which such permanence is sought. It makes it possible for future generations to inherit what their ancestors took to be foundational. *Iliad* and *Odyssey,* seen in this light, are not centrally about wars but about maxims, instantiated by memorable personages and happenings. These epics are preclassical "emblem books" in an age before books, designed to make each telling of the tales more authoritative by repetition and dissemination. The tales themselves are integrally associated with Greek religion and so become part of a sacred text to be consulted in times of doubt and trouble. To be a Hellene, then, is not only to speak a special language but to speak about a certain set of values and principles; to conduct important affairs according to received formulas; to be able to comprehend and thus more naturally enter into momentous social and communal events, because one knows the rules that govern them.

If this is the central role of the epic in general, then the more defining role played by *Iliad* and *Odyssey* can be gleaned from the contents. Less important at this juncture is deciding whether what has been adopted is a developed principle of justice *(dikaiosune)* or a *method* that is itself regarded as just *(dike).* Perhaps, as Havelock and others have suggested, it was only by the time of Hesiod, with the Greek world having turned literate, that it became possible to treat "justice" abstractly, since written language then made it abstract. Nevertheless, the preliterate Homeric age still displayed not only a judicious ("straight judgment") method of resolving conflicts, but a quite developed sense of the sorts of conflicts warranting the application of this method.

Room for interpretation is inevitably wide in such matters. One might defend the notion that the preliterate world of the Greeks had developed the usual ritualistic modes of settling disputes as an alternative to trial and battle. With the "wise men" properly identified (on the basis of age, or experience or just good memories for tribal customs), justice arose as nothing more than fidelity to tradition combined with mnemonics by which the details of tradition were preserved. Later, on this same theory, thanks to the more subtle hermeneutics required by written rules and judgments, the concept of justice became extricated from myth and ritual. Needed now were wise judges, known less for total recall of the rites and rituals and more for the practical wisdom *(phronesis)* needed to apply customary practices to unforeseen and evolving conditions. Through it all, however, the emphasis remained attached to something akin to legal procedure, which is itself the echo of formulaic rites. Rendered at once more abstract and more general by written language, procedure on this construal now took on a life of its own. Once universalized by the propositional resources of language, it surfaces not as custom but as something that seems to transcend any and all experience.

A theory of this sort must take it as simply mistaken to consider principles of justice as somehow inherent in the very rationality of the human race, rather than the inevitable effect of discursive refinements on what initially are essentially behavioral habits and performances.[11] It will be necessary to say more about this theory later. For the present it is important to keep in mind that the usual distinction between legal rules and moral rules not only begs one of the foundational questions in jurisprudence but may itself reflect something of a merely cultural penchant.[12] It might be argued, for example, that the very recognition of the need for settled procedure arises from the essentially *moral* judgment that like cases should be dealt with in like manner. Evident among at least some of Homer's protagonists is an emerging conception or principle of equity (the notion that comparable cases should be dealt with comparably; that losses should be compensated comparably; that punishments should somehow match up with the gravity of offenses). What is evident further, in the very transcription and official repetition of these poems, is the recognition of a duty to the future and, more specifically, a recognition that the duty in question includes the transmission of judicious methods of resolving conflicts.

To address the "why" questions above, then, if only obliquely, it is perhaps prudent to be wary of radically linguistic theories of cognition. The power of language to shape concepts must not mask the power of thought to find, as it were, the right words to express itself. The dialogue contains cognitive prospects totally lacking in the dance, but the dialogue itself arises when the most thoughtful and creative participants understand that the ritual takes for granted much that must be reexamined. Method or principle? Is there finally any fundamental difference between such alternatives? To adopt a method is to make a choice based on a set of objectives; to adopt a method for settling disputes is already to begin to appeal to a principle. For all the appeal of theories that ground legal principles in the latent resources of literacy, the challenging fact is that written language is only used for such purposes when the purpose is already conceived and widely adopted.

The Greek world boasts no burning bush or god-given decalogue, even if archaic commentators were satisfied that law is a gift from the gods. It was the Hellenes who sought out Solon. They did so not because he had a better memory of the past or a special link with Olympos. The past no longer served the more fully discerned interests of justice, and the gods were, to say no more, too remote to be consulted. A person such as Solon was prized, it would seem, because his judgment was straight in the sense of yielding the shortest route to the right principles. Moreover, he held to these principles without reservation *(eutheos)*. In any case, within the Homeric epics, as well as later in Hesiod and later still in the Solonic reforms of Draco's laws, the Hellenes record their recognition of the relationship between law and psychology; between principles that are binding because of the psychological capacity of rational beings to be *bound by principle*. Conditions that defeat this capacity mitigate the law's otherwise unavoidable burdens. Recognized too are those fundamental maxims that make any rule of law possible, even amidst the numerous and various customs of different communities. In the fourth century B.C. Aristotle reaches what he takes to be the obvious conclusion that "the principles of equity are permanent and changeless, and . . . the universal law does not change either, for it is the law of nature."[13]

If this is obvious to Aristotle, it is partly because Hellenes centuries earlier had already established methods of ensuring equity; methods of honoring "the straight" because it is changeless.

How then are these considerations to be judged in light of the widely shared thesis that abstract conceptions of justice either depend upon or merely rediscover the abstractions immanent in written language?[14] It is clear that both the preliterate and the written prescriptions of law strive for clarity and consistency. What is "straight" *(ithys)* is better than what is curved *(scholios)*, but better in what sense? The answer is obvious to Hesiod: wild beasts *(thersi)* must answer the summons of nature and devour each other because the gods have not ordained them to live in accordance with *dike.* They do not have it within them. Human beings, on the other hand, possess *dike* as a very condition of their humanity, and this is the best by far *(pollon ariste)*.[15] The best man is one who considers things for himself while seeking the good counsel of others, in a manner such as to ensure that he and his future generations prosper.[16] All this is prefigured in Homer, of course, nor is there any reason to think that something special about the written word creates the unique means by which to exhort others to think for themselves. What is essential, however, if there is to be a jural perspective, is the recognition that something within—something that matches up with the concept of *dike* whether in practice or in principle—permits a recognition of the straight, the crooked, and the right.

The Hesiodic fragment that urges persons to think for themselves stands in conflict with yet another school of interpretation inclined to withhold self-consciousness from the archaic Greeks and from primitive man in general. In a now classical work, Bruno Snell insisted that the hero in Homer "does not yet regard himself as the source of his own decisions." Lacking the tools of abstract thought, the primitive is tied to concrete experiences and has no reliable means by which to fashion an I-Thou barrier. Events are thus more or less visited upon him, including those actually arising from his own actions, for these too are in some sense called forth.

This is a theory much indebted to C. G. Jung and more recently taken to quite surprising limits by Julian Jaynes, who regards Homer and his heroes as victims of hallucinations![17] Jaynes argues that the cerebral hemispheres in Homer's time had not yet begun to function in integrative fashion, and as a result, Homer's hero "had a part of his nervous system which was divine, by which he was ordered about like any slave, a voice or voices which indeed were what we call volition."[18] What this theory fails to explain, however, is that three and four centuries after Homer the Delphic Pythia was still alone in being able to hear Apollo, and Euripides along with his contemporaries did not think her power was a sign of hallucination or madness. Rather, the gods have found in oracles yet another means by which to convey their wishes and prohibitions to man.[19] It may not be beside the point to recall, in the face of such intriguing speculations, that communities in the Nile basin and Middle East, many centuries before Homer's Greek world, had elaborate schemes of taxation, records of payments and defaults, and countless other evidences of "unicameral" minds.

The very distinction made by Homer's characters between actions attributed to divine influences and those not thus impelled can only come from persons self-consciously in touch with their own volitions. The religious orthodoxies exemplified in these epics and still evident in the modern world can be thoroughly fatalistic; this does not mean that believers need to hallucinate or abandon self-consciousness and the concept of personal agency. One can accept, for example, that the divine will is ultimately determining, but that one is nonetheless obliged to play one's part, to do one's duty and otherwise to act *as if* one's actions could prove to be decisive. All this, too, is similarly ordained by the gods. Consistent with this is adherence to a standard of conduct circumscribed by the law. In holding themselves responsible to this standard, the Homeric Greeks give ample testimony to their belief in individual autonomy.

In discussing the first appearance of *nomos* (law), Martin Ostwald has observed that the Greeks themselves never seriously attempted to date a given *nomos*. Animals prey on each other without any concept of justice, whereas human beings regulate their affairs through the gift of *dike*. The term *nomos* in reference to the behavior of animals can mean only customary behavior, whereas human beings have the sense of "an abstract 'ought', commended but not enforced by social pressures." As Ostwald goes on to say, "There is no idea of development, no thought that there may have been a time when a given *nomos* did not yet exist . . . The norms of life have been decreed from time immemorial and for all time to come."[20]

The road to virtue, says Hesiod, is rough, long, and steep, made more accessible only by practice and the cultivation of habits guided by *dike*.[21] Some four centuries later, Aristotle would summarize this view of the human condition as follows: "A social instinct is implanted in all men by nature, and yet he who first founded the state was the greatest of benefactors. For man, when perfected, is the best of animals, but, when separated from law and justice, he is the worst of all."[22]

It is worth noting further that none of the ancients themselves thought of this inner standard as in any way tied to writing. For many decades after Draco and Solon the Spartans refused to codify law in written form. The distinction common in the ancient record is between those possessing *dike* and the actual or *de facto* "wild beasts" who did not. When Agamemnon or Helen seeks exculpation, some sort of possession theory is invoked to establish the method by which *dike* was suspended or lost or neutralized. One can be overcome by a "wolf's rage" *(lyssa),* deceived by the gods, or invaded by imps and dream-demons sent by the gods. Victims of such conditions are as powerless as are the *thersi* (later *theroi*), whose physiological needs drive them to destructive but undeliberated behavior. The question of guilt or innocence arises, then, only after there is reason to believe that, in the circumstance, the actor had possession of those defining marks of mind by which human beings might remove themselves from the bestiary. In some cases, the potential dupe actually asks his assailant whether he is a god in disguise, presumably to determine whether personal initiative holds out any hope of success. Again, this makes sense only on the assumption that fatalists, even extreme fatalists, are able to consider those all too few and narrow fields on which personal initiative still makes a difference. Where this is so, one of the necessary assumptions of law has been satisfied, though nothing need be written.

How or if or in what sense a written language serves as the necessary precondition for abstract justice must, alas, remain debatable. So, too, must be the question of the priority of procedure over principle in the evolution of legal systems, for the very demand for uniform procedures already establishes the widespread adoption of principles sanctioned by carefully thought out judgments of wise persons. This attachment to the counsel of the wise is recorded not only in the "proto-legal" world depicted on the shield of Achilles but also much later in Plato's *Statesman,* where the Athenian Stranger makes clear to Socrates that legal procedure can never supplant the wise counsel of the just man. The leader who must legislate for the masses "will not be able, in enacting for the general good, to provide exactly what is suitable for each particular case."[23] As "no art whatsoever can lay down a rule which will last for all time," it becomes obvious that "the best thing of all is not that the law should rule, but that a man should rule, supposing him to have wisdom."[24] Neither fixed rules nor fixed procedures will ever be sufficient. Rituals and habits in general can only fail to satisfy the particulars of the given case. Written language achieves much, but not all that is sought by a just state. The appearance of literacy does not fully explain what will come to be the defining marks of the just state. It does not, for example, explain the impulse to justice itself.

Less controversial in this regard would appear to be the implicit logic of every system of law: that the reach of law extends only to creatures able to comprehend its terms and abide by its prescriptions. By this very logic, being human is not enough, for some human beings are so lacking in comprehension, so possessed by the ruling power of another, and so destitute of personal powers of self-control as to be indistinguishable from wild beasts or mere tools. Ancient Greek and Roman law fully respected this logical and conceptual relationship and thus made provision for legal defenses based on claims of diminished capacity. Far from making a mockery of justice, such defenses are implicit in the concept of justice itself. None of this is plausibly at issue. Instead, seeds of controversy are sown once different criteria of diminished capacity are pleaded and methods are developed to identify cases worthy of exculpation.

Absent an adjudicative record, however, it becomes necessary to rely chiefly on statutory language and on understandings expressed outside the law itself; understandings found in that larger context of science, philosophy, and public discourse in which the notion of insanity received its meaning. Legal texts may retain set phrases for generations, even as later commentators, adopting a different *Weltanschauung,* give new meaning to the same words. In the present context, it will be sufficient to identify those widely shared classical values and beliefs that were incorporated into Roman law, moving on in the next chapter to the problems faced by an officially Christian world, which retained the laws while rejecting many of the values and beliefs that inspired them.

An explicit recommendation for the law's treatment of the insane is given in Book IX of Plato's *Laws.* In it the Stranger explains how the laws of Athens deal with issues of motivation and competence. He notes that laws have been enacted to deal with those who rob from the gods, who commit treasonous actions, and who manipulate the laws to their own ends. Such crimes may be committed

> in a state of madness or when affected by disease, or under the influence of extreme old age, or in a fit of childish wantonness *(hybris),* himself no better than a child. And if this be made evident to the judges elected to try the cause, on the appeal of the criminal or his advocate, and he be judged to have been in this state when he committed the offense, he shall simply pay for the hurt which he may have done to another; but he shall be exempt from other penalties, unless he have slain some one and have on his hands the stain of blood. And in that case he shall go to another land and country, and there dwell for a year.[25]

A year's ostracism is ordered for murder even where the defense of insanity has been successful. Moreover, considerations of fairness require aggrieved parties to be fully compensated, though the defendant caused this damage while under the influence of madness, or disease. And then, of course, the stain of blood cannot be eradicated by the (mere?) fact of mental illness. The reason for this, quite obviously, is that whatever degree of rationality is necessary for a homicidal act to be perpetrated, it is sufficient for the actor to be stained by guilt *no matter what else he suffers at the time.* In the same dialogue, careful attention is given to medical and philosophical adumbrations of insanity and diminished capacity as the participants consider what the laws should be in the ideal *polis* of Magnesia. Medicine, philosophy, and law must work together to shed light on the extent of the defendant's willful and competent contribution to the crime. The fundamental canons of justice and the seasoned reflections of the wise judge still remain dispositive in such cases.

In the hands of the philosophers, this conservative position on the nature and exculpatory force of madness would be subjected to finer analysis and to conclusions not especially helpful to those carrying the daily burdens of legislator, judge, and citizen. It is just because of this, however, that something further can be learned about the more general perspective by examining these philosophical challenges. The principal source here must again be Plato, not only because of his sustained interest in madness, discussed in several of the dialogues, but also because of the changes his views on this subject undergo in dialogues of different periods.[26]

The official or standard view is developed unremarkably in *Republic.* In Plato's last work, the *Laws,* the position defended is less the standard one than a more technical, analytical, medically informed position that was less likely to be fully adopted by jurists of the fifth century B.C. (Today's jurists would embrace it, surely.) But it is a "classical" position nonetheless. That dangerous alloy of reason and passion—man—needs to be shaped and controlled, lest a nearly divine creature sink to the level of the worst and most destructive of animals. Good examples are required from the earliest stages of moral development, augmented by the right sort of education, by harmonious and elevating music, and by careful insulation against the corruptions of poetry and all other celebrations of the sensual and the mythic. Reason is like the charioteer who must control and coordinate two strong steeds, one good and one defiant, volition and passion. Where reason rules, the journey is direct and the destination sound. Everyone, *ceteris paribus,* wants this to be the case but fails to achieve such integration and control because of bad rearing, bad habits and ignorance. Through the cultivation of virtue, through the steadfast refusal to become hostage to one's emotional and non-cognitive nature, the good life is within reach and is protected by the good state. Those mentally too weak or mad to be reached by such civilizing influences should simply be kept at home and denied all access to the life of the *polis.* Families failing in this duty should be heavily fined.[27]

In *Phaedrus,* however, the standard or "classical" view is abandoned as Socrates composes a veritable paean to madness. Of the two forms of desire, the rational and the irrational, it is the latter that is the power of love (*Phaedrus,* 238). And love is a noble form of madness; one of four such forms. Another, prophecy *(mantike),* is not only etymologically linked to madness *(maniche)* but has (divinely inspired) madness at its foundation (244). It liberates the individual from "the yoke of custom and convention" (265), allowing the soul to attain heights of insight and revelation. Of the four divine forms of madness—the prophetic, the initiatory, the poetic, and the erotic—the madness of love is best, anchoring the lover to beauty and the harmonious life. And madness, too, can expiate a relentless blood-guilt that has ravaged generations: "Again, where plagues and mightiest woes have bred in certain families, owing to some ancient blood-guiltiness, there madness has entered with holy prayers and rites, and by inspired utterances found a way of deliverance for those who are in need" (*Phaedrus,* 244).

Phaedrus ends interestingly, even somewhat incongruously, with a discussion of rhetoric and argumentation and the recognition that written laws are not enough: "even the best of writings are but a reminiscence of what we know . . . only in principles of justice and goodness and nobility taught and communicated orally for the sake of instruction and graven in the soul, which is the true way of writing, is there clearness and perfection and seriousness, and . . . such principles are a man's own and his legitimate offspring;— being, in the first place, the word which he finds in his own bosom" (*Phaedrus,* 277–278). It ends, that is, with the affirmation of intuition as the wellspring of knowledge. As with all that is implanted in man by his very nature, the writings in the bosom are the most trustworthy and authentic. Madness has authenticity and the power to reject the conventional and trite and to find its way to the object of its desire. This philosophical analysis of madness imbued it with value and preciousness, elusiveness and subtlety, even as it recognized its destructive force.

Where jurists and legislators had developed workable solutions to the problems created by the behavior of the insane, the philosophers raised questions about the validity of those very standards by which madness itself might be gauged. There is no evidence in the ancient sources that this philosophical inquiry, any more than prevailing medical theories of insanity, yielded exculpatory consequences in the arena of adjudication. What is clear, however, is that, from the earliest times in Western jurisprudence, there has been a tension between the law's recognized duty to expose and punish the guilty, and those medical, philosophical and psychological theories concerning the determinants of human conduct. The ancient courts, with what seems to be a nearly heroic indifference to the emerging philosophical conundrums, took the criminal act itself as evidence of mental capacity and saw to it that damages were compensated, crimes punished, and society protected against the deeds of the mad. In this connection, Aristotle offers the interesting distinction between the solemnity of the court of the Areopagus and other courts. In the former, the disputants are never permitted to speak of nonessentials or to go beyond the provable facts of the case. "This," he says, "is sound law," for it is wrong "to pervert the judge by moving him to anger or envy or pity—one might as well warp a carpenter's rule before using it" (*Rhetoric,* 1354a 20–27).

To state the matter perhaps too generally, it may be said that the perspective of the ancient jurists quite carefully partitioned explanation and exculpation. Just why a felon committed the foul deed was of marginal importance relative to the proof that he did it. It is true, however, that the ancient Greek archons and juries, at least from the time of Draco, paid close attention to questions of intentionality and premeditation. The homicide law of Draco actually begins with reference to unintentional *(ek phronoias)* homicide. Michael Gagarin, after a careful study of it, concludes that Draco's law provided for two categories of crime—the intentional and the unintentional—and that changes from the time of Draco to the time of Aristotle were not substantive. Nonetheless, there were but these two categories, and the courts seemed content to avoid any finer-grained analysis.

Indeed, even where a subtler analysis was performed, the burden of guilt still attached to anyone for whom the presumption of wrongdoing was credible. In the *Nichomachean Ethics,* for example, Aristotle delineates the number and range of factors of which an actor would have to be ignorant to qualify for forgiveness. He offers six conditions: The actor would have to suffer ignorance of the agent (of agency) himself; of the act; of the thing or person affected; of the instrument that brought the result about; of the effects of the act; of the quality (gentle, violent,and so on) of the act. Having delineated these mitigating factors, he then concludes that only the mad *(mainomenos)* could be ignorant of all these together. (*Nich. Eth.* 1111a). Put the other way around, Aristotle would take this number and range of ignorances as providing the criteria of a madness that would be exculpatory.

The ancient record, then, appears to warrant the conclusion reached by W. J. Jones: "the Greeks long felt unable to delve into men's mental states for the purpose of distinguishing different degrees of guilt. . . . And as long as almost any sort of homicide brought pollution upon the killer and others connected with him, the problem of causation was evaded. The only defence seemed to be that the accused had not in truth killed the deceased at all."[28]

If this attitude appears plain by contemporary standards, it should be recalled that ancient jurists were closer in time and perhaps in temperament to the assumptions permitting the veritable invention of the rule of law. Those laboring in the patrimony of Draco, Solon, Lycurgus, and the rest were fully cognizant of the great range and number of factors inclining citizens toward unlawful conduct. They were as great as the conditions promoting disease and death. W. J. Jones has drawn the parallel between the healthy body and the body politic in ancient thought, with Solon seeing himself as keeping hostile parties from destroying each other. Faction thus becomes "a wound in the body politic." Contrary to Hesiod, who speaks of injustice as having nearly magical effects, Homer has it "starting a train of consequences as ineluctable but also as calculable as the results of any violation of the laws of physical health in the human body."[29]

Though thin, the statutory evidence from the ancient Greek world is not without both revealing and surprising features and, in any case, is a useful prelude to considerations of Roman law.[30] The term "statute" itself is worth tracking in this regard. In the preclassical period, *nomoi* refers to the timeless principles by which conduct is guided. By the time of Aeschylus, however, *nomos* increasingly indicates a *statute,* even if Olympian in origin. By the conclusion of the fifth century B.C., *nomos* is virtually synonymous with statute in the sense of enacted law. *Nomos* in the postarchaic period has become prescriptive, referring now not only to practices once appearing as customary but to rule-governed behavior to which punishing sanctions are applicable.[31] What has taken place is the gradual abandonment of the notion of eternal verities and standards, and the recognition of the political community as the source of obligations, at least in the daily sphere of social and commercial life.

At yet another level, these man-made *nomoi* are needed in ever greater number and variety by a society now too complex to be portrayed on a shield. Military success and security, combined with international commerce and the creation of personal wealth, required ever more delicate means for settling disputes and reaching equitable solutions. Consider the laws (*nomoi* in both senses) of testation. In the archaic period, the social unit was the family (*oikos*). Property was passed down from father to eldest son. Wives inherited nothing. Where no male children existed, the property remained within the *oikos,* stewardship falling to the nearest relative. If that happened to be a woman, she became an heiress (*epikleros*), but only *pro tempore,* keeping the property in a kind of trust until she remarried.

Among the reforms introduced by Solon in the sixth century was the right of a childless testator to name an adopted son in his will, a measure by which he averts timeless custom in designating his own heir. But of course this created possibilities probably unimaginable in simple societies. Women without property could encourage aged and childless men to adopt their sons. Peevish men might capriciously choose (adopt) heirs for spite. In this one area, then, the growth and complexity of Greek society made recourse to the customary *nomoi* less than helpful in particular cases. A newly enacted *nomos* might be called for to achieve ends deemed desirable by the *polis* at large.

Nomos as both statute and as custom also provides for specific duties within the *oikos,* not the least of which was the care offspring must give to aged parents. Yet within this patriarchal society not only did slaves and women enjoy few of the benefits of law, but children especially fell almost entirely beyond the bounds of legal protection. Until the time of Solon, fathers could sell their male offspring into slavery, and even in post-Solonic Greek law it was still permissible to do the same with a daughter who had lost her virginity out of wedlock. Infants and children, with few exceptions, were not even accorded the usual burials and funereal rituals and gifts. Cremation was common, at least in Athens, where even in death the person's status within the community was ceremonially acknowledged.[32] The relevance of this here is based on the tendency of ancient law to regard insanity as akin to infancy, a tendency still extant as late as the seventeenth century. The *furiosus* was as removed from the domain of legal actions as the *infans,* and like an infant was entrusted to the *cura* of his *gens* or next of kin. And, as Leage observed, this *cura* functioned as a kind of *potestas,* controlling the person and the property of the *furiosus.*[33]

The earliest written laws in Greece continued the centuries-old tradition of treating homicide as a phratric affair, the murderer having to come to terms with the clansmen of the deceased. The relevant passage (in Michael Gagarin's translation) states: "Even if a man unintentionally kills another, he is exiled. . . . If there is a father or brother or sons, pardon is to be agreed by all, or the one who opposes is to prevail. But if none of these survives, by those up to the degree of first cousin once removed and first cousin, if all are willing to agree to a pardon; but the one who opposes is to prevail."[34]

In the matter of insanity, ancient Greek law is predictably explicit when considering just such issues of contract, property, and testation. One of the few sources of actual judicial proceedings here is Isaeus (ca. 420–350 B.C.), the rhetorician and metic who may have numbered Demosthenes among his students. Of some fifty court appeals he prepared for clients eleven survive, all of them pertaining to matters of contract and testation. The mental state of those entering into such matters is often referred to by various claimants. It is useful to consider briefly several of these cases.

Regarding the estate of Cleonymus, who died childless and whose will benefited relatives who were not next of kin, the claimants insisted that Cleonymus wrote the will "in a misguided moment of passion." Other claimants then declared that if this was true, the will should be set aside on the grounds that Cleonymus was insane *(paranoian)*. Again, in the matter of the estate of Menecles, whose adopted son would properly be beneficiary, it is part of the son's burden to argue that Menecles "was not insane or under the influence of a woman, but was in his right mind *(eu phronon)*" at the time of the adoption. In still other cases consideration is given to senility and seduction as grounds on which to overturn a will. Thus a man who adopts a son, says Isaeus, will have the adoption invalidated if it is shown that the action was taken "because of madness *(paranoia)* or old age or drugs or sickness, or under the influence of a woman, or compelled by force or restriction of liberty."[35] Here the expected and expectant beneficiaries (the next of kin within the *oikos*) protect their interests against impulsive, late-in-life actions by the childless testator eager and desperate for a male heir.

Considering only the special provisions introduced to identify and punish *hybris,* one discerns uncommon vigilance on the part of ancient legislators. They seemed to be especially attentive to the subtle psychological and social conditions able to mould or transform the human character, regarding law itself as especially potent in this regard. They were, then, quite strongly opposed to having the law's directives and teachings masked by that learned but generally conflicting discourse emanating from medicine and philosophy.

Of course, the record of ancient cases is frustratingly incomplete. That ancient Greek and Roman law made specific provision for the insane is amply documented. As early as Rome's *Twelve Tables* it is commanded that "When no guardian has been appointed for an insane person, or a spendthrift, his nearest agnates, or if there are none, his other relatives, must take charge of his property."[36] Still, there is no surviving adjudicative record to establish the criteria testators or criminal defendants were required to meet.[37] The very categories used to partition defendants in Roman law—*non compos mentis, fanaticus, ideotus, furiosus*—indicate both the sincerity and the refinement of ancient law in this area.

It was common for statutes pertaining to, say, conditions that invalidate a contract, to refer to infants (children) and the insane in the same context. A senile and childlike father, successfully charged with insanity *(paranoia)*, could be legally stripped of control of his estate by his son.[38] Rome's *Twelve Tables* identified the madman *(furiosus)* specifically, and required nearest relatives to take over the management of his affairs if no guardian *(cura)* had been appointed. Nonetheless, the Institutes of Justinian (hereafter, *Institutes*), citing Ulpian, traces to a time even before the *Twelve Tables* laws that interdict the transactions of a *prodigus* or spendthrift, noting however, that the *furiosus* was not thus interdicted, "and what he did was valid if he was not mad at the particular time when he did it."[39] Prodigality, regarded as something of an uncontrollable or obsessional disposition, is constrained by the laws of contract, whereas some forms of madness are taken to be episodic. During sane intervals, the transactions of a *furiosus* are valid, presumably even where the *cura* has not been a party. But when a *furiosus* was without remission, Roman law conferred no validity whatever on any transaction entered into by such a person.

How are such practices to be understood? The Greek *mania* and *paranoia,* like the Roman *furiosus,* arise within the broader framework of ancient conceptions of normal civilized life, and these conceptions were not static. It can be said, however, that they invariably include the idea of human life as something of an alloy of the rational and the bestial, ever needful of the discipline first of family, then of *polis.* As rationality is the crowning faculty or power *(dunamis)* of human nature, so the wise man is the crowning rational authority of the community. At the level of the *oikos* this is the father, who, like good laws and good judges, makes decisions pleasing to the gods and useful to the *polis.*

Children, to the extent that they have any status at all, are in a limbo of sorts, nurtured (if not invariably loved) because of the responsibilities they will one day assume. But these potentialities never confer an independent standing at law. Only the censors could infringe on the otherwise limitless powers parents had over their children. In patrician families, where education was highly valued, fathers would pace boys through the *praecepta paterna,* readying them for lives of influence and power. They would retain Greek tutors for sons and even for daughters, all this before (and during) the formal education provided by pedagogues, and the lifelong education conducted by the relentless Stoic moral philosophers.[40] But all this shaping and tutoring and discipline had one object as its goal: the production of worthy civic leaders, sources of pride to their families and security for the state.

The very rule of law, recognized as reason's cardinal gift, is available only to and for rational beings and rational purposes. What the *infans* and the *furiosus* have in common is just this absence of rationality that would otherwise grant them legal status. Hence both have their affairs and interests placed in custody, the *cura* being either the *pater familias* for the *infans* or a near-relative or appointed *cura* in the case of the *furiosus.* But the law never defined insanity. It regarded it as a matter of fact, to be settled according to the folk-psychology of the community.[41] Absent a ruling theory of mental illness, ancient juries recognized that the onset of lucid intervals restored the *furiosus* to full legal authority over his own affairs. Any further reversion to the status of *furiosus* would then strip him of this same authority and restore it to his *cura,* no further adjudication being required.[42]

One need not agree with Henry Maine's famous dictum about the ancient Greek's total aloofness to the issue of free will and determinism to accept the fairly nontheoretical manner in which ancient Greek law dealt with madness as a practical matter.[43] As it happens, Greek society showed a quite robust recognition that certain actions were controlled either by the gods or by factors beyond the actor's control, and others by the actor's own deliberate choices. Indeed, the most influential medical writers of the classical period, the members of the Hippocratic school, were at pains to argue for naturalistic theories of disease, including mental disease. This was taken to be no more (or less) divine than any other malady. Differences and alterations of personality, when not traceable to environmental and cultural sources, were explicable in biomedical terms. Thus, in the celebrated treatise on epilepsies, the Hippocratic author calmly insists that the cause of this and of many of the graver illnesses is to be found in the brain: "From the brain, and from the brain only, arise our pleasures, joys, laughter and jests, as well as our sorrows, pains, griefs and tears. . . . It is the same things which makes us mad *(paraphronimos)* or delirious . . . and [causes] acts that are contrary to habit. . . . The brain is the interpreter of consciousness."[44]

In *Airs, Waters, Places* the same scientific approach is adopted to account for national differences. Commenting on the greater diversity and vitality of Europeans, when compared with Asiatics, the writer notes that the European seasons are various and daunting. "In such a climate arise wildness, unsociability and spirit. For frequent shocks to the mind impart wildness, destroying tameness and gentleness. . . . For uniformity engenders slackness, while variation fosters endurance in both body and soul."[45]

In his *De Medicina* Celsus (b. ca. 25 B.C.) summarized Greek medical theories of insanity and therapies that had been employed for centuries. One form, called by the Greeks *phrenesis,* is the acute derangement caused by fever. In this state, "patients are delirious and talk nonsense." In extreme cases, when the condition does not pass quickly or respond to treatments for fever, the patient's mind comes fully under the control of illusions and imaginings *(mens illis imaginibus addicta est)*. Additionally, some people's insanity is expressed in the form of sadness or hilarity, violence and rebelliousness. Of the violent ones, notes Celsus, some may be impulsively harmful, others may even be "artful" *(etiam artes adhibent),* seeming to be entirely sane only to reveal their madness in mischievous acts. The violently insane must be fettered, even as they show meekness in order to be freed from physical restraints. "The ancients generally kept such patients in darkness, for they held that it was against their good to be frightened, and that the very darkness confers something toward quieting the spirit."[46]

But Asclepiades reasoned otherwise, and Celsus can find no basis for choosing light over darkness, each case presenting idiosyncratic features. In all, his discussion is sound and sensible, his review of the Greek theories making clear that ancient doctors and commentators appreciated the many natural causes of insanity.

Why, then, were such conclusions not routinely included in discussions of crimes or wills or the law in general? Surely part of the answer lies in the ancient Greek concept of nature *(phusis)* itself, according to which it was no less natural for man to live in society under the rule of law than for digestion to take place in the stomach or for birds to build nests. If man's defining human nature was so ravaged by disease or denuded by the gods, the afflicted person was thereupon excluded from the discourse. To be a wild beast was, as it were, to leave the *genus* and to be located in that part of the taxonomy for which the law had neither concern nor remedy. In this regard, it mattered little whether the cause originated on Olympos, in the cranium, or in the climate.

This is not to say, however, that Greek law did not consider the overall character and disposition of the actor in determining guilt and proper punishment. Although accounts of the "insanity defense" *per se* are lacking, there is a fuller record of adjudications involving the offense of *hybris,* which came under the law covering assaults. Demosthenes cites the law: "If anyone treats with *hybris* any person, either child or woman or man, free or slave, let anyone who wishes . . . submit a *graphe*. . . . Whoever the Eliaia finds guilty, let it immediately assess whatever penalty seem right for him to suffer or pay. . . . A man who attempts to act with *hybris* wrongs the state, not just the victim."[47]

The hubristic act reveals the character of the actor. The arrogant mode of abuse, the clear intention not merely to hurt but to dishonor the victim, established the perpetrator as a threat to the *polis* itself, because he apparently regarded the other citizens as of less consequence than his own vanities. Douglas MacDowell has compared simple assault with offenses coupled with *hybris,* noting how the Athenian concern for personal honor required special legal remedies if that honor was diminished. And N. R. E. Fisher has shown how the dishonor arising from the hubristic act was widely perceived as a threat to the very fabric of Greek society. The difference between simple assault and hubristic assault arises from the attitude and disposition of the offender. If Smith strikes Jones out of sudden anger or in a tantrum, the action is for simple battery *(aikeia).* "But if he hit him because he considered himself and his own wishes more important than the rights and esteem of his victim, that was *hybris,* a much more serious offense."[48]

Greek jurors were keenly interested in states of mind (as these were revealed in actual conduct) and states of character, but did not regard either as falling within the narrow province of science or medicine. Yet if there was no single ruling theory of mental illness in Greece or Rome, there was in both an undisputed conception of duties to the state. The law was structured to make these duties ever more salient, adherence ever more orthodox. In the end, terms such as *paranoia* and *furiosus* conveyed a deviation so extreme as to make the afflicted person incapable of intelligible contact—even in the form of open defiance—with the public good. What the madman shared with the infant was not a recognized disease or malady or measured deficiency. It was, rather, the unfitness of both for citizenship, and the fact that punishment would do nothing to improve them. At the close of Book I of the *Laws,* when the Athenian Stranger speaks of insobriety as a good test of virtue, he is acknowledging the common-sense belief that alcohol and other drugs will not strip the genuinely virtuous of all self-control; that significant actions are not determined in such a way as to render the actor unfit for the law's regard.[49] The citizen who has benefited from the discipline of law becomes worthy of the freedoms so revered by the classical Greeks, for this is a person who can be counted on even under conditions of stress; even under the mind-robbing powers of drink. All this assumes the capacity to be thus disciplined. The Roman *infans* has the capacity for such nurturance but, of course, has not yet been nurtured. The profoundly retarded *(ideotus)* lacks the capacity itself. The *furiosus,* if he ever did have the capacity and the nurturance, has now lost his rational power and has reverted to a state of infancy in all matters of moral and legal consequence.[50]

Apart from this, however, was that ubiquitous sense of fitness in the worlds of ancient Greek and Roman alike; fitness as *harmonia* and balance and straightness. An offense, whatever the underlying causes and however understood, disturbs the peace of heaven. It inflicts on the rational order of things some foreign and malignant element that must be purged. Purifications, which were such a common feature of ancient religious rituals, were embodied in the law itself, sometimes explicitly but always as the background of the laws of equity and compensation. An offense against persons, the squandering of an estate, the neglect of parents, the failure to prepare children for a civic role, disrespect toward the gods, wantonness and arrogance, cowardice and treason, theft and slander—what they have in common is a disruption of the intended order of things. Accordingly, even if the perpetrator is mad or senile or drunk or out of sorts, what he has done must be undone or repaired or expiated by sacrifice, purgation, purification, recompense. To have done something out of madness was to have done it nonetheless. The ancient jurists were never distracted from the interests of the *polis,* even as they acknowledged the misfortunes that drove some to lawlessness or irrational extremes.

The development of ancient Rome's own political and legal institutions was itself a gradual one, built partly on earlier Greek and Etruscan models, but then taking new directions dictated by the unprecedented success of the empire. Each of the major developmental phases reflects a characteristic conception of human nature and furnishes the law with fresh problems and possibilities. If all of Roman law can be reduced to legal statements about persons, possessions and actions, then in the ancient Greek homicide law one can begin to locate the pre-Christian conception of persons. Clearly, from the time of Draco and until the Christian era, persons derived their essential identity from the (Greek) *phratry* or the (Roman) *gens* and belonged to it in the fullest possessory sense. It is not the state or the larger community that is offended by murder but the next of kin, and they, once agreed on appropriate cash settlements, have the power of complete pardon. Murder surely offends all in the sense of creating a blood-guilt on the land itself, which can only be purified by appropriate purgations and propitiations. But the cash settlement was between private parties, the value of the lost life being set by that phratric body from which it had been taken.

In the laws and customs covering testaments the same attitude is dominant. Even after the reforms of Solon, which gave Athenians the right to have the terms of their wills honored at law, a firstborn male could not be disinherited. The same was true in Rome long before the *Twelve Tables.* And, although later provisions for disinheritance were made, the aims of testation in the ancient world seem to have had nearly nothing to do with what is now described as "private property" or individual rights of ownership. It was, instead, the means by which landed families preserved themselves *as families.*

The global protection granted to testators by the *Twelve Tables*[51] was long ago recognized by Henry Maine as the source of testamentary power for the plebeian class—the same power the patricians had always enjoyed in their Comitia Curiata.[52] What was passed on through instruments of testation was nothing less than the *familia* itself, this referring not only to the testator's property but to the full range of his powers, duties, debts, and ancestral rights. The technical term for the beneficiary was *emptor familiae,* the buyer of the family. In earlier Roman law this was usually the male offspring. Once lawfully handed down, the *familia* was now irrevocably granted to the *emptor familiae,* though the testator might be in the prime of life.[53] Within the patrician class, the will clearly did not aim to secure the wishes of an individual property-owner but rather the continuation of the *gens* of which the testator had been but an extension or instrumentality. Although technically they could claim no *gens,* the plebeians shared this outlook and used the law to express it.[54]

There is a striking difference between the modern psychological notion of persons and personalities and the ancient conception—which was not especially psychological—of the same. More will have be said on this in later pages. It is necessary here, however, to devote more than a little space to ancient Greek and Roman conceptions of personal identity. Against the background of this depiction the subtle and then not so subtle changes in outlook become more apparent and suggestive.

At the outset, it is important to recall the special standing the ancient world conferred on a "house" or tribe or clan, for it is from such a collective that the ontology of the person arises. Homer recounts how curses befall such collectives and leave their individual members in the clutches of destiny—which they can try to fight, though usually resistance turns out to be futile for all the heroism.

It is, after all, the House of Atraeus that has been condemned to do battle in Troy. Guilt and shame and redemption are the properties of phratric enclaves whose individual members derive their duties and their rights from the collective. The primary duty is to the collective: to its enrichment and its perpetuation.

In the more developed society of imperial Rome the law, through its terminology and ponderous methods, concealed the rich and primitive foundations of its own rationale. Consider the *universitas juris,* the technical term referring to the total *legal* personality *(persona)* of the *paterfamilias.* It is the totality of estates, obligations, commitments, and vulnerabilities acquired not only by personal actions but by successions that might date back over several generations and reach ahead to several others. It is all of this that is passed on by a will, and it is the *persona* that the successor-beneficiary absorbs, develops, and bequeaths in turn. As Henry Maine remarked in connection with the testamentary provisions the *Twelve Tables,* its wording returns to a more primitive age when property was possessed by a family which itself was governed by a citizen, so that "the members of the community do not own their property *and* their family, but rather own their property *through* their family."[55]

Speaking more generally of these ancient societies, Jerome Hannan gives this informative summary:

> Every man is regarded first as a member of the tribe or state; then as a member of an order or caste; then as a member of a *gens* or clan; and finally as a member of a family. The family was the most nearly personal aspect in which the law regarded him. . . . When the head of a family died, he was regarded by the law as not dying at all. For was he not the family? The person who succeeded him would be the family, identified with it in every respect, in the place of the man who died.[56]

That pathetic isolate in Homer—the "clanless, lawless, hearthless man"[57]—is emblematic of the ancient citizen's worst fears; a life cut off from the phratry and the *polis*. Such a life is not merely lonely and risky but is less than human. It is unnatural and defective in a way akin to the monstrous and deformed. One's identity is familial; just as one's own life contributes to the recorded achievements of the family (tribe, *polis, gens*), so does one inescapably share in the disgraces heaped on one's ancestors.

When asked by vain and eager Croesus to say who is the happiest of men, Solon recounted the accomplishments of Cleobis and Bito. Rather than arrive late to Hera's festival, the two young men placed themselves under the oxen's yoke and pulled their mother's cart over five miles of rocky roads. In awe did the Argives witness the arrival of these great young men at Hera's temple, where their mother prayed that these noble sons be awarded the greatest of mortal blessings: "God showed forth most evidently, how much better a thing for man death is than life. . . . Her prayer ended, they offered sacrifice, and partook of the holy banquet, after which the two youths fell asleep in the temple. They never woke more, but so passed from the earth."[58]

Cleobis and Bito are ranked as the happiest of men because they are held to be great by their clansmen. They died in a sleep that followed a triumph; their reputations added lustre to the glory of the *polis*. They not live long enough to dim the brilliance of their accomplishments. This understanding was the case in ancient Greece as a matter of custom and in ancient Rome often as a matter of law. One's personality, then, was not just subservient to one's standing within the community but was essentially identical to how one was remembered, his *monumentum*.

The same ruling outlook is exemplified in the Roman *paterfamilias* whose rights and powers over spouse, offspring, and slaves strain the credulity of modern readers. He could put his own infants and young children to death, sell them, or have them adopted by more solvent families within the *gens*. Even as late as the Lex Pompeia, Rome's homicide laws covering murders within extended families still ignored a father's lethal assaults on his offspring. Under the *patria potestas,* so long as the father was alive a man might live out his entire youth and early middle age without enjoying the benefit of personally owned property. All of his acquisitions immediately were added to the *familia* of the *paterfamilias.*

A century ago, asking how the Romans, with their vaunted respect for law, justice, and equity, could not only tolerate but venerate such a system, the classical scholar James Hadley attributed it to their "profound impression of family unity, the conviction that every family was, and of right ought to be, one body, with one will and one executive. The *paterfamilias* was . . . the embodiment of its interests and the organ of its activity."[59] As such, and quite in the spirit of Cleobis and Bito, the *paterfamilias* was to compile a record of achievements that would redound to the good name of the *gens* and *familia.* His power over others was for them repaid by the *monumentum* in which they shared and which could not possibly be as great without him. His "personality," like those under his *patria potestas,* was drawn from historical sources and would have remote effects. As with the Imperator, so too with the *paterfamilias;* both the head of state and the head of family occupied positions that were the bequest of a timeless process; a long unfolding narrative which, for all its organicity and catastrophic punctuations, took place under cosmic laws which ultimately would prevail.

If modern sensibilities are to be accessible to ancient conceptions of madness, a fuller appreciation is needed of the daily expectations, the communally imposed pressures, the now legendary stoicism that characterized life within the patrician families. Mattingly has listed the ancient virtues alphabetically, providing just a hint of the culturally imposed qualifications facing that *paterfamilias* possessing such formidable *potestas:* he must be a free man in possession of estates *(abundantia),* of equability and calmness of mind *(aequitas).* He must have the qualities of mercy *(clementia),* amity *(concordia),* happiness *(felicitas),* faithfulness *(fides),* and cheerfulness *(hilaritas);* be disposed toward uprightness *(justitia)*, joy *(laetitia)*, and courtesy *(liberalitas)*. He has full independence *(libertas)* through financial means *(moneta)*, and deploys them with liberality *(munificentia)*. He lives a life marked by serenity *(pax)*, devotion *(pietas)*, foresight *(providentia)*, health *(salus)*, hopefulness *(spes)*, repose *(tranquillitas)*, fecundity *(ubertas)*, conquest *(victoria)*, and courage *(virtus)*.[60] Only the state committed to these virtues can and should prevail, and will prevail when led by men of such a stripe. So, too, with respect to the *gens*. What is special, therefore, about the *paterfamilias* is not the autocratic power he enjoys—which is common throughout the ancient world—but the standards of conduct and character he is routinely expected to meet. In keeping these standards alive, he keeps his clan alive. With the support of all such similarly constituted *gentes*, the state perpetuates itself.

Anomalies coexisted with consistencies in this special world. The authority of the *paterfamilias* was virtually unchallengeable, but he could not make himself curator of an insane wife. A magistrate also reserved the right to remove him as curator of a son who was *furiosus* or *mente capti* if, in the judgment of the court, the curatorship was being abused. If Roman civil law seems now and then indifferent to personal affairs within a family, it is because nothing in the Roman world was entirely private in the modern sense of that term. All of the powers and options enjoyed by citizens were understood to be conditions of citizenship itself, special gifts of the rule of law which the law could suspend or revoke. The restraints on curatorships in cases of insanity are informing in that they make clearer what is otherwise somewhat disguised by the nearly tyrannical perquisites enjoyed by heads of families. It is just because the *paterfamilias* is less an "individual" in the contemporary sense, and more a link in the long chain of the *gens* and *familia*, that the interests of the latter are subject to the consideration of the magistrate. And this in turn further illuminates the assumed condition of the *furiosus*: he is one who is beyond the summons of citizenship and thus needful of custodial magistracy.

The point might be made in yet another way. Beyond the formal limitations applied to, say, curatorship, the *paterfamilias* also confronted a persistent check on grandiosity: his spouse's candor, which often took the form of undisguised incitement. This was not merely tolerated but expected, as was her management of the entire estate in his absence.[61] The wives in patrician households were employers and supervisors, accountants and managers, teachers and partners, often taking on these duties for long periods without the help or the presence of the *paterfamilias.* It is not surprising that one such wife would dream that half her face was bearded.[62] Nor is it unusual for the sarcophagi of such families to portray domestic cohesion, respect, deep affection and, above all, *concordia.*

An elusive social theory reveals itself in these practices. From the very fact that women habitually were entrusted with the management of great estates, often for very long periods, there is no doubt but that their abilities were fully acknowledged and respected. Thus their *legal* position must reflect something other than the actual estimation of their worth. What it reflects is just this classical conception of *persons* not as atomic or corpuscular units separable from hearth, *gens,* and *civis,* but persons as participants in a continuing familial biography which assigns duties and powers in such a way as to preserve the whole.

Returning now to the matter of individuals and personal identity, and how it bears upon the standing of the *furiosus,* the ancient legal attitude becomes at once clearer and strikingly different from the modern. The Greek and Roman theories of the person were not individualistic without qualification, but only after some foundational requirements were satisfied; and then only insofar as the greater good of the community was served. Given the wide range of responsibilities undertaken not only by women but by slaves, it is safe to conclude that their standing as what now would be called "persons" was never in doubt. Rather, their status was ordained by customs and laws faithfully answerable to the larger aims and needs of society. It was more important to preserve the hierarchic organization—even in the face of injustices—than to tamper with the natural order of things merely to serve the narrow interests of this or that woman, this or that slave, this or that infant.

Within this context, the *furiosus* stands simply and totally excluded from matters of this sort as one who can take no responsibility at all. He is discounted in the affairs of state, and it is with these that the laws are concerned. The management of his estates, the disposition of his property, and the protection of others from such damage or injury as he might cause mark the beginning and end of the law's interest in him. His status is that of a beast, and a wild one at that, except to the extent that his appearance within one of the cycles of his *gens* creates the need for certain administrative measures lest the *gens* itself suffer. Beyond this, the *furiosus* may be of concern to medicine or might surface as a topic within speculative philosophy, but the law is concerned with him no further.

If more explicit, the law was not unique in dismissing the madman from its purview. Arguably, in dramatic literature and philosophy "madness" presents itself either as folly or as a tragic flaw in character or as some impulse answering to the forces of destiny. In these renditions, however, the subject of the story is recognizable as a fellow citizen, the member of a family, a participant in the life of his community. The element of *agency* is present throughout. What, after all, is so tragic in the saga of Oedipus is his steadfast resolve to defeat the horrific prophecy by leaving those he takes to be his parents, and the city he takes to be his own. He is tragically caught up in a drama in which his agentic powers fail, strong though they are. Similarly, in the "divine madness" of love, as the philosophers of the *Symposium* and *Phaedrus* examined it, the victim has been taken in by his own passions which have waged a successful battle against the calm and calculating objectivity of reason. It is not a *furiosus* who surrenders to the claims of beauty, but an otherwise rational being pulled by another side of human nature, no less natural for its conflict with reason. But again, the *furiosus* is simply not part of any of this; not part of that natural order within which art and life and law find their places and parts.

Committed to the philosophical teachings of the Stoics, the aristocratic families of Rome at the height of its civilization were paragons of a self-discipline designed to preserve the aims of nature. In Justinian's *Institutes* this whole arc of thought would be neatly summarized in a classic statement of that now elusive doctrine, natural law theory: "The law of nature is that law which nature teaches to all animals. For this law does not belong exclusively to the human race, but belongs to all animals, whether of the air, the earth, or the sea. Hence comes that yoking of male to female, which we term matrimony; hence the pro-creation and bringing up of children. We see, indeed, that all the other animals besides men are considered as having knowledge of this law."[63]

On this view, the dominant tone of life and thought in the ancient Roman world, well into the era of "late Rome," was conservative, restrained, temperate. Before its final descent, this privileged society, for all of its rigidity, promoted what Peter Brown has described as "a graciousness, a tolerance, and a matter-of-factness that vanished in medieval Byzantium and in the Catholic West."[64]

As late as the fourth century, the Theodosian Code, which meted out severe punishments to adulterous women married to men of consequence, paid virtually no attention to common women guilty of the same behavior.[65] The reason becomes clear within the social context and further illuminates the rationale behind the law's regard of *furiosi*. Not every human being is a full participant in the great scheme of things. Some are temporarily exempt by virtue of their tender years; others because of their enfeeblement. But then there are those who are more difficult to locate within that rule of human law which is itself located within the rule of natural law—slaves, women, certain aliens, some of the aged (some of the time). What these classes revealed was not unlike the revelations of the animal kingdom: that even the most illustrious of citizens carries within him elements that are common to the infant, the brute, the wild beast. It is by dint of a good upbringing, of developed character and constant application that one suppresses this inferior side of one's nature, as Rome herself through law "hast made a city of the once wide world." Reflecting on the second century of the Christian era, Peter Brown observes, "The young man's father did not need to be a Christian to insist that his son behave in public with a puritanical rectitude, which was closer to that subscribed to by men in a modern fundamentalist Muslim country than to our modern, romantic fantasies of a 'decadent' Roman Empire."[66]

The ancient Roman state placed the highest premium on duties within a family, in part because of the recognition of the family as the source of the state's own continuity, but also on the view of the family as an ordered state in its own right, to be governed by principles of justice. Provisions for children, the aged, and the insane were clear, humane, and rigidly applied. The curator of a child, called into service because of the insanity of the child's father, must fully represent that child's interests or later be sued for damages. Justinian ordered that one who cared for a neglected parent who was not his own would become the lawful heir of that person's estate. There were also special provisions for the care of insane or retarded children.[67] In all, the laws of Rome merged with and refined the ageless customs of the indigenous peoples, and then those of the conquered world, to produce a social climate that was reasonable, predictable, flexible, and progressive. These attributes are not to be denied because of the well known and ultimately fatal weaknesses of that civilization; weaknesses that became especially apparent once emperors took on divine status and began to dictate the laws. Instead, these good qualities help explain the staying power of a state that exercised hegemony over much of the settled world for more than half a millennium.

It is all too obvious that the collapse of such an empire pervasively affected the nature of legal understandings and relationships within and between communities. The fate of the western reaches of the Roman empire took a different turn from that of the East, once Constantine had relocated the center of power and administration in the fourth century. And even though Justinian's *Digest* (and, even more so, the *Institutes*) still were cited and used, the Roman law available by the sixth century was already debased and distorted.

The set formulas and well rehearsed terms would remain in use, even in remote places, but even by 200 A.D. legal decisions were increasingly *ad hoc* and ever less illuminated by the perspective of seasoned jurists firmly in control of the principled foundations of the law.[68] It is to be recalled that from the time of Augustus and the emergence of a renewed republican Rome, emperors participated in the development of law as lawyers, some of them quite distinguished in this regard, and all of them lending the weight of imperial authority not only to the letter but (more importantly) to the spirit of the law and the standing of lawyers. Augustus himself devoted hours to service on the tribunal and availed himself regularly of the soundest legal scholarship, an example which continued to be followed even as the Principate was replaced by the Dominate and as the royal succession included now and then reckless and debauched emperors.[69]

Rome had united the peoples of Europe, North Africa, and western Asia; indeed, many of them over the course of centuries come to enjoy great gains beneath the sway of Roman law. It was no secret among the waves of invaders that the laws of Rome as much as her legions had grounded its success. The general understanding is captured in a panegyric of the fifth century A.D. in which Rutilius Namatianus celebrates his return to Rome in a composition written six years after Alaric had sacked the city: "Thou hast made of alien realms one fatherland; / The lawless found their gain beneath thy sway; / Sharing thy laws with them thou hast subdued, / Thou hast made a city of the once wide world."[70]

The division and collapse of this "one fatherland" transformed the legal understandings that had lasted a near-millennium. The mere words of Roman law were hurled into contexts increasingly unable to employ them with precision and discernment. In the Greek-speaking eastern empire, even in the time of Justinian, only simplifications and redactions of Roman law were available in Greek, these generally lacking in the intellectual foundations set forth in the *Digest*. In Italy the Lombards soon undermined the authority of Roman law. In Gaul the monetary fine was twice as much for a homicide that claimed the life of a Frank than for the killing of a Roman.[71] Romans themselves were loyal to Roman law in regulating commerce with each other, wherever they found themselves on the large field of shifting borders, but Gauls, Goths, and Lombards were burdened by no such scruples. Thus by the ninth century, commenting on a situation that had deteriorated steadily over the years, the Bishop of Lyons claimed that an assembly of contesting parties would invoke as many laws as there were parties to the dispute.[72]

2

IMMORTAL SOULS, MORTAL CITIES

A long and spirited controversy surrounds the question of the continuity of Roman law in early and late medieval jurisprudence.[1] Apart from the uncertainty about how well or accurately the classical texts were conveyed and understood, the central fact was, in Paul Vinogradoff's words, that "no State of this period was strong enough to enforce a compact legal order of its own, excluding all other laws, or treating them as enactments confined to aliens."[2]

At least from the time of Constantine, and even with the seat of empire moved to the East, there was no frontal attack on Roman law by the Christian world. Rather, in what now must seem like a remarkably brief time, its core principles were systematically absorbed into the larger political and social objectives of the Christian Church; so much so that, beginning with the *Corpus Juris Civilis,* it becomes difficult to identify any fully independent lines of development of canon law, common law, or, for that matter, the laws of contemporary western democracies. The "natural law" theory in which all of them are grounded was bequeathed by Greek philosophers (chiefly Aristotle), taught by Greek teachers, and adopted and promulgated by Rome's legal writers (chiefly Cicero).

However, the early Church did not catch up with this bequest immediately. Changes of a subtle nature were imposed on the older tradition once the adaptations were officially undertaken. There were twists and turns in the single line, and these reflect some of the profound differences in outlook between classical writers and those of the early Christian centuries. Indeed, most of the attempted adaptations would of necessity be incomplete, for Roman law, though foundational for the canon law of the Christian Church, was not predicated on all of the assumptions and aims of Christianity. Where classical juridical reasoning and procedure avoided theoretical inquiries into the private recesses of conscience and belief, these were precisely the domains of greatest concern and interest to the Church. Accordingly, much closer attention was paid in practice to the aspects of mental life and its special vulnerabilities to which classical jurisprudence had been nearly officially aloof.

The present chapter examines the interplay between ancient foundations and Christian dogma in the progress of law as it pertains to questions of mental competence. The story is cluttered, of course, for the emerging Christian world was more diverse in culture and custom—including legal custom—than either the Greek or Roman world had been. Barbarian princes, at once seeking to publicize their Christian orthodoxy and the respect for Roman law, would issue statutes not entirely consistent with either set of values and presuppositions.

This contrast between the laws Rome had carefully crafted over the centuries and laws that arose when members of alien cultures attempted to absorb them is particularly vivid in the instance of Lombard laws. The record of Germanic invaders in Italy and Spain is varied, more so in virtue of the undeveloped conception of a political state among these people. Contact, even by way of conflict with Rome, worked to refine this conception. Nonetheless, if promulgated laws are a valid means of assessing progress in this sphere, the influence was incomplete to say the least.

The Ostrogoths had secured their position in Italy by 491. Justinian was tireless in his attempts to reclaim Italy, having been successful in his campaigns against the Vandals in north Africa. In 554 he declared that the imperial laws once again ruled Italy, a decision that created constant strife during decades of ultimately unsuccessful military engagements. The seventh century would find Italy hosting large Aryan and Christian communities, the Lombard dukes and kings generally more faithful to Germanic custom than to Christian teaching. To make matters worse—or at least significantly different—the well-established judicial functions of Roman emperors now devolved upon barbarian kings whose preparation for such an office was negligible. The Christian Church in Rome, still a repository of much of Roman law, presented to such kings an irksome need for shared responsibility, not to mention an official theology that was unintelligible to some of them. On the whole, and with notable exceptions, governance remained an expression of timeless and unwritten Germanic customs, some of which were compatible with Roman law.

In 636 the newly elected Duke of Brescia, Rothair, undertook to codify and promulgate Germanic laws as custom had yielded them. The contemporary reader can gauge the jurisprudence thus installed in Italy from a study of Rothair's 338 Edicts.[3] Numbers 48 to 124 record the separate penalties ("composition" for damages) assessed for assaults against specific parts of the body: Thus, (50) "On cutting off lips," (52) "Concerning the molar teeth," (69) "Concerning big toes," (70) "Concerning second toes," (71) "Concerning third toes," (92) "Concerning fourth fingers," and so forth. The juridical calculus employed by Rothair is revealed by fines of twenty solidi for cutting off someone's lips, and 1,200 solidi for murdering an innocent wife. According to edict 176, the leper who is quarantined by exile cannot transfer his property to another, "because on the day that he is expelled from his home, it is as if he had died."[4]

Note that, under Roman law, only exile as a punishment for grave offenses stripped one of such rights of disposal. But in the time of Rothair an illness such as leprosy was no longer simply a physical condition. This becomes clear in edict 180, the first to mention mental illness:

> Concerning the girl who becomes a leper after her betrothal. If it happens that after a girl or woman has been betrothed she becomes leprous or mad or blind in both eyes, then her betrothed husband shall receive back his property and he shall not be required to take her to wife against his will. And he shall not be guilty in this event because it did not occur on account of his neglect *but on account of her weighty sins and resulting illness.*"[5]   (Emphasis added)

As for Roman solicitude toward those judged mad, Rothair's edict 323 contains both the theory of mental illness and the law's judgments: "On madmen. If a man, because of his weighty sins, goes mad or becomes possessed and does damage to man or beast, nothing shall be required from his heirs. If the madman is killed, likewise nothing shall be required, provided; however, that he not be killed without cause."[6] Nor must an owner pay for damages done by his own mad dog, or expect to be compensated should the animal be killed (edict 324).

It is not coincidental that the Christianization of Germanic law would connect madness and kindred infirmities to the sins of the sufferer. There is no comparable reasoning behind Roman laws touching on such subjects. A culture of sin and redemption that takes life after death to be the life of central concern cannot be completely reconciled to a Stoic culture of law, order, and the civic virtues. Belief that a personal God enters into and causally brings about all that is—a God of justice—carries with it the implication if not the resolute conviction that all misfortune is somehow earned and thus deserved. Rothair's edicts are quite clearly informed by such beliefs.

This legislation marks a recognition of the actions proceeding from sudden impulses and the need to distinguish between pre-meditated and spontaneous offenses. According to edict 198, for example, one who in a rage accuses a girl of being "a harlot or a witch" avoids customary punishments if he can "offer oath with twelve oathhelpers to the effect that he accused her . . . in wrath and not with any certain knowledge."[7] And punishment awaits him who kills another man's slave on the grounds that she is a vampire *(striga),* because "it is in no wise to be believed by Christian minds that it is possible that a woman can eat a living man from within."[8] But with the same sobriety Rothair forbids men fighting a duel to arm themselves with witch's herbs (edict 368).

Between A.D. 713 and 736 King Liutprand would authorize 153 additions to Rothair's edicts, these even more explicitly tied to the King's acknowledgment of himself as "This Catholic Christian Prince," whose judgments owe nothing to his own powers but come about "through the wisdom and inspiration of God." This is so because "the heart of the king is in the hand of God."[9]

Pretensions of this sort were not uncommon in the Dominate of polytheistic Rome, but even then the sheer weight of Roman jurisprudence had at least something of a leavening effect. But the heady mixture of early Christian dogma and older Germanic legend now produced a different conception of human nature and thus a different conception of law itself. Lombard kings and feudal lords, once under strong Christianizing influences, regarded their edicts as divinely inspired, their mission a divine service. To the law's traditional function of regulating commerce and preserving peace and order within the community a new element was added: vigilant concern with sin and its consequences. When Liutprand gets around to the matter of witchcraft and sorcery, he not only orders that the judge and *schultheis* command offenders to cease or be sold into slavery, but goes on to explain the special importance of prosecutions in such cases. Just as officials must not be neglectful of the King's causes, "so much more ought they not to be guilty of neglect in inquiring into the cause of God, who is greater."[10]

Such reasoning, and the reprisals arising from it, were not regional but general, as Germanic and Frankish kings undertook to absorb Christian doctrines into their customary practices. The body as the temple of the Lord could only generate fines and punishments proportioned to the extent to which it had been defiled. Thus the Salic laws of the early sixth century penalized a freeman 600, 1,200, 1,400 or 1,800 denarii depending on whether he had touched a freewoman's hand, arm, elbow, or breast. A fine of 2,500 denarii was assessed against witches whose spells caused sterility; 8,000 denarii or death if the victim died. And, whereas 2,500 denarii had to be paid by one whose charge of witchcraft proved to be libelous, 8,000 had to be paid by the witch who ate a man.[11]

Records from Carolingian Europe, covering the period 830–832, provide a similar picture. Lothar, judging Gerberga to be witch, "tortured her for a long time and then executed her by the judgement of the wives of his wicked counsellors." Lothar's own passion for Waldrada was also taken to be caused by witchery. And, in order to preserve "the peace of the Church," Charles promulgated in 873 laws that put to the ordeal all suspected of witchcraft.[12]

This new duality of the temporal and spiritual, the hidden and the revealed, was to some extent part of the legendary heritage of the barbarian, but it was also central to the teachings and beliefs of the now dominant school of thought, Christianity. Informed itself by the philosophical and broad cultural achievements of ancient Greece and Rome, the Church was also cognizant of the fragility and impermanence of these merely human creations. The collapse of Rome as the repository of ancient greatness made it clear to others besides St. Augustine that there is only one eternal city, and that is the City of God. In that city it is not just the overt actions, far less the outward bearing or standing of a person, that determine the fate of the immortal soul. It is what is in the heart. There can be sin where there is no crime, and crime where there is no sin. The Christian martyrs were, after all, saints in heaven even if (or just because) they were treasonous felons in Rome. Civic duties and burdens are part of what is "rendered unto Caesar." It is the pure heart that must be rendered unto God.

Even as Lombards and Visigoths struggled to come to terms with the Church's teachings and authority while attempting to secure their rightful portions of the fractured empire, the Church itself was absorbed in problems generated by points of conflict between Roman law and the Gospels. The great weight of Roman juridical reasoning had been devoted to the civic virtues displayed in social commerce and service to the state. Rewards and punishments were granted by the laws on this basis and took the palpable forms of coin and acreage. The perpetual subject and object of the law's concern was the state itself, constituted as it was of the hereditary succession of first families. The original tribal and phratric identities were camouflaged rather than erased by the evolution of law in Rome. At its conceptual and procedural heights, this law still took the "personality" to be the *gens,* and the specific persons to be points along the endless cycle of the Roman state.

Christianity from the first was at odds with nearly all of this, except for the profound belief that human law expresses in a local way what the order of the heavens reveals in a cosmic way: namely, that a rational principle is the source of all things. This signal point of agreement made it possible, even inevitable, not only that the canon law of the Christian Church would be richly indebted to Roman jurisprudence, but that it would in time succeed in preserving its essential character.

For the canonist and Christian moralist, the issue of insanity and diminished capacity was far more complex than it was in the ancient world, for both practical and theoretical reasons. First, there was the question of the validity of sacramental rites when either conducted or received by those judged to be insane or incompetent. Then there was the need to distinguish between (merely) legal offenses and those that are genuinely sinful. Bound up with this was the biblical (textual) authority for the belief that certain debilitating conditions, including insanity, were visited upon certain persons as a punishment for their sins, such that these conditions—far from conferring immunity—add further evidence of guilt! In the matter of evidence, still greater burdens were created by the need to see into the heart and soul of the defendant: that realm of interior life in which guilt and innocence find their ultimate standing.

When Roman jurists concerned themselves with *mens rea,* the matter was more or less disposed of by the very nature of the offense. By identifying an intelligible motive and locating reliable witnesses, the court was able to conclude its business. The impoverished mind of the *mente capti* or *idiotus,* and diminished power of conduct of the *furiosus,* it may be safely assumed, were so transparently obvious as to require no subtle inquiry. But what of one who had sinned in his heart in a community now won over to the view that "there cannot be a sin which is not voluntary,"[13] and that, in any case, "only a divine power . . . can show man what the truth is"?[14]

The very early Middle Ages not only converted much of the traditional discourse on crime and punishment into the idiom of sin and retribution, but at the same time suffered an impoverishment of the medical and physiological concepts which had provided at least background considerations for classical jurisprudence. If anything, conditions in the Western empire were even worse in these regards.[15] In the Eastern empire Christianity would soon benefit from the teachings of Galen and from the naturalistic traditions of the classical world, but in the Western empire such sources were rarely consulted and only partially known. Even when consulted, such authorities were not used in any discerning way when conditions such as *phrenitis* and lunacy were addressed. When such maladies were discussed in quasi-scientific terms, there was no larger sense of how they might bear upon questions of adjudication.[16] The regnant theories of the early Middle Ages were theological, not naturalistic, and the perspective on law followed in kind. The rational structure was bequeathed by centuries of Roman law, while the spiritual aims were dictated by the Fathers of the Church.

On the whole, this situation worked a special hardship on insane or mentally retarded defendants. St. Ambrose, St. John Chrysosthom, and St. Augustine all lent their authority to the proposition that the insane cannot justly be punished for their actions. Augustine speaks for them all when he says,

> We have known certain individuals suddenly unbalanced who, with club and cudgel, stones and bites, have injured many, and even killed some people, who, nevertheless, when seized and brought before judges, were not found guilty because of the fact that they had done these things unknowingly and not freely, but by the impulse of some force, I know not what. For how can a man be called guilty who does not know what he has done?[17]

Serious infractions were not fully exonerated on these grounds, however, for there was still the view that some form of penance was in order even when the act was the product of an insane mind.[18] Behind this reasoning may stand either or both of two suppositions: first, as a living residual of Stoic philosophy, the conviction that an offense creates an imbalance or upset in the order of things, and that only some sort of penitential response will redress the balance; secondly, that the victim of insanity may not be entirely guiltless in the matter of the insanity itself. It has been suggested that Gratian, in the portions of his *Decretum* addressed to this point, might have thought of cases in which the defendant was responsible for his own insanity. R. C. Pickett has challenged this, finding the rationale for the ordinance to be at once the element of doubt in all such cases, and the sense that, if the murderer was unencumbered by penance, "many of the faithful, not appreciating his mental abnormality, would be scandalized."[19]

Pickett's interpretation of the ordinance, which was passed by the Council of Worms in 868, is probably correct and also revealing. For the worrisome room for doubt to exist in such cases, the evidence of insanity must have been less obvious than that displayed by the ancient *furiosus*. And the same can be said if, indeed, the faithful did not appreciate the mental abnormality. When madness is depicted by ancient dramatists or discussed by philosophers, the symptoms are indubitable and are external, whatever the theory of aetiology. There is a great difference between a moral order in which judgments are based nearly entirely on such outward and public manifestations—manifestations regarded as bearing upon the interests of the collective—and judgments that seek to penetrate the innermost precincts of conscience.

The Christian world came to adopt a voluntarist theory of criminal liability, thereby narrowing to some extent the range of punishable offenses where the mentally afflicted were involved. It also enlarged the range of moral offenses constitutive of sin, some of them becoming tied to mental disturbances assumed to be of the sinner's own making. Inevitably, this perspective attached to mental illness the heavy burdens of shame and concealment which, in the ancient world, seem to have been remarkably lacking. Theory was replacing matter-of-factness, and with mixed results. Pope Gregory I (590–604) ruled that "he is not to be ordained a cleric who has at any time been a victim of insanity."[20]

The clear implication of a taint is conveyed by this edict, as there is in the ruling of the Council of Toledo (675) that "those possessed by devils or suffering from similar afflictions" must never have anything to do with the holy sacraments. But Cassian, the Egyptian monk of the fifth century, rejected such exclusions and proposed that the sacrament be administered every day. He and his fellow monastics were satisfied that the very existence of insanity established the reality of demons and possessions, but they reasoned that this ability to possess persons is connected with the angelic part of human nature. Thus even the "fallen angel" can make this sort of contact and establish an influence.[21]

Cassian is illustrative of the generally more tolerant (if no more enlightened) attitude in Eastern Christianity. If the Western empire saved itself somewhat later and for a time from superstitious excesses by means of scholasticism, the medieval Arabic world was spared centuries earlier by the authority of ancient Greek natural science and medicine. In his study of early medieval attitudes toward insanity and demonic possession in the Byzantine Middle East, Peregrine Horden has shown the matter-of-fact acceptance of such conditions and the application of practical and fairly humane methods of dealing with them.[22] Though the saints and holy men of the period (ca. sixth and seventh centuries) performed exorcisms and were regarded as the last best hope for those beset by demons, it is also the case that many sufferers learned to live with their conditions. Many communities made provision for them. And possession, regarded as an abiding affliction, tended to be taken as but another malady to which the flesh (or, at least the spirit) is heir. As for the saintly healers and exorcists, the record is mixed. Maro the Syrian avoided the possessed, fearful that his successful treatments would result in sinful celebrity for himself. "His asceticism would be thus compromised. So he feigned dementia and had himself bound to a stone in his monastery."[23]

Of course, it was just these saints and holy men whom the evil spirits were zealous to offend. There was widespread belief that demons possessed the innocent so that, in the process of being exorcised, they could heap shame and abuse on the exorcist in revenge for the relief of the victim. Such a theory is compatible with an attitude of sympathy toward the possessed. At the least it challenges the competing theory according to which the sufferer's own sins invited possession.

It was also generally assumed, even from the earliest medieval period, that demonic possession varied in frequency, in its physical consequences, and in its severity. The more naturalistic the commentator, the more fully is demonic possession absorbed into a general theory of health and disease. Accordingly, one victim of demonic possession might be driven insane, but another might have no more than a welt raised on his forearm. And, as the affliction of possession could itself be abiding, there was no need to suspend important undertakings to deal with it. "On at least one occasion Theodore offered only temporary alleviation rather than cure of possession—so that the harvest could be gathered."[24]

Given the range of conditions that might be brought about demonically, it was not uncommon for healers to dispute whether, in a given case, possession or a purely natural disease was involved.[25] Moreover, the lore of demonology was enlarged by epidemics, by hereditary disorders, and by the sudden bad fortune that might follow in the wake of communal indiscretions. Just as the ancients often regarded such events as divine visitations, medieval Christians of the Eastern empire, shaped by Scripture rather than Homer, found otherworldly culprits. Thus the demons of the period were brought into the folklore and into a more general if innocent epidemiology that would explain plagues, natural disasters, and other inexplicable and unwanted occurrences. Nonetheless, at least in the Eastern empire, demons are neither the first nor the chief suspects when forms of mental illness arise. The influence of Aristotle's natural science and Galen's medical treatises long equipped the Byzantine world with alternatives to undiluted spiritism. "Witness," writes Horden, "the vigour of the whole Galenic tradition . . . that set what we now distinguish as mental illness firmly in the context of somatic diseases . . . sometimes explicitly in opposition to alternative aetiologies involving diabolical interference."[26]

The medical writers and major philosophers of classical Greece had understood such disorders as epilepsy, retardation, and certain forms of insanity as entirely natural. They generally scoffed at demon-theories of the "divine madness," even as they made progress in distinguishing among various forms of epilepsy and nonepileptic variants of convulsion, palsies, and states of confusion and unconsciousness. As Owsei Temkin observed in her now classical study of the history of epilepsy, the ancient Greek physicians were remarkable in their attitudes toward mental disturbances. They not only explained somatic illnesses on the basis of somatic disturbances, but were inclined to account for disorders of the mind in the same terms. "It remains a cause of wonder that they attempted a theory of psychic afflictions which was not only rational and natural but was mainly based on somatic factors."[27]

These Greek influences were strong in Byzantine medicine. They would become nearly hegemonic in the Islamic world of the later Middle Ages, when the *bimaristan* surfaced as a veritable psychiatric hospital. In such places insanity was thoroughly "Galenized" in comparison with the Byzantine world, where it had been somewhat (but rather harmlessly) "demonized."[28] It might have been expected that once this same tradition was recovered and launched in the West, it would have progressed more or less without retreat. The ensuing centuries of witch-hunts and executions are proof enough that this was not the case.

Several major factors worked against the wide acceptance of classical and Islamic naturalistic theories. Perhaps most important is that the Islamic medical community had prospered from the outset as a community of secular professionals, identifying themselves with the traditions of Greek medicine. This same tradition was, of course, not only native to the West but still available to it. Yet by the end of the second century A.D., the early Christian world view had been added to it. The two would come to coexist in an unsteady peace for centuries, and then would begin to merge in a most destructive fashion.

At the outset, there were two competing traditions in place for understanding and dealing with exceptional cases; the one so thoroughly developed by Galen as to come to be known as Galenic, and one that had been fashioned by the Church Fathers. The New Testament account of Jesus ridding a young boy of unclean spirits (Mark, ix, 14–29) may be used to highlight these orientations. As understood by the disciples of Galen, the youth was the victim of a diseased brain; his lunacy was cured by Jesus, who restored the brain to health. Origen's version, ever faithful to the New Testament, is different: "Physicians may offer natural theories. . . . We, however, also believe the Gospel in the point that this disease, in those affected with it, is obviously brought about by an unclean dumb and deaf spirit."[29]

The sect that will rid the world of depravity may not scruple over the needs of the insane. That *alienatio* or estrangement of mind by which Augustine has the mind of the believer surrender to the divine leaves room for the mischief of Satan, too. Thus it mattered to the mentally deranged where they found themselves in the early Christian world. It was one thing to be living in a part of the world whose thinking had been shaped by Hellenistic natural science; a part of the world exposed to a Galen who would claim, "I have given the demonstrations proving that the rational soul is lodged in the encephalon; that this is the part with which we reason."[30] And it was quite another matter to be ruled by an austere volitionist theory which, in a manner of speaking, has even diseases arrive by invitation. The Syrian (Messalian) monks, so highly praised in the *Book of Degrees* by its fourth-century author, are not like the Christian "Righteous" who murder all the local lunatics.[31]

The classical traditions surviving in the Christian West were thus systematically assimilated into an already developed theory of human nature in which satanic and demonic elements were included; a theory of human nature according to which distinctions between and among scientific truth, revealed truth, and canonical reasoning were neither sure nor sharp. Compromise was possible nevertheless, and was achieved throughout the Middle Ages. Witches and witchcraft had their place not only in the religious teachings of Christianity but in the folk medicine of the period. Resisting paganism in all its forms, the early Church came to condemn sorcery and "black magic" but still remained faithful to the scriptural accounts of satan's ways and works. At law—whether Germanic, Roman, or an amalgam of the two—proper penalties, some severe, were assessed against offenders, but nothing approximating a witch-hunt appears in these centuries.

With the development and increasing authority of canon law and the ever more widespread appearance of heresies of one sort and another, the issue of witchcraft gradually took on greater theological significance. By the ninth century the celebrated *Episcopi Eorumque* was promulgated, condemning any teaching incompatible with the omnipotence of God. This, of course, would include the belief that demons could thwart the will of God or subvert the natural order that He ordained. Those who espoused such views were declared by the canon to be not of God but of the devil. As H. C. Midelfort astutely observes, this canon—"by which the Church judged witchcraft well into the eighteenth century"—removed offenders from the category of insane and deluded visionaries and placed them squarely in the domain of infidels. Carlo Ginzburg, in his close study of primary sources in connection with the *Canon episcopi,* which grew out of these developments, observes that all the references are to women; women able to concoct potions capable of inducing love or hate; women who take nocturnal rides with or on animals, and so forth.

All of them feature . . . expressions used in the *Canon episcopi: retro post Satanam conversae (XIX. 158); certis noctibus equitare super quasdam bestias (X. 29; XIX. 60); terrarum spatia . . . pertransire (XIX. 159); noctis silentio (XIX. 159).* These formal parallels underscore an indisputable unity of content. The target

is not isolated superstitions, but an imaginary society in which
the followers of the goddess consider themselves participants
. . . and for which they tried to gain new followers.[32]

In light of the rationale on which this canon was based, it becomes
less surprising that during the centuries of witch-hunts, trials, and
executions, the insanity defense is virtually absent in trials for
witchcraft itself.

For all the powers that might be attributed to satan, the Church
remained resolute in denying that the devil could rob persons of
their free will. Were this otherwise, the very grounds on which
eternity is spent in heaven or hell would be removed. Satan's power
can extend only as far as God allows, and the line is drawn at man's
moral freedom. On this understanding, then, the possessed are not
passive victims but willful collaborators.

Thomas Aquinas would develop the rationale more fully.
Faithful to patristic teaching and Scripture on this point, he accepted the existence of demons and of even more remote (astrological) influences on perception and conduct. His own teacher,
Albertus Magnus, had written authoritatively on the difference between sound and useful astrological predictions of events subject to
natural causes, and predictions of events not thus determined.
Those who would seek to foretell the latter were deceivers to be
shunned.[33] In this same naturalistic-scientific tradition of medieval
Aristotelianism, Thomas Aquinas approved of astrological applications to medicine and meteorology, but stopped short of accepting
judicial astrology. Any theory that took significant human actions
to be determined independently of the moral autonomy of the
actor was to be opposed. If one presumes to predict the future
actions of persons, thereby denying free will and treating human
rationality as if it were causally determined in the manner of physical events, "he does so falsely. In this sort of prophecy the activity
of demons is called into play."[34]

Of course, the notion of demons being called in carries with it the implication of a *pactum implicitum* whereby the powers of satan are summoned to suspend the otherwise natural order of things. Commenting on this, Erik Midelfort concludes: "The scholastics, in analyzing the pact between man and devil, brought together the secular and religious conceptions of magic and witchcraft, seeking to forge a unity where none had existed. The key to this genuine contribution to witchcraft theory was the view that all magic was demonic."[35]

It was, indeed, the very naturalistic outlook that Thomas Aquinas and his near contemporaries adopted that required the participation of supernatural forces in magical or unnatural events. These, alas, were either God's or the devil's. In the latter instance, there was at least the presumption of a *pactum* entered into by those able to bring about or invite or predict such events. Whereas churchmen in the preceding centuries tended to relegate sorcery and magic either to the category of superstition or that of unavoidable possession, "in the thirteenth century, all magic became heresy."[36]

Overall, in the matter of the sacraments, the Church's earliest positions departed in a number of places from Roman law. Marriages in Rome could be readily dissolved as a result of the insanity of one of the partners. The very purposes of marriage in the Roman world necessitated mentally competent mates. But marriage in the early Christian world was validated by a sacramental blessing that reached beyond the temporal affairs of family and state. On this Pope Nicholas in the ninth century was explicit: "In the case of those who contract marriage in health, and one later becomes a victim of insanity or madness or any other affliction, the marriage may not be dissolved on account of the affliction."[37]

But the period under investigation was a complex and an evolving one. Facing imminent death, a frenzied and mute madman, once heard by witnesses to want the sacraments, shall have the Eucharist put in his mouth; nor are the insane to be barred from confirmation in the faith by the hands of a bishop.[38] Should a lunatic, totally uncomprehending of the very meaning of a sacrament, be baptized? Again, the mixture of theology, psychology, and juridical reasoning yielded interesting results, generally consonant with canon 13 promulgated in 441 by the Council of Orange: "Amentibus quaecumque pietatis sunt conferenda."[39] Whatever is in the nature of piety is to be conferred on the insane, and this would surely include the saving sacrament of baptism.

By the twelfth century, maxims of this sort were subjected to that analytical rigor for which scholasticism would become so famous, and infamous. When Innocent III (1198–1216) was asked this same question, about the baptizing of a lunatic, he distinguished between original and actual sin: the former attached itself to man *qua* man as a result of his fallen nature; the latter arose from the knowing consent of the actor. The original sin is expiated through the very power of the sacrament *(per vim Sacramenti)* without any need for consent *(sine consensu),* for consent had not played any part to begin with. But actual sin, arising from the sinner's volition, can be expiated only by consent, of which contrition forms a part.[40]

A religion of sin and redemption, drawing philosophical inspiration from Plato, Aristotle, and the Greek Stoic teachers of Rome, and coming to have such political hegemony as to judge offenses and mete out punishments in the temporal realm, must be ever at pains to locate the volitional boundaries within which personal responsibility is established. And, after these are set, the religious doctrine must draw the even more ambiguous boundaries of a responsibility diminished by uninvited circumstances and conditions; then come those clearer boundaries within which the infant, the profoundly retarded, and the unreachable mad bear none of the moral weight of their actions. By the later Middle Ages (1150–1400), the era of the Scholastics, these elements and functions had generated a substantial and subtle theory of human nature and how it should be theologically and juridically regarded.

The more recent scholarship devoted to correcting the once received judgment of the later Middle Ages as regards witchcraft and insanity is examined in the next chapter. Only a summary of main points is needed here.[41]

To begin with, it is clear that most of the influential writers of the patristic period (including Tertullian and St. Augustine) had incorporated demonic possession into Christian teaching, relying for authority on New Testament accounts of Jesus performing exorcisms. Nevertheless, the notion of madness as the result of witchcraft and possession is far less common in the psychological and legal treatises of the later medieval period. It is sufficient to recall, following Naomi Hurnard, that English records before 1307 yield not a single case in which the King's pardon was requested on the grounds of demonic possession.[42]

To be sure, at the level of folk wisdom, attempts to explain madness rely on demonology, astrology, and witchcraft, but these were taken for granted in a more or less matter-of-fact way, viewing the victim in a manner comparable to one who "fell ill with urinary troubles and infections."[43] There is ample evidence of official attempts to rein in such views, presumably because of their challenge to the volitionist position that was basic to the Church's moral teachings. In 1398, for example, the Faculty of Theology at the University of Paris condemned a full panoply of superstitious beliefs. The wording adopted by the faculty to explain their action— "Perceiving, therefore, that the nefarious, pestiferous and monstrous abomination of false insanities with its heresies has developed more than usual in our times"[44]—is instructive. Note that at the time—the close of the fourteenth century—there has been a fearful proliferation of such heresies and "false insanities." In the XVth Article the faculty specifically rejects "that it is possible by such arts to force the free will of a man to the will or desire of another."[45] Another of the articles (XXI) finds such practices to be an error in *natural philosophy,* while Article XXVII condemns the view that "our intellectual cogitations and inner volitions are caused immediately by the sky, and that by a magic tradition [they] can be known, and that thereby it is licit to pass certain judgments on them."[46]

Moreover, although for several centuries (the eighth to the eleventh) the medical and scientific knowledge of ancient Greece and Rome was unknown, ignored, or neglected in the western reaches of the empire, it was duly transcribed, studied, and disputed by Arab and Jewish scholars in the Moslem world. As Jerome Kroll notes, the locus of scholarly interest shifts again to Europe in the twelfth and thirteenth centuries, the result being the reintroduction of (Galen's) naturalistic and physiological theories of mental disease. Equally important was the revival of jurisprudence within the context of Lombard law by scholars once again thoroughly acquainted with Roman jurisprudence.[47]

As the later medieval period more completely recovered both the classical treatises and, through them, something of the classical approach to jurisprudence, Roman law again became the standard against which regional statutes were judged. Moreover, with the tensions and competitions between popes and emperors becoming ever sharper, judicial review was often the only alternative to strife and sedition. In Lombard Italy, the fusion of Roman law and Germanic codes endured into the late Middle Ages. But first at Ravenna, and then at Bologna, schools of Roman law were established.[48]

It was one of the signal intellectual achievements of the high Middle Ages to apply in a relentless and disciplined way logical rigor to propositions that had for centuries flourished in the form of revealed truths, rank superstitions, unimpeachable *ipsedixits.* In law, this achievement expressed itself most clearly in the recovery of classical jurisprudence. The renewed attention to the *Corpus Juris* in the eleventh century was not accidental. After the pivotal year of 1000 A.D. there occurred a period of reorganization and renewal.

In law, as Paul Vinogradoff wrote, the books of Justinian for the doctors of the new study "were sacred books, the sources of authority from which all deductions must proceed."[49]

In such a climate, the insulation of the law from the more primitive understandings of the peasantry and the faithful was nearly complete. Those venerable demonic entities and satanic influences still pervaded the popular imagination in its darker hours, but the restoration of classical legal procedure and modes of legal proof and argumentation offered an effective if less than perfect buffer. It is no surprise, then, that the scholastic period in Western intellectual history was relatively free of witch-hunts and of the persecution of mentally disturbed citizens, even though such luminaries as Thomas Aquinas accepted the reality of satan's work in the world.[50]

But in this very same period of otherwise sober and detailed analysis, foundations were set for the dreadful excesses of later centuries. The gradual and then accelerated laying of these foundations was the result of several factors interacting in a complex way. The main effect was that the scientific and theological perspectives of the period began to converge in the thirteenth century in such a way as to foster dogmatic positions. The abandonment of an essentially juridical outlook within the law itself, and the appearance of the "expert," were two the more significant consequences. But the convergence of scientific and religious tenets alone would not have been sufficient to generate the epidemic of witch-hunts that overcame Europe between 1400 and 1700. Also necessary were those very developments in legal procedure just noted. In returning to the developed law of the *Corpus Juris,* both the secular and the ecclesiastical courts adopted the accusatory mode of adjudication in place of the early medieval trials by ordeal, battle, and compurgation. How these otherwise worthy developments would help support the witch-hunt fervor of succeeding centuries is considered in the next chapter. But it should be noted that at least as early as the twelfth century the insane were taken into the private homes of the peasants of Gheel, and by the fourteenth century the financial burdens of this care were underwritten by a number of municipalities such as Elbing and Hamburg.[51]

With no desire to modernize or glorify the insights and judgments of the period, it is still fair to say that late medieval scholarship in the matter of insanity was classically informed and guided far less by superstition than by the now rigorous canonical principles of the Roman Catholic Church. By the conclusion of the thirteenth century, and largely as a result of the writings of St. Thomas Aquinas and the more general revival of Aristotelianism, medieval theories of mental illness were increasingly naturalistic. On such matters as the validity of sacramental rites, Aquinas carefully distinguished between insanity from birth and that occurring later in life; and between insanity without remission and that in which lucid intervals are common. The point of these distinctions is to establish the conceptual and moral dependence of sin and guilt on rationality and consent. The fineness of these distinctions is conveyed by his discussion of marriage covenants and insanity: "Present consent is sufficient for mortal sin, but the matter of the betrothal contract requires consent bearing on the future. A greater degree of discretion, however, is required in a matter regarding the future than in one having to do with only a present act. And, therefore, a man can sin mortally before he can impose upon himself some future obligation."[52]

The concluding sentence in this passage is, *"et ideo ante potest homo peccare mortaliter, quam possit se obligare ad aliquid futurum"* ("and this is why one has the capacity to commit a mortal sin before he can obligate himself to anything in the future"). This formulation clearly recognizes that there are gradations of madness, and that incapacity as regards one class of thought or action may not extend to another class. Passages like this one are strong evidence of the Church's thorough absorption of Roman juridical reasoning into its own canonical context. How unsurprising, then, that Bracton borrows freely from Romanists and canonists (Bernard of Paivia, for example) in compiling his *De Legibus . . . Angliae.*

It is of interest in this connection to consider how canon law, under the inspiration of Scripture but everywhere beholden to Roman law, dealt with specific cases involving questions of mental competence. The growing canonical authority of the Pope resulted in any number of such issues being brought to Rome for settlement. The mode of settlement was adjudicative, in the sense that cases were disposed of according to carefully gathered evidence (such as depositions), settled law, well established precedents, and (papal) interpretations in hard cases. R. Colin Pickett has summarized a number of cases occasioned by allegations of insanity, of which the following is illustrative.[53] A monastic priest, just before he died, declared to witnesses his intention that his earthly belongings be conveyed to the monastery, thus excluding the local church as a beneficiary. This resulted in a conflict of interests between a bishop and an abbot. In this dispute, the Bishop of Nevers insisted that the deceased had been insane at the time he expressed his intentions and should therefore be regarded as having died intestate.

In deciding the matter, Innocent III (1198) ruled that such cases rest upon the presumption of sanity, and the resulting burden of proof is imposed on those who would challenge the validity of testaments. But what of cases in which one declares himself to have been insane at some earlier time; for example, a priest seeking relief for some offense on the grounds that he had been entirely beside himself *(extra se positus)*? Again, canon XV had long established the nullity of vows taken by the insane, but Innocent III introduced this modification: the burden of proof now shifts to the claimant, again because of the presumption of sanity.

With few exceptions, the canon law pertaining to testamentary capacity was beholden, *mutatis mutandis,* to the developed Roman law on the subject. In Rome it was possible for a child to become *paterfamilias,* but the law regarded him as legally competent only when he reached the age of fourteen. For girls the age was twelve. Otherwise, for legal purposes, such children were infants. The same ages were accepted by ecclesiastical courts from the time of Justinian in the matter of wills. In the English courts throughout the Middle Ages these criteria were honored even when legal infants wrote wills with parental consent.[54]

In the matter of criminal responsibility, both ecclesiastical and secular courts routinely exonerated defendants judged to be insane or mentally retarded. Although the families of victims had, under English law, the right to appeal such pardons, "the idea of executing such people was so detestable that prosecution of an appeal by the victim's relatives was almost inconceivable."[55] Beyond England, similar considerations prevailed. Records from Florence before the witch panic indicate the same lenient and even casual approach to the manifestly insane. In 1415 Anastasio di Ser Domenico di Ser Salvi Gai killed his mother with a stick, but because he was "mad and insane, and therefore according to law his penalty should be mitigated," was sentenced to life imprisonment; he was released in 1428, having fully recovered his sanity in prison.[56]

In the middle of the thirteenth century Bracton would summarize English law in this area in a phrase that could have been found in Aristotle and defended by Justinian: "For no crime is accomplished except that the desire to harm intercede."[57] Canonists had reasoned similarly far earlier, but in climates less congenial to such views. The early Church, an amalgam of Platonism, Scripture, prophecy, local customs, and legends, had yet to fashion an intellectual center for itself during the very centuries in which the classical centers were overrun. The conception of human nature, Donne's "dregs of Adam's race," was in transition. But as the ultimate reality was itself otherworldly, the ultimate identity of the person was itself nonempirical and immaterial. "Mind," in one way or another, was taken to be the sign and symbol of this, and the disordered mind was therefore a thing to be abhorred, purged, prayed over, detested, exiled.

As an immaterial entity, it was, of course, vulnerable to spirits and demons, which is why such attributions in the early medieval literature have a nearly clinical ring. But why is one mind chosen and not another, if not on the basis of affinity or desert? In some communities, the mentally retarded and deranged were not only beset by their disorders but condemned and blamed for them as well. The Church in its official documents and canonical reasoning did nothing to encourage this view and gradually defeated it, even while laying the foundations of a "witch theory" that would wreak havoc in later centuries. But solicitude toward the mentally disturbed was possible only with the civilizing of the European communities themselves; a task undertaken by great kings and good clerics. Perhaps the most vivid outward sign of the process was chivalry, the humanizing influences of which were broad and deep.

One class of beneficiaries of such influences included the mentally infirm and afflicted, who routinely enjoyed the possibility of acquittal in the age of Bracton and who, as early as the reign of Edward I, might expect release from custody when judged to be no longer dangerous. Provision was routinely made for those released on bail to be placed in the custody of their families or even of *mainpernors* appointed by the Crown for the purpose. There is no doubt that in the thirteenth century and earlier the courts were sensitive to the mental states capable of promoting violent behavior—states that could vary in frequency, intensity, and duration, and so unpredictably as to call for long-term custodial care and caution.

The record of the late Middle Ages reveals a reasonable measure of compassion and skepticism. Then as now, courts were fearful of being gulled. Nonetheless, in the highest councils of thought, rationalism had again become the dominant psychological theory, such that horrendous crimes were readily judged as only arising from utterly deranged minds. Naomi Hurnard has noted that although in homicide cases resulting in acquittal insanity might not have been accepted as a defense, offenders thought to be mentally deranged generally enjoyed pardons and custodial care. And where pardons failed, it may well have been because families chose not to have the burden of such care.[58]

Pollack and Maitland observed long ago "the very high standard of liability" the early Christian penitential books imposed on the faithful, due in part, they conjectured, "to that nervous horror of blood."[59] The nervous horror of blood was the echo of the Stoic moralists whose predictions of the fate of unreasonable empires had been confirmed. The early Church had found the way to the Eternal City—which was, alas, not Rome—and had the sad task of instructing the catechumen in how hard and unforgiving a journey this must be.

The leavening effect of nobility, which would be the most significant bequest of medieval chivalry, was centuries into the future.[60] As it appeared and spread, it would supply the affairs of Church and state, at least for a time, with a corrective for that unblinking earnestness endemic to both in their earlier days.

3

POSSESSION & WITCHCRAFT

At the age of seventy, charged with impiously mouthing the Holy Eucharist, Barbara Rüfin was arraigned on the charge of witchcraft. After five days in custody she was accused of using salves to kill cattle and poisons to murder her own son. The testimony of neighbors came down against her, her own husband even admitted that over the years and when angry he would call her a witch. About a week later, her denials disregarded, she was stretched on the rack twice in one day. Still denying her guilt, she was tortured again two days later, whereupon she finally admitted not only to the desecration of the host but to sexual intercourse with the devil, with whom she had entered into a pact. Her spiraling mental anguish and confusion only encouraged her tormentors to continue their questioning. The nightmare ended five weeks after her arrest when she was executed by sword.[1] This all took place in the spring of 1611, in the German city of Ellwangen, with the full benefit of developed legal procedures and at a time when Shakespeare, Galileo, and Descartes were all alive.

The centuries of witch-hunts and persecutions in Europe and America mark off a significant period in the evolution of legal concepts of insanity. Indeed, the very theory of witchcraft effectively denied defendants access to the insanity defense, though the defense was otherwise available. The special nature of witchery called for alterations and even the suspension of trial procedures that had become settled features of law, for the powers and attributes ascribed to witches created the need for specialists better able to identify the guilty and far less prone to devilish deceptions. Finally, after the persecutions had run their course, the reaction against the vile and relentless torments and executions took an increasingly scientific and medical turn, thus laying the foundations for modern psychiatry and medical jurisprudence.

Belief in occult powers, demons, witches, and demonic possession is a veritable fixture in human history; one that has been totally abandoned only recently and perhaps still only by a minority of the world's population. In legal history, as early as Rome's *Twelve Tables,* one finds the following threat to practitioners of the occult: "Anyone who, by means of incantations and magic arts, prevents grain or crops of any kind belonging to another from growing, shall be sacrificed to Ceres" (Table VII).[2] In the Homeric epics the fearful hero asks whether a challenger is a god in disguise. In the *Iliad* recall Agamemnon attributing his own less than commendable behavior to divine possession, and Zeus dispatching dream-demons to invade the sleeping mind. Centuries later, Greek dramatists would serve up an even wider assortment of tormentors and furies. Bennett Simon, discussing the *Eumenides,* memorably describes one type:

They are something like Gorgons: they are like disgusting Harpies who snatch and contaminate the food, only they are wingless. They are black and disgusting. Their breath drives one away. Their eyes drip foul ooze, and no human beings would claim them for their own. . . . And, of course, madness is their specialty:

"Over our victim
we sing this song, maddening the brain,
carrying away the sense, destroying the mind."[3]

It is more apt, of course, to refer to "beliefs" rather than belief, for different ages and peoples have had quite different conceptions of the nature and influences of the occult. The reasoning and general context that led to the torture and execution of Barbara Rüfin cannot be neatly merged with sacrificial propitiation of Ceres or the exculpatory rhetoric of Agamemnon. Rather, a given age or culture adapts its inherited folk wisdom to changing conditions, bequeathing yet other versions that will then be transformed anew by the flux of history.

In the ancient worlds of Greece and Rome, ordinary citizens readily accepted that some persons possessed exotic powers or might be chosen by the gods to be the medium for divine stratagems. It was understood that practitioners were able to perpetrate evil through a "black magic" harmful to others *(maleficium);* or that they might employ a benign "white magic" to cure illnesses and bring about good weather or a decent run of luck. The *Twelve Tables* threatened only those guilty of *maleficia*. Healers, prophets, tricksters, and kindred devotees of the arts of "white magic" did not suffer the severe penalties of law.

Such superstitions have always become mixed and modified over long stretches of time, and with the complex influences of trade, imperial expansion, and the centralization of power within ever more pluralistic societies. Depending on the special political and cultural climate in which these folk beliefs and practices occur, they may come to be celebrated, rendered "official" and promulgated, or condemned as heresies and ruthlessly suppressed. In either case, the laws and adjudicative outcomes of an era disclose as well as shape all such widely held convictions.

As the power of ecclesiastical courts increased, along with the pronounced urbanization of European communities late in the Middle Ages, the adaptation of Roman law to Christian purposes was ever more vigorously pursued. Ancient distinctions between "black" and "white" magic were dissolved, and all witchcraft was now taken as proof of a covenant with satan. These effects would come to be catastrophic in many European communities, but only after the merging of secular and religious thought. Given the very nature of the still undeveloped scientific outlook of the Renaissance, it becomes less paradoxical that the greatest excesses of witch-hunting would take place well into the modern era.

The accusatorial procedures of early medieval law required that complaints and charges originate with the aggrieved or injured party. It was not the judge or the jurisdictional authority who prosecuted. Rather, the authorities heard the charges brought before them, weighed the evidence, and then ruled. Where the weight of evidence was insufficient to support a ruling, the contestants in a criminal action were called upon to face some ordeal. In a criminal or a civil action, they would engage in hand-to-hand battle; or, if a nobleman, the accused might simply summon reliable oath-helpers *(compurgators)* whose ritual utterances and attestations of his veracity might well vindicate him. The ordeal of toting red-hot objects some specified distance or of immersion in cold water—the innocent would sink, the guilty would float—was customary. But the accuser in such actions faced severe penalties were his charges to prove groundless; severe enough to discourage frivolous or spiteful litigation. The rationale behind the ordeal was that divine assistance must be solicited in hard cases. In cases where the defendant protested his innocence and the evidence against him was not fully convincing, a higher authority must be consulted. The assumption on which such "trials by divination" depended, of course, was that God favors the innocent and punishes the wicked.

With the evolution of more refined procedures (adapted from classical law) and the greater centralization of power, the accusa-

torial method was replaced by the inquisitorial, the judge now centrally involved in trying the case. Ancient Roman courts had found
no need for divine signs or interventions. The Roman magistrate
closely queried the parties to the dispute, saw to it that relevant
evidence was presented, and reached a judgment more or less indifferent to the fraction of the citizenry that might declare the defendant to be a man of transparent goodness! As the various parts
of the later medieval world adopted their own versions of these
procedures, the participation of the judge came to include both
inquisition and disposition. The jury system of England was an
exception here, accounting to some extent perhaps for the smaller
number of prosecutions and convictions of witches than would
occur on the Continent. But with these developments the burdens
imposed on accusers were now all but eliminated. A court finding
the charges at all credible would take up the case, the officers of
the court having the power to obtain and weigh the evidence,
determine guilt or innocence, and set the penalties.

Prior to the witch panic, the net effect of these developments
was salutary, for the rules of evidence were clearly biased in favor
of the defendant. Successful prosecution required either admission
of guilt by the defendant or two eyewitnesses to the offense vigorously examined under oath. The major gain in these procedural
developments was the elimination of savage and juridically meaningless practices, and their replacement by rules of evidence applied
by competent jurists acting in behalf of Church or Crown. But the
major liability, during the long season of the witch-hunt, was that
a successful prosecution of a crime such as heresy or the white
magic of witchcraft—which often had neither victim nor eyewitness—would require the defendant's confession. Moreover, a defendant no longer had the option of countersuit.

The means by which confessions would be secured soon reached
the level of the macabre, as heresies multiplied and as witchcraft
was taken to be a species of the same. But long before these mea-

sures became dominant, the attitude toward demonic possession and magic was more or less dispassionate. The full weight of the law hung over any and all who would harm others by practicing black magic, but the witch-hunt itself was still a century or so into the future. Furthermore, the corrupting influences of superstition were kept a safe distance from the special academic centers now entrusted with the development of law, medicine, philosophy, and theology. Scholastic rationalism, notwithstanding its (often exaggerated) innocence to the contrary, afforded practical guides to the courts, even while reserving a place for whatever demonic figures Scripture required.

At the University of Paris in the time of Albertus Magnus and Thomas Aquinas, and next at Oxford where Robert Grosseteste and Roger Bacon would promote experimental science and naturalistic theology, the demons and the stars were both given their due. If rationality and volition are not themselves material entities, then the force or power of celestial bodies—which can work only on similarly physical bodies—can have no direct influence on the mind. There may, however, be indirect influences, for the mind is clearly affected by bodily conditions, and these are vulnerable to cosmic forces. That is also the case with demons. Once summoned, they can deceive and promote evil, but they might also influence the course of medical therapies through their control of the body. Lurking behind this rationale was the possibility of a scientific method of exposing the devil's disciples.

For Roger Bacon the possibilities were immense and warranted energetic exploitation, even if officially proscribed teachings had to be consulted. Suggesting that this may have had something to do with his Franciscan superior's decision to imprison Bacon, Theodore Wedel has traced out the larger consequences of these developments:

> The Church, fearing perhaps that it had dealt too leniently
> with astrology in theory, gave evidence that it would be all

the more severe with it whenever in practice it meddled with magic or with fatalistic doctrines. It was ostensibly on these two counts, at any rate, that the Inquisition condemned to the stake its first astrological heretic, Cecco d'Ascoli, professor of astrology at the University of Bologna in the first quarter of the fourteenth century.[4]

In an awkward and persistent march of thought, leading clerics and secular scholars alike found themselves committed to a "natural magic" that might account for witchcraft in scientific terms. Within the evolving Christian theory of human nature were numerous subsidiary and corollary theories, among them one that Christina Larner dubbed "the Christian witch theory." She offers three reasons to account for the gruesome consequences of the theory in practice. First, it was a product of the ruling classes, whereas in earlier times there had been "a fairly sharp contrast between village credulity and intellectual skepticism." Also, the very codification of the laws against witchcraft sanctioned an enlargement of the powers of punishment. "The other reasons are connected with the theory itself. The logical conclusion of the idea of the demonic pact was the abolition of the traditional distinction between black and white magic. The power of the witch sprang from the demonic pact and was therefore evil, whether it was used for healing or harming."[5]

Why, after all, should it matter whether the witch did good or evil if, to do either, the propitiation of satan was involved? In the end, for any good that might arise from the pact, there would be a final accounting. Brian Levack reduces the logic of the thesis to the faultless proposition that "demons did not provide services without demanding something in return."[6]

The melding of the civil offense of *maleficium* with that of heresy greatly enlarged the pool of potential suspects. Predictably, the hardships wrought by these developments would be greatest for those whose medical or social or psychological conditions resulted in signs or symptoms not readily explicable in the primitive medical idiom of the day. Even now it is not easy to distinguish between physiological and essentially psychological factors in the overall pattern of symptoms a patient might display. The difficulty inherent in such distinctions reveals itself most fully where natural causes are not to be found, and where the symptoms themselves are most mysterious. Epileptic seizures, various movement disorders, hysterical and neurological conditions that mar the body or modify memory, thought, and consciousness are illustrative of diseases that would prove to be especially congenial to demon-based or possession-based explanations. But possession never carried the burden of crime or of sin that would be assigned to the witch. To be possessed by demons was to be a victim. To be a witch was to be a willing participant.

As for the recovered classical approach to law, the declared witch again lost out. The crime of witchcraft was the *crimen exceptum* for which standard procedures were ill-suited. The wiles and resources of the devil being what they are, ordinary rules of evidence or testimony from citizens and relations were simply not up to the task. All this was, again, a departure from the past. The earlier policy, even if it punished witches severely, required authorities to treat such cases in the same way the law covered other infractions. The laws of England, at least in this respect, are representative of the more general state of affairs during the early medieval period. Thus the seventh century *Liber penitentialis* compiled by Theodore, Archbishop of Canterbury, requires one to ten years of penance of those who sacrifice to demons, and excommunication of magicians and enchanters. Under King Withraed (690–731), a husband making offerings to the devil is fined. Later, Ecgberht, the Archbishop of York (735–766), demands of the woman who casts spells that she fast, and that if her spells cost a life, the fast continue for seven years. In the reign of King Aethelstand (925–940) one charged with killing through witchcraft is "liable in his life," but if he denies the charge, he is sent to prison for 120 days and must compensate the King and the kindred of the deceased. With Ethelred (975–979) nothing less than exile faces the "soothsayers, magicians or whores" who might also be killed "unless they desist, and the more deeply make bot". During these centuries in England, "very few prosecutions for witchcraft took place in any of the civil courts of justice. Magicians and witches were classed as heathen and heretics."[7]

Policies were less cordial on the Continent, particularly in the south of France, where Albigensian and Catharist heretics appeared as early as 1012. The sect was not actually centered in Albi but in Toulouse and Limousin, though in time "Albigensian" was the official term covering the entire movement. The heresies from the outset were grave. The *cathari* (purified) insisted (as Manichaeans had centuries earlier) that an evil principle stands behind the affairs of terrestrial life, satan's powers being just below those of God's own. Dubbing themselves the "good men" *(bons hommes),* they rejected the baptismal waters—these, too, tied to earthly things— and insisted on baptism by spirit. John the Baptist was himself rejected on just these grounds. The heresy of admitting an anti-God capable of thwarting God's own will was intolerable, but the rejection of it still raised theological problems, for it now became necessary to accept certain evils as occurring through the will of God. On this account, the rationale was developed that the devil's doings are permitted either to test the faithful, or to make room for an even greater good.

The Council of Toulouse (1119) enlisted the reluctant support of a heretofore quite tolerant nobility to suppress the Cathars, but they continued to enjoy both princely sufferance and popular enthusiasm. The demands of papal legates were scorned by the Albigensians themselves, who regarded the papacy's arrogant claims to authority as heresies in their own right. Finally, Innocent III, all patience spent, authorized a Cistercian crusade (1209) against the Cathars, thus engaging the noble houses of France in open warfare. With the Treaty of Paris (1229) came the end of the wholesome political independence of the southern provinces, and a more or less free hand for the inquisitors of the next two centuries. The precedent was now firmly established by which secular courts, including the royal courts, would be expected to work hand in glove with ecclesiastical authorities, not only in crushing heretical movements but also in accepting the ecclesiastical rationale for prosecutions. The medieval Inquisition, brought into being by Pope Gregory IX in the thirteenth century, was specifically directed against the Cathars. As such heretical movements (as well as the Reformation and the Counter-Reformation) came to preoccupy a whole succession of popes, the procedures and rationale of the medieval Inquisition proved ever more serviceable. The severity of various versions of the Inquisition tends to reflect the size of the challenge as perceived by the Church authorities. The same Innocent III who launched the crusade against the Cathars in 1209 put an end in 1212 to the practice of ordeal in the trial of heretics. But then, denied the illumination allegedly obtained through ordeal, the ecclesiastical jurists argued for the remedy of torture, the practice of which was officially approved by the Lateran Council of 1215.

Even where one might have assumed insanity on the part of a great many defendants in the various witch trials, the overriding rationale ruled this out in all but a negligible number of instances. Carlo Ginzburg offers the instructive example of a sermon by Bishop Nicholas of Cusa, in which Nicholas reviews the case of three old women brought before him in the 1457 trial at Bressanone. Ginzburg relates how this great and progressive thinker concluded that the women were deluded, half-mad *(semideliras)*. Alas, the defendants themselves disagreed! He thus had to sentence them to penance and jail, explaining that his leniency had meant to discourage belief that the devil is more powerful than God. Even here, the "insanity defense" was not raised, but was unsuccessfully proposed by the judge. Rejected by its potential beneficiaries, the defense never got off the ground in the first place. In this same connection, the celebrated Inquisitor Nicolaus Eymeric, whose manual *Directorium inquisitorum* was based on his twenty years' experience, rejected the claim that witches actually flew on the backs of animals, and other such phenomena. Nonetheless, their fantasies established them as "wicked women . . . seduced by demonic illusions." Where physicians were consulted, the cases of possession and those of alleged witchcraft were kept quite separate. D. P. Walker has noted in this connection that medical experts in witch trials were called upon to examine the accused for the devil's mark or to determine if there were supernumerary mammaries with which to nourish the demons. But the doctors were not asked whether the witch was insane.[8]

In the thirteenth century either secular or ecclesiastical court might apprehend those charged with witchcraft, though the maximum penalty was probably not carried out often. It was still the open heretic who attracted the most ferocious and diligent response, and the theory that tied witchcraft and heresy together made progress only slowly at this time. The trials and executions in the sixteenth and seventeenth centuries are thus all the more vivid by contrast, and all the more revealing of the complex, stubbornly maintained, and weirdly evolving theories that made such practices nearly inevitable. These same excesses and the ever widening circle of suspects would encourage the "natural magician" to protest his objectivity, his indifference to theological disputes, his total innocence of any compact with dark forces or the minions of Satan. In the heady dialectic of Renaissance and Reformation, the metaphysical foundations of modern science were being clumsily and fitfully laid by those seeking to manipulate the physical world without inviting the attention of the witch-hunter and inquisitor. The rhetoric of scientific objectivity predated its metaphysics.[9]

Within the arena of adjudication, once the assumption was en-dorsed that those charged with witchcraft did not qualify as "de-fendants" in the accepted sense, standard trial procedures were abandoned. The infamous *Malleus maleficarum* (1486) of the Do-minican Fathers Heinrich Kramer (Institoris) and Jakob Sprenger carefully noted the special procedures that had to be adapted and applied to such cases.[10] Where there is *maleficium* there, too, is the devil. Injuries and great damage result, calling for the vigilant at-tention not only of the Church but of the secular courts as well, now properly informed by those who can tease the devil from his lair. More will need to be said below about the *Malleus.* In time, the secular courts would have the monopoly of witch trials, many jurisdictions coming to declare witchcraft to be a secular crime on the order of treason. Indeed, there is a rough proportionality be-tween the number of prosecuted and executed witches and the degree of dominance enjoyed by secular courts which the clergy now assisted.[11]

The use of torture to extract confessions initially rested on a congeries of interpretations of Roman law and tight scholastic ar-guments that also imposed unequivocal limitations. These latter would be gradually disregarded by the less patient judges of later centuries. Until well into the thirteenth century, however, the con-straints on torture were tight and rarely relaxed. Medieval courts were genuinely fearful of convicting the innocent. Citing the Apostle in *Romans* (vii. 23) who detects *"another law in my members, fighting against the law of my mind,"* Thomas Aquinas underscored the conflict between the dictates of reason and the *fomes* or sensual demands of the body.[12]

Clearly, torture can compel its victim to abandon rationality in order to preserve the flesh. There must be limits on so powerful a device. Thus in most jurisdictions throughout the high Middle Ages repeated torture was prohibited, as was the torture of a preg-nant woman, or of any defendant in a case not involving an actual crime. And in all cases it was necessary for the court to arrive at the warranted presumption of the defendant's guilt, usually through eyewitness accounts, before ordering torture. Judges were specifically enjoined to avoid questions that might lead the defendant to avoid torture by opting for self-incrimination. To this same end, no confession made in the torture chamber was admissible as evidence; rather, the same statement would have to be given freely in the courtroom. Needless to say, had each of these provisions been steadfastly honored, there could have been no witch-hunts at all. But by 1631, perhaps unmindful that there ever had been a limit on repeated torture, the hangman of Dreissigacker could confidently promise this fate to a defendant who happened to be pregnant: "I do not take you for one, two, three, not for eight days, not for a few weeks, but for half a year, or a year, for your whole life, until you confess: and if you will not confess, I shall torture you to death, and you shall be burned after all."[13]

It is not easy to determine the relative severity of Roman Catholic and Protestant punishments from the data, though they do support the general claim that prosecutions were more common and executions far more frequently ordered by magistrates in Catholic countries.[14] The Reformation was filled with charges and countercharges as each side struggled to define and defend its true confession. It was in such an atmosphere that Catholics would judge the Reformation itself to be the very wellspring of witchery, while Protestants dismissed the Catholic clergy as magicians. The intense and bloody conflicts in France between Catholics and Huguenots would seek vindication in biblical sources and in medical or quasi-scientific treatises, each side declaring itself to be on the path of righteousness. Tests of orthodoxy extended to one's position on and beliefs about witchcraft, the consequence being ever firmer positions on both sides and with little to choose between them. Celebrated cases drew huge crowds which assembled to observe not only the antics of the demonically possessed but the shrewd devices invented by the clergy to determine whether Beelzebub was the culprit. The famous Marthe Brossier, who proclaimed herself possessed in 1598 at the age of twenty-five, appeared before many and large audiences as her family traipsed her through the villages of the Loire. The Bishop of Angers was unconvinced, however, when he was able to precipitate convulsions by seeming to read from the Book of Exorcisms when in fact he was reciting the first lines of Virgil's *Aeneid*.[15]

Surely Luther himself acknowledged witchcraft and considered it as, at best, "a mixture of natural reason and the devil's aid." He regarded the traditions of genuine natural science as prefigured in the Old Testament, pursued by the prophets and wise men of Judaea, and nurtured later by the scholars in Persia and Arabia. "But then, as happens with knowledge and learning, swine and numskulls invaded the field, deviated far from the right course, and adulterated that noble knowledge with their trickery and sorcery. . . . The devil has retained much of this knowledge and at times uses it through the magi, so that magus is now an ignominious name and refers to those who prophesy and work miracles with the aid of the evil spirit."[16]

The "sharp contrast between village credulity and intellectual skepticism" withered in the heat of Luther's rhetoric, the "pagan" teachings of Aristotle and his modern worshippers were exposed to ceaseless ridicule. So, in his own way, Luther also secularized the phenomenon of witchcraft, taking it to be a mingling of natural science and devilish designs. Here again an argument was in place for the proper use of "experts" in attempts to locate the evil core within the body of quasi-naturalistic happenings. Additionally, the success of the Reformation and the recognition that it could no longer be reversed resulted in a more inward-looking Roman Catholic institution in the sixteenth century. It was now committed to the elimination of all superstitions and pagan vestiges. Hence it is after the Council of Trent that the Church devotes its energies to an especially harsh and relentless pursuit of witches and sorcerers. The highly visible and public activities of the Inquisition are to be understood in this context. In vigorously Catholic Venice, for example, where policies had been as lenient as those in England, the Counter-Reformation led to an upsurge in witchcraft prosecutions, but with heresy the focus rather than felony *(maleficium)*.[17]

The *Malleus maleficarum* is the primary text to consult in order to understand the "witch panics" that overtook Europe between 1400 and 1700. This book was not simply the work of two diligent Dominicans. It was the official handbook, authorized by the Pope, approved by the theological faculty of Cologne, and accepted as authoritative by Maximilian, "most August King of the Romans, Archduke of Austria, Duke of Burgundy, of Lorraine, of Brabant, of Limburg, of Luxemburg and Guelderland, Count of Flanders."[18] The papal bull (*Summis desiderantes affectibus,* 1484) issued to fathers Kramer and Sprenger carried forward the urgent tradition of fighting the devil and defending the faith, and declared that any who opposed this war on witches would bring down upon himself the wrath of Almighty God. *Malleus maleficarum* was *the* book. The theological positions presented in it were "correct"; the scriptural research and interpretation sound and accessible. If it broke no new ground in hermeneutics or natural science, it carefully reviewed the best productions of both and integrated them into a practical manual of extraordinary influence. In its many editions it would be the acknowledged scholarly reference work to be consulted on all matters pertaining to the identification, trial, and sentencing of witches.

The work is divided into three parts and covers thirty-five questions, ranging from the ontological status of witches to the appeals procedures available to them after conviction. All questions are dealt with in a sober and thoughtful manner, the overall tone of the work being scholastic, juridical, and conservative, notwithstanding an occasional expression of passionate orthodoxy. Against the teaching that belief in witches is itself a superstition incompatible with belief in God's goodness and omnipotence, the authors clearly establish that in fact such teaching is itself heresy. Kramer and Sprenger cite not only Scripture and canon law, but also ancient Roman civil law as taking special notice of sorcerers and magicians. To say that the manifestations of witchcraft are fantasies is beside the point, for "fantasy cannot be procured without resort to the power of the devil."[19] In response to those who insist that only God can create and, therefore, that witches with or without satanic assistance cannot bring about new forms, the authors refer to both Thomas Aquinas and to the recent efforts of the alchemists. True, devils cannot be creators as such, but through their mastery of various arts they can (like the alchemists) produce things very much like the original.[20]

Throughout the work, there is this mingling of scientific (secular) and theological considerations. Agreeing that trials by ordeal are generally to be avoided, they note the special limitations of this practice in dealing with witches:

> And it is not wonderful that witches are able to undergo this trial by ordeal unscathed with the help of devils; for we learn from naturalists that if the hands be anointed with the juice of a certain herb they are protected from burning. Now the devil has an exact knowledge of the virtues of such herbs: therefore, although he can cause the hand of the accused to be protected from the red-hot iron by invisibly interposing some other substance, yet he can procure the same effect by the use of natural objects.[21]

Similarly, Kramer and Sprenger merge the functions of ecclesiastical and civil courts in these cases: "although in the case of simple heresy those who are penitent and abjure are . . . admitted to penitence and imprisonment for life; yet in this heresy (witchcraft) . . . the civil Judge can, because of her temporal injuries . . . punish her with death."[22] Moreover, customary trial procedures, rules of evidence and the grounds of legitimate suspicion, and statutes of limitations are all challenged and revised. A defendant might be facing charges based on alleged bewitchments occurring ten or fifteen years earlier.[23] Nor is it the defendant who names her advocate, but the court. As for the advocate, if he "has wittingly undertaken to defend a prisoner whom he knows to be guilty, he shall be liable for the costs and expenses."[24] Even in the absence of a complaint, the judge is free and even encouraged to summon for trial the children of the accused and other members of the household, "for these are generally found to be infected."[25] As for the possibility of rebutting the testimony of witnesses, this too was greatly diminished. Given the alleged powers of witches and their penchant for vengeful attacks against those they have come to hate, it would be perilous to witnesses to give their names or to appear in person. Citing the authority of Pope Boniface VIII (1294 to 1303), Kramer and Sprenger advise thus:

> If in a case of heresy it appears to the Bishop or Inquisitor that grave danger would be incurred by witnesses or informers . . . he shall not publish (their names). . . . It is more dangerous to make known the names of the witnesses to an accused person who is poor, because such a person has many evil accomplices. . . . And if the accused again and again insists that she should know the names of the witnesses against her, he can answer as follows: You can guess from the charges which are made against you who are the witnesses.[26]

The most vulnerable members of the community were predictably the most frequently arraigned. Vagrants, the destitute, foreigners, and especially unmarried or widowed women were the commonest targets. Where data have been at all reliable, the ratio of women to men among those accused of witchcraft is as high as four to one.[27] As for the benefit of the doubt, a prisoner might enjoy it only so far as it "involves no scandal to the faith nor is in any way detrimental to justice."

How an interrogation proceeded, therefore, depended on just what was taken to be a "scandal to the faith." One benefit of doubt that might have been extended to deluded or hallucinating defendants (of which there must have been many) was withdrawn by the official theory. When Kramer and Sprenger consider such phenomena (Part II, q. 1, ch. 8), they draw examples from sources as divergent as Homer, the Old Testament, and St. Augustine; examples including the comrades of Diomedes occupying his temple in the form of birds; Nebuchodonosor living as an ox for seven years; Circe's transformation of Ulysses' companions into animals. How are such events to be understood? Here the authors distinguish between a "glamour" and an imaginary vision. In the case of a "glamour" there really is an external object, but it is seen as something quite different from what it really is. With imaginary visions, no external object is present. The distinction duly noted, Kramer and Sprenger then conclude that the devil uses both forms of deception. A defendant is no less guilty for suffering one of them rather than the other.

During the interrogation and examination, judges are to use various devices to trick the devil and reveal the compact. One technique, though not unfailingly successful, would have the judge test for true tears and prevent the flow of false ones: "Let him place his hand on the head of the accused and say: I conjure you by the bitter tears shed on the Cross by our Saviour the Lord JESUS Christ for the salvation of the world, and by the burning tears poured in the evening hour over His wounds by the most glorious Virgin MARY His mother . . . that if you be innocent you do now shed tears."[28]

Heaping further indignities on the marginally defended accused, the courts then might undertake to have "hair shaved from every part of her body . . . for in order to preserve their power of silence they are in the habit of hiding some superstitious object . . . even in the most secret parts of their bodies which must not be named."[29] A sixteenth-century French observer in Rome commented on the spectacle: "When I hear their frightful cries and see the upturned whites of their eyes, my hair stands on end and words fail me; but when I see a monk spouting Latin, fondling them belly and breast, this fright passes and I must laugh."[30]

It is clear that the authors of the *Malleus maleficarum* are aware of the difficulty of teasing out those effects which an emerging natural science is able to produce, and those that come about through the intervention of dark forces. Eager to avoid the taint of heresy themselves, they withhold from satan any of the creative powers properly reserved to God, but still must account for the transmutation of persons into animals or one species of animal into another. Such problems call for subtle conceptual analysis and the use of the different senses of "making," "likeness," and "created." No, the devil cannot make a *perfect* creature (such as man, sheep, horse, and so on), but he can create such imperfect ones as serpents, frogs, and mice, for these "can also be generated from putrefaction."[31] Science, having established by its own arts that such events can come about, it is obvious that the devil's arts can achieve at least as much. Doctors may use dreams in their diagnostic work because dreams sometimes reveal natural underlying conditions. The "choleric" man dreams of fire, just as dreams of water are common to the phlegmatic and those of flight to the sanguine. But there is all the difference between the use of these natural signs and processes in medicine, and summoning the devil to assist in foretelling and affecting the future.

If one is to make the necessary distinctions between scientific and satanic practices, it becomes important to know about each genre. Kramer and Sprenger refer to information that has been gleaned by direct experience; to findings that have been reported in medical (Galenic) or naturalistic settings; to Aristotle's scientific analysis of the prophetic power of dreams—a power based on the ability of the imaginative faculty to record states of the body that might indeed portend disease. Further distinctions are made between healing based on mere superstition (as in believing in the power of Saturn over lead) and that based on witchcraft. In this, too, the *Malleus* served as a prod to a kind of objective science; a prod to those engaged in medical and naturalistic studies to make clear the purity of their inquiries. Indeed, by absorbing a wide range of suspect behaviors into orthodox theology, the *Malleus* in effect left the remainder for the natural scientists. But in either category the disorders of this special interest called for a differential diagnosis: for explanations informed both by science and theology and for an expertise otherwise unheard of during earlier centuries of adjudication in the patrimony of Roman law.

Even as the witch-hunts proceeded, scientific workers and commentators, loyal to the ancient traditions of natural science, made their own contributions to theories of insanity and possession, sometimes with the added motive of defending one religious orthodoxy against challenges from another. In the earlier era the birth of Christianity added a powerful motive to debates about the causes of human behavior, as the Church Fathers and apologists of the new religion labored to defeat its intellectual and cultural competitors. Of the latter, the most formidable included both Platonists and Stoics, Epicureans and Aristotelians, all providing useful arguments with which Rome's leaders might wage bloodless war against the Christians. In the third century, as Emperor Julian worked to eradicate Christian sects, partly by appeals to the more venerable religions of Rome and Egypt, Origen wrote his *Contra Celsum* to expose the weaknesses and pitfalls of these very religions. It is helpful to pause over this work briefly, for it was authoritative for many centuries and was regarded as foundational by Renaissance scholars (for example, Ficino) trying to reconcile the claims of religion with an emerging, though still hopelessly defective, scientific outlook.

The precise identity of Celsus remains elusive, though the work that elicited Origen's *Contra Celsum* can be dated with some confidence as being completed a half-century earlier, between A.D. 177 and 180.[32] It is thanks to Origen's many and lengthy quotations that Celsus' work can be reconstructed, if only incompletely. Undoubtedly, though, Celsus' aim was to challenge the basic tenets of Christianity by showing them to be lapsed and distorted versions of older religious teachings, bequeathed by the Egyptians and later corrupted by the Jews. As a result of the corruptions, the new sectarians now insist on a dangerous and even treasonous separation of religion and government, while promoting practices and beliefs appealing only to the most ignorant and superstitious classes in the empire—those who are the natural prey of charlatans who employ "magic and sorcery and invoke certain daemons with barbarous names . . . (to) bamboozle people."[33] Forcing an issue that will require the Church to reaffirm God's omnipotence, Celsus accuses the Christians of blasphemy in their witchery and exorcisms: "They make a being opposed to God; devil, and in the Hebrew tongue, Satanas are the names which they give to this same being. At all events, these notions are entirely of mortal origin, and it is blasphemy to say that when the greatest God indeed wishes to confer some benefit upon men, He has a power which is opposed to Him, and so is unable to do it."[34] He goes on to compare the power of the ancient gods and demons to punish blasphemies with the failure of the Christians' Son of God, "who lived a most infamous life and died a most miserable death," even to defend Himself.[35]

The Egyptian beliefs and customs revered by Celsus were revived again by the Hermeticists of the Renaissance as well as by some of the most accomplished neo-Platonists of Florence, not to mention the nobility and educated classes of *quattrocento* Italy.[36] The figure and legend of Hermes Trismegistus lurked in the shadows or actually moved to the forefront of Renaissance science, even in its greatest achievements. In his *De revolutionibus orbium caelestium,* for example, Copernicus stops to acknowledge the perfect connection between the location and the function of the sun, and how ancient wisdom has long respected this fact: *"In medio vero omnium residet sol. Quis enim in hoc pulcherrimo templo lampadem hanc in alio vel meliori loco poneret, quam unde totum simul possit illuminare?"* (The sun sits in the center of everything. What other or better place within this most beautiful temple to put this torch than where it can illuminate the whole?) Then, after noting how informed persons take note of this by the names they give to the sun, he concludes, *Trimegistus* (sic) *visibilem deum.*[37] (Hermes Trismegistus calls it the visible god.)

Copernicus at least liberated his mathematics from Hermeticism, even if ancient mystical elements still guided his overall perspective on astronomy. Giordano Bruno, however, an ardent defender of the heliocentric theory, would show, in the words of Frances Yates, "most strikingly how shifting and uncertain were the borders between genuine science and Hermeticism in the Renaissance."[38] Bruno was sympathetic to Hermeticism specifically and, more generally, to the proposition that the "oriental" wisdom of the Nile valley was purer and more powerful than all the systems it spawned. For him the march of ideas resulted in successive dilutions and corruptions. The movement toward truth should proceed from Aristotle back to Plato, to Socrates, to Pythagoras, to Aglaophemus, to Orpheus, and ultimately to that great priest and prophet, Hermes Trismegistus, three times great.

The Renaissance did not make a sharp distinction between natural science and natural magic, for it did not have a developed conception of the former. What is instructive in the writings of the greats and the near greats of this period are just those "shifting and uncertain borders" cited by Yates. The scholar Pico della Mirandola was threatened for possible heresies in his *Conclusiones* and *Apologia* by one Pope (Innocent VIII) and warmly welcomed by his successor (Alexander VI), all within a matter of a decade. Within this span (1486–1495) one can see the borders shifting again in favor of the *magia naturalis* of Hermeticism. The greater the tolerance of the Church toward the view that natural magic is both compatible with and useful to the teachings of the Church, the greater will be a movement toward explications based on natural phenomena, and the greater will be the freedom to manipulate and transform such phenomena in ways no less "magical" for all their "naturalness."

In 1466 the faculty of the University of Paris was deputized by the King to determine whether a collection of magic books was "consonant with the Christian faith." The judgment went against the books owing to their inclusion of "many superstitions, many manifest and horrible conjurations and invocations of demons."[39] Two years earlier, on orders from Cosimo d'Medici, his patron, Marsilio Ficino, completed his translation of the *Corpus hermeticum,* a work laced with superstitions, conjurations, and respect for the work of demons. Indeed, in *Asclepius III* of the *Corpus,* Trismegistus tells Asclepius that man is not merely rational but has the marvelous ability to create divine nature—to make gods; *"homo divinam potuit invenire naturam."*[40] The ancestors of Trismegistus, though unable to make immortal souls, did discover how to fashion divinities by invoking the souls of demons and placing these within created and otherwise lifeless statues. The original Asclepius is one of these, godlike in his powers of healing. And why would such gods or demons or angels take up residence among human beings? "They are induced, Asclepius, by means of herbs and stones and scents which have in them something divine. . . . These things are done to the end that, gladdened by oft-repeated worship, the heavenly beings who have been enticed into the images may continue through long ages to acquiesce in the companionship of men. Thus it is that man makes gods."[41]

The famous translator of this work would write in a separate work that man, too, is something of a god; one who rules over animals, who provides for both the living and the lifeless, who instructs others. "It is also obvious that he is the god of the elements, for he inhabits and cultivates all of them. Finally, he is the god of all materials, for he handles, changes, and shapes all of them. He who governs the *body* in so many and so important ways, and is the vicar of the immortal God, he is no doubt immortal."[42]

Ficino distinguished between two kinds of magic: one practiced by those who merge with demons through religious rituals, and the noble sort practiced "by those who seasonably subject natural materials to natural causes."[43] Even among these there are mere inquisitive types who show off with ostentatious tricks. But there is also the necessary form of natural magic joining medicine with astrology, which is as compatible with Scripture as is essential to the development of knowledge.

Amidst these shifts and uncertainties, leaders of thought in the sixteenth and seventeenth centuries still had to reconcile the un-equivocally pagan nature of cabalistic and hermetic teaching to the strictures and orthodoxies of a Christian world. In matters of the mind, the reconciliation took the form of a reassuring if philo-sophically awkward dualism. Like the natural gods of the *Corpus hermeticum,* man is at once fire and clay, spirit and matter. The immortal soul cannot be made, but through the proper rites and the use of the essential herbs, scents, and stones, it may be invited to stay longer as a good companion. Writing to his friend in 1544 about the morbid illness of the Marchesa di Pescara, Girolamo Fra-castoro recognizes that the subtle union between mind and body cannot endure the tyranny of either: "I should wish for a physician of the mind to be found, who should minutely calculate and justly balance all the Marchesa's actions, giving to the master what is his and to the servant what belongs to him. And this physician must be wise and of so much authority that her Ladyship would believe and obey him, like the most illustrious and most reverend Cardinal of England."[44]

Actually, the physicians of the mind had already begun to appear, some in the fearsome garb of inquisitor and witch-pricker, others in the long gowns of cabalistic shaman and magus, still others in the stained and singed tunics of the herbalist, alchemist, the hermeticist; a few in the modest role of the diligent doctor, willing to admit ignorance and eager to enlarge his knowledge through the study of actual patients. The excesses perpetrated by the first of these were condemned by the rest. Reformation and Counter-Reformation spawned volumes of martyrologies, each side declaring itself the true and persecuted Christian Church. It is likely that one of the unintended benefits of this literature was a mounting aversion to the reasoning and the methods by which martyrs are produced in the first place. Superstition itself, along with its dogmatic foundations, gradually lost the support of even the less educated as it had never fully won over the most enlightened.

Pico's nephew, Giovanni Francesco, would speak for a new generation of forward rather than backward-looking thinkers when he condemned those credulous scholars in the thrall of Egyptian astrology and Orphic mysteries. His wide readership included that most forward looking physician, John Weyer, whose *De praestigiis daemonum et incantationibus ac veneficiis* saw six editions between 1563 and 1583. By this date, such defenders of orthodoxy as Peter Binsfeld, Bishop of Trèves, declared that only "a few medical men, advocates of the devil's kingdom" deny that witches have intercourse with the devil or fly in formation to their rendezvous, but the camel's nose was already in the tent. In France the Huguenots insisted that Catholic exorcisms were an out-and-out fraud and rallied medical facts to support the charge. Increasingly, village credulity came to yield to the urbanity of a changing world.[45]

Even Weyer, however, occupies a position of characteristic uncertainty and wandering perspective. He never denied the reality of satan, nor did he rule out the participation of demons in mental illness. Rather, he considered the weakened mind of the aged and the psychologically distressed to be something of a devil's workshop wherein all varieties of illusion may be crafted. Some things were facts of nature. Of course women tend to float, given their lighter constitution, a fact known since the time of Hippocrates and lacking any and all spiritual implications. He observed that drugs such as belladonna, opium, henbane, and tobacco enhanced the effects of illusion and could produce them in their own right. Again, forms of mental disorder did not require the participation of occult forces or beings. The poor souls who regard themselves as possessed and admit to being witches are, he reasoned, generally suffering from melancholia. They need the attention of a physician, not an inquisitor.

Inevitably, the Catholic Church put Weyer's name on the *Index;* meanwhile, his book was burned by the Protestant faculty of Marburg. At about the same time, the progressive Queen Elizabeth enacted in the twenty-eighth year of her reign a law against witchcraft and sorcery, threatening death to those who cause a death by "witchcraft, enchauntment, charme or sorcerie . . . invocations or conjurations."[46] Here then was more shifting, more uncertainty, but the center of gravity was moving discernibly in the direction of science and medicine.

The law, too, which recovered its Roman roots in the later Middle Ages, had been gradually catching up with older understandings as it undertook to establish *mens rea* in doubtful cases. Contrasted with the severities of earlier centuries, the legal treatment of children charged with criminal offenses was relatively benign by the time of Edward I, the *ad gratiam* remand being replaced by direct acquittal. Comparable leniency was displayed in trials of those judged *furiosus* or mentally defective. By the thirteenth century there was little enthusiasm for executing the insane, no matter how grave the offense,[47] and by the fourteenth century the care and treatment of the insane had become an accepted duty within a number of municipalities.[48] As early as the reign of Henry III, the patent rolls of England recorded any number of acquittals on the grounds of *furiosus* or *amentia* or *fatuitas.*[49] Thus "Richard of Brent, son of Adam Thurbern, accused of larceny, comes and defends all of it and puts himself upon the country. And the twelve jurors and the townships of Brent, South Brent, Limpsham, and Burnham say that they do not suspect him, save of a fowl which he took in his madness at a time when he was lunatic. Therefore let him be under pledges until more be known."[50]

By the middle of the thirteenth century Bracton could summarize the law's understanding with his customary succinctness as he addressed the very nature of justice: "Remove will and every act will be indifferent. It is your intent that differentiates your acts, nor is a crime committed unless an intention to injure exists; it is will and purpose which distinguish *maleficia*."[51] Applying this reasoning to commercial transactions, and citing the *Institutes* (3.19.8–10) as authoritative, he concludes that a *furiosus* cannot legally participate in any transaction, nor can infants who, after all, are not much different from the insane *(qui multum a furioso non distat)*.[52]

These early developments moved only gradually and haltingly. They were of no benefit to the victims of the witch panics between 1400 and 1700, chiefly because the principle of the *crimen exceptum* remained official even as progress in medicine and in law worked to the advantage of those judged insane. Nonetheless, the medical perspective on insanity grew in prominence during these very centuries, and juridical reasoning progressively conformed to it, even when the most obviously disturbed defendants failed to win clemency.

The trial of Hacket, Coppinger, and Arthington (1592) is illustrative. The three were charged with conspiracy, Hacket having declared himself King of Europe and that "the Queenes Majestie had fortfaited her Crowne." In reporting the details of the case, Richard Cosin set down the grounds of an insanity defense as English courts understood it at the end of the sixteenth century.[53] The principal categories affirmed by "the best writers" on the subject were *Furor sive Rabies, Dementia sive Amentia, Insania sive Phrenesis,*

Fatuitas, Stultia, Lethargia, & Delerium. The condition of *furor,* as Cosin discussed it, is that of the venerable *furiosus,* whose mind suffers "full blindness or darkening of the understanding," the actor knowing not at all what he is doing or saying. *Dementia (mente captus)* is an unremitting insanity, distinguished from *insania* in its severity. With *insania* the sufferer, though "braine-sicke, cracked-witted . . . or hare-brained" is still fit for social life and is not entirely void of understanding. *Fatuitas* is the condition of the "natural fooles," though with *stultia* the victim is not included among the *idiotes.*

When Cosin turns to the question of the defendants' guilt or innocence, he acknowledges that their plans and reasoning were "fantasticall, unadvised, & most fond and unlikely," but in this they share the defects of "all such fanatical fantastiques, schismatiques, heretiques, or malecontented treasonable conspirators whatsoever." Thus, although Cosin's taxonomy is clearly informed by medical knowledge and the opinions of "the best writers," the courts still hold all perpetrators responsible who are not totally mad. The three defendants in this case revealed their purposes. In the very framing of purposes and undertaking to realize them, Hacket and the others displayed sanity enough. Note, too, Cosin's merging treason with heresy and fanaticism. All such conditions are "fantasticall" and unadvised, but punishable nonetheless. Accordingly, the progress of medical opinion within the jural domain could not yet work to the advantage of the accused witches.

The law would continue to avail itself of muted forms of the witch theory throughout the reign of James I, whose own shifting convictions about demonology have been discussed. As the King's Solicitor, Francis Bacon must make clear to jurists in lower courts how the law pertaining to witchcraft is to be understood: "For witchcraft, by the former law it was not death, except it were actual and gross invocation of evil spirits, or making covenant with them, or taking away life by witchcraft: but now, by an act of his majesty's times, charms and sorceries in certain cases of procuring unlawful love or bodily hurt, and some others, are made felony the second offense; the first being imprisonment and pillory."[54]

It is not to be assumed that Bacon was simply doing his job, believing all the time that the theory behind the law was groundless superstition. A man of his time, Francis Bacon looked to science as the court of ultimate appeal on matters of fact, but accepted at least some of the Renaissance natural magic. His *Sylva sylvarum or A Natural History* was published in 1627, the year after his death, and contains many hundreds of scientific conjectures and proposals for experimental research. The powers of witches are discussed in connection with Bacon's theories about imagination. He does not deny that some people may have the ability to control the imagination of others, by means of their suggestibility. He reasons, however, that such influences, when they seem to be remote, probably have corporeal and personal intermediaries, the influence operating from one person to the next, *seriatim*.[55] As for the well-known influence of the moon on mental life, here again the causes are probably natural, the lunar phases being able to alter the moisture of the brain through tidal forces.[56]

He then goes on to devote many pages to the natural causes of mental illness, including astrological forces (which *incline* but do not *compel*), aging, heredity, diet, blood chemistry, habit, social life, discontent, cares, anger, jealousy, and the compelling power of imagination and credulity. Charms and spells, no less than salves applied to offending weapons or the superstitious ministrations of "mountebanks and wizards" all effect cures, and the reason is not hard to find. It is the patient's confidence in the healer; the confidence "which Avicenna *prefers before art, precepts, and all remedies whatsoever. . . .* Why does one man's yawning make another yawn if not by the power of suggestion?"[57]

Bacon's position on such matters exemplifies the most influential thinking of the Jacobean period. By this time, and for all of its enormity, the long season of the witch-hunt had become as a parallel but self-contained activity which, at least by the seventeenth century, followed a set of understandings ever less defensible or even intelligible within the emerging scientific context. Early in the sixteenth century Paracelsus (1493–1541) wrote his brief treatise *On Diseases That Deprive Man of Health and Reason,* noting in the preface that the European clergy attribute these diseases to "ghostly beings," whereas "nature is the sole origin" of them.[58] In this work he would oppose the Galenic theory, adding a medical theory of his own but, with all this, still reserving a category, the *obsessi,* to the devil's handiwork. On the account developed by Paracelsus, the loss of reason reveals itself in four principal forms. The *lunatici* get the disease from the moon and react to its phases; the *insani* are born with the malady, insanity being part of the family heritage; the *vesani* suffer from toxic reactions to food, drink or poison; the *melancholici* become insane, losing reason in the course of a lifetime. Any number of natural diseases can have insanity as a residual or corollary. With the *obsessi* the remote causes are not natural, but there are natural mechanisms involved nonetheless. For Paracelsus, the composition of man creates wider latitude for pathological processes. The clay God used—the *limus terrae*—has cosmic components which confer something of the heavenly on the human form. Accordingly, "there are two kinds of disease in all men: one material and one spiritual. . . . Against material diseases material remedies should be applied; against spiritual diseases, spiritual remedies."[59] Remedies work by opposing the offending agent. Once it is discovered, for example, that a person has been taken ill by eating a cat's brain, the remedy to be applied should be that herb which is known to kill cats. But if the malady resides in the *spiritus vitae*— as, for example, when bewitched potions have been consumed— these natural measures will be of no avail.[60]

It was some forty years later that Johann Weyer published his *De praestigiis daemonum* (1563), a foundational work in psychiatry.[61]

Like Paracelsus—whose "worthless opinions" he is at pains to refute[62]—Weyer attempted to explain in a scientific way the black and white magic of mentally troubled persons. His own medical education had exposed him to the teaching of such pioneering figures as John Fernel and Jacques DuBois, the latter the "Sylvius" of the brain's *duct of Sylvius*. He was probably personally acquainted with Andreas Vesalius, and fully sympathetic with the progressive scientific thinking of this leading age of anatomical and physiological research. Still, he is a man living on the edge of two worlds. The intellectual master of his student days, Cornelius Agrippa, who had written tempestuously against the self-serving and superstitious excesses of the witch-hunter, had also lectured lengthily and admiringly on Hermes Trismegistus. Weyer, though moving calmly away from Agrippa's Hermeticism, nonetheless accepts that the devil does indeed tamper with the affairs of the world, but can do so without the aid of mortals; that those owning up to witchcraft must simply be deluded (by the devil) into thinking themselves responsible.

It was Weyer's perceptive thesis that the symptoms often mistaken as signs of witchery were but those of melancholy to which older women were especially susceptible. Again, he does not deny satanic influences in the world; only that these are routinely expressed through complicity with human beings. Sensitive to the legal implications of his thesis, he explicitly denies that the "insanity" defense should be available to those whose sorcery actually harms others, but insists that those who seek to execute harmless witches *(lamiae)*, "deluded by the demon, their imagination impaired, harmful to none," merely "thirst[s] for innocent blood." It is outrageous to punish these deluded persons and absurd to consider them the causes of such events as no one can bring about, given "the structure of the universe and the condition of the elements."[63] It ought to be that "nothing is legally possible if it is naturally impossible."[64]

By the turn of the century this naturalistic perspective had made even greater progress. As a result, the courts would begin to consult physicians directly in ambiguous cases. When Elizabeth Jackson was tried in 1602 for bewitching Mary Glover, doctors testified in her behalf that the victim's fits were caused naturally. Justice Anderson, a firm believer in witchcraft, was unmoved by their testimony, insisting that, "Divines, Phisitions, I know they are learned and wise, but to say this is naturall, and tell me neither the cause, nor the cure of it, I care not for your judgment: give me a naturall reason and a naturall remedy, or a rash for your Phisicke."[65] Nonetheless, they were heard, were accorded the attention reserved for those, like "divines," judged to have relevant and expert knowledge. Nor were the doctors and the divines all that different in their perspectives at this time of transition. Weyer's tolerance of the witch theory has already been noted. As for Dr. Edward Jorden's famous arguments favoring a medical understanding of cases such as Mary Glover's, it should be noted that Judge Anderson was not so much hostile to the notion of medical proof as he was quite correctly aware of its absence in the instant case.[66]

In the early decades of the seventeenth century this conflation of unnatural magic, natural magic, and natural science would be common even among the more forward looking leaders of thought. The merging of the secular and the theological would lead ultimately to the reliance on pseudoscientific methods of proof and discovery as the Inquisition took on its most deplorable features. Thus experts were retained to locate the "devil's mark" on the body of the suspect, usually a woman, now with her body shaved as specialists probed meticulously in search of the telltale region of insensitivity. James I of England was of two minds on the subject of demonology and possession. Though his enthusiasms later cooled, his first forays into the subject were intense and enthusiastic. In his widely read and influential *Daemonologie* he supplied his readers with the best thinking of the day, going so far as to outline the technical methods useful in the detection of witches, methods which had not changed in the century since the best selling *Malleus:*

> Judges ought to beware to condemn any but such as they are sure are guilty. . . . (T)here are two other good helps that may be used for their trial: the one is the finding of their mark, and the trying the insensibleness thereof. The other is their floating on the water: for as in a secret murder, if the dead carcass be at any time thereafter handled by the murderer, it will gush out blood, as if the blood were crying to heaven for revenge of the murderer, God having appointed that secret supernatural sign . . . so it appears that God hath appointed (for the supernatural sign of the monstrous impiety of the witches) that the water shall refuse to rescue them in her bosom, that have shaken off them the sacred water of Baptism, and wilfully refused the benefit thereof. No not so much as their eyes are able to shed tears (threaten and torture them as you please) while first they repent. . . . (A)lbeit the women-kind especially be able otherwise to shed tears at every light occasion when they will, yea, although it were dissemblingly like the *Crocodiles.*[67]

King James himself would conduct tests on the alleged witch or victim of possession, proudly displaying his prowess in unearthing frauds. In time he would more or less disabuse himself of the witch theory and the law would place even greater stress on the need for the soundest judicial procedures in such cases. James's own warning to judges illustrates his continuing commitment to principles of legal procedure and what must be assumed to be a sincere desire to see justice done. The nature of the commitment varied from region to region, however.

In her careful examination of trials for witchcraft in Venice between 1550 and 1650, Ruth Martin has reviewed hundreds of trials, noting the care inquisitorial courts took to preserve settled procedures. Those charged with the offense were provided with canon lawyers to assist in the defense, and time to draw up said defense. Generally, the approach was to establish malice on the part of accusers. But, with all this, "in no case of witchcraft did the presentation of a defense prove a defendant's innocence." And, as she also observes in the matter of these trials, the chief problem faced by Venetian tribunals was distinguishing between illnesses allegedly caused by witches and those that were naturally occurring. Accordingly, in lining up witnesses, "Priests . . . were frequently called . . . as were the doctors who had been treating the sick."[68] In Tudor and Stuart England the same function was served by "cunning folk," the witch-finder, the witch-doctor; specialists whose numbers and methods are illuminatingly discussed by Alan Macfarlane. Their expertise may not have been uniformly acknowledged but, as Macfarlane observes, "Even legal authorities wavered. Although cunning folk could be prosecuted at both ecclesiastical and secular courts, yet their accusation was a 'great presumption' in the case against a black witch."[69]

King James's warning to judges is also redolent of the concerns of ancient jurists to spare the innocent by fairly weighing evidence systematically gathered and heard with judicial disinterest. The same ancient courts had permitted the use of torture in cases of treason or comparable *infamia* (for example, adultery and incest), or in determining whether a slave's accusations against his master were valid. Now, the secular courts of Europe, accepting witchcraft as treason against God and as the ultimate disgrace, resorted to the same measures in meeting this new emergency. Witchcraft was not the only *crimen exceptum,* of course. Torture was also permitted in trials for parricide, rape, counterfeit, uxoricide, and murder. But the focus of methods of torture on the witch was special and sustained. Henry Charles Lea was among the first to consider the justification of torture in the witch trials as the secularization of the reasoning behind the ordeal. The latter rested on the assumption that divine intervention would rescue the innocent; the former assumes that a voluntary agent will endure just so much before admitting to guilt, and that by this admission will again enjoy the prospect of salvation.[70] How different thinking was by 1628, when Robert Burton's *The Anatomy of Melancholy* could offer nearly a thousand citations of writers, doctors, and theorists, ancient and contemporary, who had contributed to what Burton now took to be the soundest position on the whole range of mental disorders.[71] Traces of the venerable superstitions can be found—Ficino and Hermeticism are respectfully considered. But the work in its totality is a veritable textbook of early scientific psychiatry, written by a man who playfully takes "Democritus Junior" as a pseudonym and skepticism as a working hypothesis. The authorities for his work were many, stretching back to ancient times but also appearing in numbers from the late fifteenth century to Burton's own time.[72] For Burton, the evidence was complete enough for an objective scholar to declare that diseases of the mind "have their chief seat and organs in the head," and that the diseases arising from the brain proper include "*phrenzy, lethargy, melancholy, madness, weak memory, sleeping-sickness,* or *insomnia.*"[73] Those especially prone to madness and melancholia include both sexes, men more frequently but women more violently; people born under the moon, Saturn, or Mercury; people with little heads, hot hearts, cold stomachs, moist brains, and melancholy parents.[74] God, of course, can cause any malady, directly or indirectly through angels and devils. Burton gives the devils their due, granting witches their traditional powers (though chiefly by deluding their victims and even themselves). In these respects, his aetiology of madness is drawn from the received wisdom of his time. But his diffidence and even impatience in the face of preternatural theories can be taken as harbingers:

> How far the power of Spirits and Devils doth extend, and whether they can cause this or any other disease, is a serious

question . . . [but] *the finite cannot deal with the infinite;* we can sooner determine with Tully what they are not than what they are; our subtle Schoolmen, Cardans, Scaligers, profound Thomists, Francastorian & Fernelian geniuses are weak, dry, obscure, defective in these mysteries, and all our quickest wits, as an owl's eyes at the sun's light, wax dull.[75]

The European witch-hunts and trials mark an important chapter in the long history of conceptions of insanity and the principles that guide the adjudication of cases involving individuals judged to be disturbed. They demonstrate in a vivid and macabre fashion the effect that coherent but untested theories of human nature can have on a juridical perspective made receptive to such theories. Political developments in the Middle Ages led to the functional integration of secular and ecclesiastical courts; to a sharing of their respective duties to the faith. The appearance and progress of heretical movements inspired predictable defensive reactions on the part of the Church. One of these was to assign even relatively harmless forms of occultism to the category of that most serious offense, heresy.

The rationale was straightforward: to the extent that magic in any form requires the suspension or manipulation of the laws of nature ordained by the Creator, only superhuman agencies can achieve it. These are either of God or against Him. Participants are not merely chosen by the evil one, but summon him and enter into a pact with him. Such deranged behavior as might result is but the consequence of this pact and not a mitigating factor at law. With satan himself identified as the adversary, the courts of the late Middle Ages and Renaissance, now equipped with inquisitorial procedures and powers, regarded conventional adjudicative measures to be insufficient. The use of torture, the refusal to disclose the names of accusers, the special burdens undertaken by now especially vulnerable advocates, and the highly specialized tests developed to obtain evidence all come about as a result of the very terms of the witch theory. That society's most vulnerable citizens, especially women, would bear the heaviest burdens of injustice was inevitable, as was the chilling effect on conduct and discourse in general.

For the general populace, who may have thought little about theories of the *pactum implicitum,* the possibilities afforded by the witch laws were of more immediate interest. Note that some of the more complete records of the American trials at and around Salem leave little doubt but that economic interests were among the many sources of motivation. One sure way of settling property or inheritance disputes is to dispose of one party to the dispute by charging witchcraft. Indeed, once the more vulnerable members of society began to accuse some of the most influential members of being the source of their vexations, elite society's attachment to the witch theory began first its gradual and then its steep decline.[76] Reinforcing the witch-hunt atmosphere were the demographic upheavals which brought rustic and urban populations together suddenly and without preparation, leading to tensions and conflicts that could only nurture xenophobic tendencies.[77]

All this duly acknowledged, it remains the case that the witch trials altered legal proceedings in ways that would prove to be abiding even as the concept of witchcraft was first challenged, then ridiculed, and at last defeated. Ancient courts, we saw, were not given to close inspection of inner motives and hidden passions of defendants. This diffidence is certainly not attributable to a general cultural disinterest in such matters, for there has scarcely been a deeper "psychological" literature than that produced by the dramatists of the classical age. As jurists, however, the ancients were content to discover *mens rea* in the act itself; in the planning, rationale, consequences, and overall organization of the events culminating in the offense. Christianity would add to such considerations an insistent probing into the conscience, the deep-seated desires of the actor, the sin in the heart. Under this influence, the courts were less inclined to take actions at face value. Heresies were less a species of conduct than of belief.

In each developmental stage the witch theory and its legal consequences built upon older practices and precedents. As early as the period of the Proconsuls of Rome it was common for parties to be dispatched to remote jurisdictions to determine whether a crime had occurred, and in the reign of Charlemagne the Missi Dominici had a similar "grand jury" or inquisitorial function, though they were constrained by the secular laws of the empire. In Anglo-Saxon law comparable bodies were established with powers of inquisition and sentencing. Indeed, inquisition as a procedure was deeply rooted in the oldest legal traditions. But the rise of Christianity as a political force added a new tension, a new competitive relationship between the secular and clerical worlds that required frequent adjustments in the balance of power. Thus to secure the needed papal coronation, Frederic II (1220) will cede to the Church full powers in the prosecution of heretics, powers thereupon entrusted to the Dominicans in 1233 by Pope Gregory. With the death of Frederic II (1250)—a formidable challenger of papal hegemony— it becomes possible for Innocent IV to issue his *Ad extirpanda* (1252) by which heretics can be dealt with anywhere and everywhere, their possessions seized and their standing determined by ecclesiastical modes of adjudication. By 1265, this policy is established as canon law under Urban IV, the inquisition now "supreme in all lands." Laws conflicting with *Ad extirpanda* are simply null and void.[78] Now the harmless "white magic" often overlooked under the rule of Charlemagne comes to be recognized as betokening dangerous beliefs, a threat to the faith, and it is adjudicated accordingly.

The category of experts gradually developed to assist magistrates would long outlive the theories that brought the concept of expertise into being. Even as this category came to include medically trained persons, the overarching theory under which their investigations proceeded could only turn their testimony into something of a travesty, conferring on such "experts" both an authority and a burden secular jurisprudence had not anticipated. Indeed, where the courts did turn to doctors for guidance, the medicine of the period was itself generally a mixture of science and superstition, and the wider population that would be instructed by such trials was indifferent to the subtle distinctions that might be made between natural and unnatural causes. In his study of Tudor religion and society, John A. F. Thomson wisely cautions "academics" against "seeing the majority of the faithful in their own image, as being concerned with nuances of doctrine." He makes clear, too, how the medicine of the Tudor period was closely bound up with folk-medicine of early and even earliest epochs.[79] The invitation to experts, then, established yet another precedent: that of taking professional credentials or titles as indicative of scientific knowledge in areas in which science itself has played no part. And so, centuries hence, when the lingering vestiges of the *pactum implicitum* were finally expunged, the courts would reserve a place for still other specialists presumed to have access to the dark mysteries of mind and spirit.

4

WILD BEASTS & IDLE HUMOURS

Cramp-rings, made from the King's silver and gold and blessed by him, were passed around as gifts among all the right people in Renaissance England. Anne Boleyn and Thomas Linacre, to mention just two, soberly distributed them to friends and acquaintances as a means of preventing or treating epileptic seizures, convulsions, rheumatism, and other ailments. Henry VIII faithfully performed his regal duties, believing the rings he blessed had "the special gift of curation ministered to the king of this realm."[1] Legend dates the practice from the time of Edward the Confessor, who gave his own ring to a strange beggar. The recipient turned up years later in the Holy Land, where he identified himself as John the Evangelist, and sent the ring back to Edward with the promise of healing powers. But science also figures in the custom of the cramp-ring, for there was already a long tradition of tying off convulsing parts of the body—"cramping" them—to confine the paroxysmal motions to the affected limb. Late in the eighteenth century and long after the last vestiges of mythology would appear officially in medical treatises, the eminent William Cullen at Edinburgh offers the following approach to the management of "maniacs" in his standard textbook: "restraint is also to be considered a remedy. Angry passions are always rendered more violent by the indulgence of the tempestuous motions they produce. . . . Restraint, therefore, is useful and ought to be complete . . . and the strait waistcoat answers every purpose better than any other."[2]

Juridical thought and legal procedure do not take place in isolation from the larger cultural context. Science, mythology, and religion have often reached common ground, as well as grounds of fierce competition, in the presence of diseases and disorders of mind and spirit, as various ages come to regard these. During the centuries of the witch panics, any number of allegedly scientific propositions were developed and defended in conjunction with and in service to theological dogmas. The consequences were inevitable once the secular courts assumed responsibility for protecting the faith. As these courts found the rationale for the suspension of customary trial procedures, pseudo-scientific texts were prepared to assist and inform inquisitors on points of evidence. It became a matter of urgency to identify the phenomena that were explicable in scientific terms and those that seemed to depart from the laws and the processes of nature.

All of this was taking place before the intellectual communities of the West had achieved what is now taken to be the modern scientific perspective. But even before the triumph of this perspective, the court of common opinion had begun to turn away from the teachings upon which theories of possession and witchcraft depended. Part of the turning away was itself connected with broad movements of religious reform. As Keith Thomas has observed, the century of Protestant teaching preceding *Leviathan* would fortify Hobbes in his conviction that the Roman Church had turned "consecration into conjuration." By 1645 even common prayer would be condemned, an Anabaptist in Essex declaring that "none but witches and sorcerers used to say the Lord's Prayer." It was not rare for commoners to feed holy bread to their dogs. According to Thomas, "the decline of old Catholic beliefs was not the result of persecution; it reflected a change in the popular conception of religion."[3] Hence the scientific perspective evolved not only from within science but also as a reaction against the dogmatic certitudes of theology and the grim practices they spawned. But the evolution would be gradual, even when driven by such monumental figures as Copernicus, Newton, and Galileo. Moreover, as the scientific mode of thought swept across Europe and illuminated every corner of the natural world, the phenomena of the human mind remained ever refractory to the new methods and perspective. The leaders of the new thought were nonetheless committed to a unity of sciences, resolute in the conviction that a Newtonian psychology was no less possible than the Newtonian astronomy already in hand. As in preceding centuries, powerful constituencies urged this increasingly official view on jurists and legislators. The reformed conception of human nature now called for legal and political reforms compatible with what was taken to be an improved understanding of mental life. This chapter examines the growth of this conception, and the effects of the new psychology on the laws pertaining to insanity.

Burton's masterpiece, *The Anatomy of Melancholy,* appeared in the same year as Sir Edward Coke's *The First Part of the Institutes of the Laws of England* (1628), a treatise that would be authoritative on various points of law for the better part of two centuries.[4] The work of a writer who would come to be regarded as England's greatest common lawyer, the *Institutes* presents a somewhat unstudied but naturalistic perspective on insanity wherever Coke addresses the matter. The perspective is an older Roman one, not at all remote from Coke's own. There is no merging of *heretiques* with *lunatiques* as was Cosin's wont. Rather, Coke's treatise moves the law toward secular understandings of all such matters, but more by the weight of past traditions than the light of the new science. According to the laws of England, he writes, "A man of non-sane memory may, without the consent of any other, purchase lands, but he himself cannot waive it; but if he die in his madnesse, or after his memory recover, without agreement thereunto, his heire may waive and disagree to the state, without any cause shewed; and so of an ideot. But if the man of non-sane memory recover his memory, and agree unto it, it is unavoydable."

Coke, following Littleton, goes on to record the legal sense of a diseased mind, and then considers the various forms of mental deficiency recognized by law:

Here *Littleton* explaineth a man of no sound memorie to be *non compos mentis.* Many times (as here it appeareth) the Latin word explaineth the true sense, and calleth him not *amens, demens, furiosus, lunaticus, fatuus, stultus,* or the like, for *non compos mentis* is the most sure and legall. . . . 1. *Ideota,* which from his nativitie, by a perpetuall infirmitie, is *non compos mentis.* 2. Hee that by sicknesse, griefe, or other accident, wholly loseth his memorie and understanding. 3. A lunatique that hath sometime his understanding and sometime not, *aliquando gaudet lucidis intervallis,* and therefore he is called *non compos mentis,* so long as he hath not understanding. Lastly, hee that by his owne vitious act for a time depriveth himself of his memorie and understanding, as he that is drunken. But that kinde of *non compos mentis* shall give no privilege or benefit to him or to his heires.[5]

Coke uses memory and understanding interchangeably in identifying the degree of psychological deficit worthy of the law's attention.[6] Although acknowledging the exculpatory nature of a temporary insanity that is interrupted by lucid intervals, he requires of insanity itself what is essentially the total loss of cognitive prowess.[7] This can come about through the misfortunes of life (sickness and grief) or be present from birth. The causes alluded to are all natural. The phrase he thinks is just right is one that describes the insane person as having *no power of mind* whatever. One might ask (as Lord Erskine would with such great effect in his defense of James Hadfield, below) whether such a person has ever existed or, in any case, could be expected to commit a crime. Coke, however, was prepared to accept the consequences of the traditional understanding; namely, that anyone successful in planning and executing a crime or entering into a contractual relationship could not be regarded as insane *for purposes of law.*

Along with his ancient sources and guides, Coke was less interested in the subtlest aspects of the interior life, reserving his attention instead for the nature and quality of the act. There is a nearly impatient tone in his recital of the forms of madness; a nearly audible relief when he settles on the one description that is "the most sure and legall," *non compos mentis.*

The next of Britain's celebrated jurists, Sir Matthew Hale, was more forward-looking than Coke and certainly more concerned to work out the subtler aspects of insanity in relation to law. Chapter 4 of his *The History of the Pleas of the Crown* (1680) is devoted entirely to this matter, and although the work was not published in Hale's lifetime, it does establish how Britain's leading jurists were coming to regard these matters by the time of Hale's death (1676).[8] Yet Hale's life and writings exemplify the divided nature of psychological thought even in this age of Newton.

Clearly, in the seventy-five years between Cosin's discussion of the trial of Hacket et al. and Hale's *History,* the scientific and naturalistic perspective had made great progress. But the private religious beliefs of men like Hale still did not wander far from the authority of Scripture. Witchcraft found no place in Hale's discussion of legal insanity, but he wrote about it both in his unpublished papers and in briefer published tracts.[9] Certain passages in Hobbes's *Leviathan* debunking belief in immaterial demons and spirits elicited Hale's strong criticism.[10] Nor did he eschew the witch theory as a judge. In 1665, two widows appeared before him indicted for witchcraft, charged with causing children to vomit nails and see animals invisible to others (6 St. Tr. 687, 1665). Among the witnesses for the prosecution no less a personage than Sir Thomas

Browne made an appearance. And, although Hale did not speak one way or another on the matter of the actual evidence adduced against the defendants, he did direct the jury to recognize the authority of Scripture as well as acts of Parliament on the matter of the existence of witches. The defendants were found guilty and executed, Hale's position on the matter proving to be influential with Cotton Mather and his Salem contemporaries.[11] But when Hale turned his attention to the law's understanding of insanity, he composed a chapter distinguished by clarity and sobriety and almost entirely unaffected by those extra-jural considerations that otherwise engaged his enthusiasms; a chapter in which the tone as much as the content had been influenced by the growing authority of medicine in this area.[12]

Hale begins with a classification of the defects and incapacities of mind other than infancy, starting with *ideocy*. Reflecting on the standards that had been set by Bracton and Fitzherbert (who took as evidence the inability to count or recognize 20 shillings, or failure to recognize one's own parents), Hale judges them to be too narrow and inconclusive. It is the jury, and sometimes the judge's own examination, that must finally establish whether this mental defect is legally mitigating.[13] Proceeding to *dementia,* Hale delineates the usual causes ("distemper of the humours," adult choler, melancholy, violent fevers and palsies, "a concussion or hurt of the brain, or its membranes or organs") and notes that these may result in either partial or total insanity. The former is not exculpatory of capital offenses, for the defendants "are not wholly destitute of the use of reason."[14]

Note that the criterion remains a total want of reason. Because of this, and because *total* insanity is exculpatory, Hale alerts readers to the importance and the difficulty of assessing the degree of damage and injury caused. The criterion of fourteen years is "the best measure" Hale can think of to guide jurors in difficult cases. Total insanity does not present a difficult case, for the defendant suffers from a complete alienation of mind that will be obvious to all. Partial insanity is difficult, for the defendant clearly is able to comprehend some things but not others. What one must ask in the latter case is whether there is sufficient rationality for the defendant to have more than a child's comprehension. Apparently, Hale would take partial insanity to be more akin to *ideocy* than to perfect madness.

Hale draws a further distinction between permanent and intermittent or episodic dementia. The fixed variety he labels *phrenesis,* the latter *lunacy,* "for the moon hath a great influence in all diseases of the brain, especially this kind."[15] In such cases, the lucid intervals come between the full and the change of the moon, at which time sufferers have "at least a competent use of reason" such that, if they commit crimes while in this state, they are "subject to the same punishment, as if they had no such deficiency."[16] Once more Hale makes clear that it is only the total loss of rational or mental power that excuses, and then only when the offense itself takes place at such a time. Those who qualify suffer the most dangerous form of dementia, identified by Hale as *furor, rabies,* and *mania,* which strips the person of reason and also adds the elements of rage and "tempestuous violence" such that the victims may no longer be reasonable creatures at all, but brutes.[17]

Hale then turns to a third variety of mental defect, after *ideocy* and the forms of *dementia accidentalis;* this is *dementia affectata*—not a true dementia but one brought on by drunkenness, poisons, and certain medicines administered by unskillful physicians. Where the defendant has been poisoned or improperly drugged by a physician and thereupon loses his understanding, he is excused as fully as one who is totally insane. But where the defendant, through drunkenness, has entered a frenzied state, he is not excused. However, the chronic drunk whose alcoholism has produced "an *habitual* or fixed phrenzy" is excused of his offenses "as if the same were contracted involuntarily from the first."[18]

Who is to make the necessary distinctions in such cases? Who can tell whether a vagrant or habitual drinker is faking a frenzied state or has actually come to suffer a diseased brain as a result of alcoholism? How is the court to decide between a severe mental disturbance (but one that spares the understanding) and a total and therefore exculpatory insanity? One might think that Hale, so willing to consider lunar effects on the nervous system, humoral disturbances, and the like, will answer these questions by turning them over to medical experts. Not so, for "the law of *England* hath afforded the best method of trial, that is possible, of this and all other matters of fact, namely by a jury of twelve men all concurring in the same judgment, by the testimony of witnesses *viva voce* in the presence of judge and jury, and by the inspection and direction of the judge."[19] Twelve men of good sense, exercising their natural reason and concurring in the same judgment, cannot be improved on in an attempt to settle such issues.

Hale offers a 1668 case from Aylebury to illustrate just how a jury is to arrive at sound verdicts in this general area. A married woman gave birth to a child and, after many sleepless nights, "fell into a temporary phrenzy, and kill'd her infant in the absence of any company." She was thereupon indicted for murder. The jury was instructed to find her guilty if, at the time of the killing, the defendant "had any use of reason." They were to consider specific factors that might have supplied motive; that, for instance, the child was not by her husband; or she had attempted to hide the infant and deny her pregnancy; or that she was moved to feign insanity. The defendant in the Aylebury case passed these tests and was pronounced not guilty, "to the satisfaction of all that heard it."[20] Hale was satisfied that jurors of good sense and normal perception could weigh evidence in this sort of case as well as in myriad other actions of a civil or criminal nature. The very jury system assumes as much, and Hale was not persuaded that real or alleged dementia called for any other mode of adjudication. In all cases, the presumption of law is that of sanity, the converse having to be proved both in civil and in criminal cases. And if it is further established that the defendant, though insane, enjoys lucid intervals, the law again adopts the presumption of sanity, the burden once more falling to the accused to prove that the act in question did not occur during the lucid interval.[21]

Where Hale cites the authority of Coke on the grave crime of high treason, it is to underscore the degree of deficit that will excuse the defendant. It must be such as to leave the defendant *"totally deprived of all compassings and imaginations . . . an absolute madness, and a total deprivation of memory."*[22] It is a madness that prevented the defendant from acting, *per electionem* or *intentionem*.[23] But what should be done with one convicted of treason who turns insane before the scheduled execution? In the time of Henry VIII such a one was executed nonetheless.[24] But this law was repealed by Hale's time on the grounds that the now insane convict is no longer able to participate in procedures that might result in a stay of execution or an appeal.

What stands out in Hale's *History* is that, by the end of the seventeenth century, British courts had done much to demystify insanity. They provided procedural safeguards for those judged to have been insane at the time of their offenses or to have become insane thereafter. The safeguards were in place even for perpetrators of that most wicked of crimes, treason. But, neither Hale nor his contemporaries found it necessary to include provision for medical specialists to inform or otherwise guide jurors, and this warrants comment.

Taking out the pardonably dated references to lunar influences, Hale's brief summary of the chief causes of dementia is not only informed by the science of his day but compatible with what might even be called the modern view. He understands the several forms of dementia to be the result of a diseased brain, biochemical (humoral) disturbances, or heredity. However, the issue at law is not one of etiology but of responsibility. The question to be settled is whether, at the time the offense was committed, the defendant was in sufficient possession of reason to be held accountable. This question can be answered independently of any consideration of the defendant's brain, bile, or pedigree. On this Hale was explicit in accepting properly instructed jurors as sufficient for the task; as participants in what he confidently called *the best method of trial that is possible* in these or any other cases. But on this question of determining responsibility he was also making room for a wide range of theories, many of them no more "scientific" than those more or less taken for granted by Hale himself.

Writing in the age of Bacon, Newton, Galileo, Harvey, and Descartes, Hale—an avid reader of medical treatises even in his youth—left the world of the *Malleus* eons into the past. On the subject of the law and insanity, his is the seventeenth century's canonical work. With Hale the jurist (though not Hale the devout Christian) the devil is out and the brain is in, even if the medical experts are still in the wings. Writing on the evolution of thought in this period Joseph Klaits observes that "although late seventeenth- and early eighteenth-century judges did not explicitly reject witchcraft as a concept, the implicit message of their reforms was that this was an area of no interest to the law. . . . The world was greatly changed. The triumph of scientific reasoning had made the critical spirit more acceptable."[25]

It remained for the eighteenth century, in repudiating every species of superstition and cant and in identifying the natural sciences (natural philosophy) as the only sure route to knowledge, effectively to launch the program of scientific psychology. The Enlightenment popularized naturalistic and deterministic theories of human action. The movement and weight of these ideas would be reflected in the law's attempts to absorb the new thinking. A sketch of the main ideas will serve as the background for the more important cases of the period.

Two years after Hale had sentenced the widows to death for witchcraft, Thomas Willis's pioneering studies of the comparative anatomy of the brain were the subject of animated discussion at Oxford. William Harvey, whose published studies of the circulation of blood appeared in 1628, had conditioned the better medical researchers of succeeding generations to consider whole physiological systems, not isolated parts. Willis exemplified this perspective. More generally, a bold group of Oxford luminaries—Hooke, Wren, and Boyle, to mention three—had been successfully carrying on the war against conventional Aristotelian science. Willis's efforts were part of this program, too, as were the philosophical and scientific works of Gassendi and Descartes in France. The overall result of numerous experiments and theoretical conjectures was the replacement of a science of "essences" with that of matter in motion; a science finding ancient roots in the atomism of Democritus and Epicurus rather than in the elusive metaphysics of Plato and Aristotle.

The perspective in Willis's hands resulted in immensely influential books and essays. All of his major publications found large audiences, his *Opera omnia* alone going through eleven editions by 1720.[26] The conclusions he reached after painstaking research and clinical observations were set forth and finely illustrated in his *Cerebri anatome* (1664), *Pathologiae cerebri* (1667) and *De anima brutorum* (1672).[27] The brain is the central organ of experience, action, and emotion. Cerebral pathologies result in identifiable psychological disturbances. Man has an "animal soul" in common with the brutes, but also a rational soul that is immortal. A pious Christian who dedicated some of his works to the Archbishop of Canterbury, Willis was never tempted by the more radical and atheistic forms of materialism. But soon, and in ways otherwise indebted to his work, medical and philosophical writers would have this animal or corporeal soul "take on a complexity of meaning and function such as to infringe significantly on the autonomy of the rational soul."[28]

The leaders of the witch-hunt mentality, in debunking and suspecting their medical challengers, were laying the foundations for a reaction in favor of science whose strength and reach would grow for centuries. By the early eighteenth century, the major medical centers of Europe were given over either to essentially mechanistic or essentially chemical theories of health and disease, with all notions of "spirit" now being cast chiefly in psychological and mental terms.

Herman Boerhaave of Leiden (1668–1738), who became a near-legend in his own time, developed a mechanistic approach to medicine and physiology so effectively that it became the model for new and progressive medical schools like the one founded at Edinburgh in 1727. His research and writing were so thoroughly successful in demystifying various diseases that the thinking of even the recent past in medicine came to look ridiculous. An orphanage in Haarlem offered one of a great many opportunities for Boerhaave to make what would become the central point of Enlightenment medical thinking. A young girl's convulsions quickly led to a wave of convulsions overtaking the other children. (One can surely imagine how this would have been explained just fifty years earlier.) Boerhaave summoned the children to a room in which he had arranged pots containing hot coals, an iron hook in each of them. He then warned them: "I do not know of any medicine to cure you. But each child, be it a boy or a girl, that falls into a convulsion, will be burned with a little hook in his arm".[29] Thus ended the epidemic of convulsions!

Robert Whytt (1714–1766), physician to the King of Scotland and a major figure in Edinburgh's illustrious medical community, was but one of the beneficiaries of the Leiden perspective. Whytt taught from the textbook written by Boerhaave's successor, Hieronymus Gaub[30]; and Whytt's own works, collected and published by his son, cemented these same traditions at what was by then the premier medical institution in the English-speaking world.[31] Though much the dualist on the mind-body issue, Whytt nevertheless provided experimental findings and sound arguments to establish the causal relationship between neurological events and involuntary behavior; relationships so regular as to overcome even voluntary efforts on the part of the animal.

Of even greater influence was David Hartley's *Observations on Man,* an explicitly Newtonian psychology based upon the assumed functions of the nervous system.[32] In his conjectures on madness Hartley reports that "the Brain is often found dry" when post-mortem examinations of the mad are conducted, though he concludes by recommending religious remedies as "being the only sure Means of restraining violent Passions." Hartley, like Willis before him, did not present a biological psychology in opposition to dualism. Rather, he elaborated it as a way of explaining how mind-body relationships actually function in mental health and disease. To propose, for example, that a temporary inflammation of the "medullary substance" is behind "phrenzy" is not to strip the sufferer of the mental aspects of frenzy; it is, instead, to identify one of the causes of such aspects.

Hartley's own piety was also representative of the age that assimilated Newton's scientific patrimony; it was an age that took the natural order to be the truest evidence of a benign and omniscient creator; an age in which John Ray (1627–1705), the founder of modern botany, would enter the Church and write his *Wisdom of God in the Creation,* and William Derham (1657–1735) his *Physico-Theology* (1713).[33] In the shuddering reaction to the witch panics, and in the emergence of the churches of Dissent organized in opposition to all superstition, Christianity took on an ever more reasonable and naturalistic bearing. The Cartesian triumph, for all its weaknesses in astronomy and physics, survived in the form of an epistemology of clarity and sufficiency available to any rational being: accept only what presents itself as a clear idea; only such claims as are able to withstand that officially skeptical posture a reasonable creature adopts in the face of propositions not sanctioned by the most rigorous logic. The Baconian triumph added to this a widespread confidence in the power of unbiased observation to supply what traditional authority and the Idols of the Den never could: a practical means of understanding and solving problems and of finding sure guides to a flourishing and principled life.

The scientific movement of which Hartley was a member was by now international. London's Royal Society, founded in 1660, quickly became the repository of the best scientific thinking in places large and small the world over. Centers of medical teaching and research, such as Leiden and Edinburgh, were attracting students from everywhere, and they returned to plant the new learning in native soil. Edinburgh's famous William Cullen, for example, wrote the most authoritative work on insanity of his time, *Nosology,* replete with a properly neurological and biological perspective on the subject. And it was no coincidence that two of the great reformists in the field of mental health would be the American, Benjamin Rush, who studied under Cullen at Edinburgh, and France's Philippe Pinel, whose first major publication was the French translation of this same *Nosology.* In it Cullen ties the various forms of mental illness to physical and neurological disturbances and dismissively concludes the discussion with the declaration, "I do not allow that there is any true Daemonamania."[34]

If France initially hosted less basic scientific research, it more than compensated with philosophical and rhetorical contributions to the increasingly "official" view. And by the early decades of the nineteenth century France would produce many of the leading figures in medical psychology. At the time of Enlightenment, however, the chief contributions from France were, in a manner of speaking, polemical. All of the *philosophes,* for whom Baconian and Newtonian science represented the final triumph of naturalism over superstition, looked to medicine and to the material world for explanations of life and mind. In declaring the soul to be an "enlightened machine"—a conclusion reached by Galen fifteen hundred years earlier—La Mettrie only added scandal to what was already commonplace among the patrons of the *salons*[35] for whom Newton was simply "that great genius" and Bacon "the immortal Chancellor."[36]

It is worth mentioning that while Hale was collecting his *History,* the University of Heidelberg named Pufendorf to the new chair in "the Law of Nature and of Nations" (1662). This was not a mere revival of Thomistic Natural Law theory, nor was it the law's version of that "classical revival" that would dominate Enlightenment art and architecture. It was both of these, but more. By 1662 "nature" had become absorbed into the framework of what, for the first time, can be called the modern scientific view; a view stripped of magic and very much tied to ordinary perception. The evidence for God is in His visible works, and these works reflect not only order but fitness and aptness. The political and social order, to survive and prosper, must aspire to the same fitness and aptness. It does this through an ever more accurate comprehension of human nature. Just as science has liberated mankind from the earth-bound if often terrifying life of the superstitious past, so will a scientific knowledge of human nature prove to be liberating. "Nature," in the late-seventeenth and earlier eighteenth centuries, was, as Basil Willey observed, "mainly a liberating principle."[37] Thus it is when the instructed mind finally comprehends its (natural) duties and obligations that the requirements of law become illuminated. As uncorrupted nature is good—because created by one who is goodness itself—so uncorrupted man (as Rousseau was at pains to argue) has an innate tendency toward goodness; a tendency that becomes habitual under laws grounded in respect for the common good. These laws work to establish what is the right and natural human order by rewarding goodness and punishing the wicked.

The philosophical foundations of this line of thought were set broad and deep by leading social philosophers of the period. For all the differences that can be found among them on one or another metaphysical point, there was a surprising degree of uniformity in what they took to be the nature of human nature. Hobbes's egoistic psychology was challenged by any number of influential writers (notably Hutcheson, Shaftesbury, Adam Smith, and Thomas Reid) who argued that owing to the very constitution of our nature, human beings possess a moral sense and the capacity to form moral judgments. Shaftesbury put it this way: "There are TWO Things, which to a rational Creature must be horridly offensive and grievous; *viz.* To have the Reflection in his Mind of any *unjust* Action or Behaviour, which he knows to be naturally *odious* and *ill-deserving:* Or, of any foolish Action or Behaviour, which he knows to be prejudicial to his own *Interest* or *Happiness.* The former of these is alone properly call'd CONSCIENCE."[38] Hutcheson, in a fever of confidence in the new science, put it even more precisely: "The moral Importance of any Agent, or the Quantity of publick Good produc'd by him, is in a compound Ratio of his Benevolence and Abilitys: or (by substituting the initial Letters of the Words, as M = Moment of Good, and u = Moment of Evil) $M = B \times A$."[39] And, for all of his skepticism toward reason as a sufficient source of moral judgment or conduct, Hume too was given to explanations based upon "the constitution" of human nature and the moral sentiments inevitably arising from it.

The settled position among the leading thinkers of the age was that the moral dimensions of human life could be (and, for most of them, should be) understood not in theological terms but in natural terms; in terms drawn from scientific studies of human nature, human societies, human history. Whether a given theorist came to emphasize rational or emotional processes, the explanation of human actions was to be generated by an ever more developed, ever more scientific psychology. The starting point of this psychology was the recognition of humankind as being part of a purely natural order, sufficiently equipped (either by the Creator or "the

Mint of Nature") to live within a moral order that is itself designed to achieve ends compatible with that human nature. Shaftesbury spoke for the majority of the leaders of thought when, a few lines after the quoted passage, he concluded that a creature having no more than a few basic affections and "a reflecting Faculty" surely must be "*capable of* VIRTUE, and *to have a Sense of* RIGHT *and* WRONG."

The achievements of science displaced traditional thinking not only in those areas in which these achievements were made, but in all areas of inquiry and speculation. Literature and art, philosophy, even theology itself gradually came to terms with the rich implications generated by "the age of Newton." And through all of this, what of the law? How would the eighteenth-century courts, equipped with precedents, with Coke and with Hale, come to accommodate this new scientific learning, this new emphasis on purely natural and medical causes of mental disturbance and violent behavior? The answer is: first grudgingly, then matter-of-factly, finally eagerly.

In 1724 Edward Arnold was tried for felony "in maliciously and wilfully shooting at, and wounding, the Right Hon. the Lord Onslow." The trial was presided over by the Hon. Robert Tracy, Justice of the Court of Common-Pleas.[40] Arnold's plea was Not Guilty. The trial was unusual from the outset, for the defense of insanity took the form of an affidavit supplied by Arnold's two brothers. Sarjeants Cheshire and Whitaker of King's counsel both protested. Had the brothers really considered Edward Arnold insane for years, they should have confined him and called for a commission of lunacy. Instead, their brother appears in court without counsel, and expects release on the basis of a letter from members of his family. In the circumstance, Whitaker remarked, the only evidence of insanity was this mode of defense itself! As for the crime, Arnold did shoot Lord Onslow in front of witnesses and subsequently gave his reasons (that Onslow sent imps to disturb

Arnold's repose and other such complaints), though he also claimed that the musket's discharge was accidental. A year earlier, the same offense would have carried a lighter penalty owing to the survival of the victim. However, an act of Parliament of 1723 had revived the older law of England which imposed a death penalty for assaults with intent to kill, so Arnold faced execution.[41]

Cheshire presented the case for the prosecution. He informed the jury that the defendant was entirely unknown to his victim. His Lordship was well known, however, as a defender of the Protestant religion "against rebels, and for suppressing clubs, and places of meeting for people's wicked enterprizes."[42] Such notable figures apparently had excited Arnold and brought him to a great enthusiasm, all to the particular effect that Onslow was an enemy of God and country and should be destroyed. But, Cheshire goes on, "Gentlemen, though he acted like a wicked man, void of reason, you will have little reason to think he acted like a madman. Every man that so departs from reason, every wicked man may be said to be a madman; but I hope that shall not skreen all that so act, and free and exempt them from punishment."[43]

The evidence against Arnold was unimpeachable. His offense was committed in the presence of reliable witnesses. Earlier in the day he had attempted to obtain even larger shot for his musket, his failure here resulting in a less than mortal wound to the victim. Mr. Flutter, in Lord Onslow's hunting party, described the crime: "When he came to my horse's head, his countenance changed pale; then I asked him, why he carried his gun in that manner? He made no answer but immediately turned short, and shot my lord."[44] When Sergeant Cheshire and Justice Tracy asked Arnold if he had any questions he would put to the witness, Arnold declined. "I don't know. Ask him yourself, if you have a mind to it."[45]

Mr. Parsons testified next and reported that Arnold, after firing and walking away, was apprehended, whereupon he threatened "to charge again" before he was completely subdued. Confronting the wounded Onslow, Arnold seemed to struggle to get at him again. Parsons had known Arnold for twenty years and testified that though he found him "a morose, ill-natured man," he never considered him mad. During this questioning Arnold spoke up and said, "I have had my gun go off several times in my hand; but never till now, had this accident."[46]

John Stuart recalled Arnold asking the whereabouts of Onslow earlier on the day of the assault and, on being told that Stuart didn't know, "he stood humming and talking to himself, swearing and cursing, and damned my Lord Onslow several times; and stood so for near a quarter of an hour."[47]

Still others testified to Arnold's sullen nature, but none of them took him to be insane. Arnold was asked repeatedly if he had questions for the witnesses, and each time declared that he had nothing to say or to add. Arnold's tailor recalled a conversation in which Arnold has asked about Onslow and whether his wife was a good woman. On learning she was, he then asked, "Why doth she not cut his throat?" Mr. Allen, a peace officer, spent time with Arnold after the fact at the house of correction, seeking to discover the motive. Arnold repeated his contention that Onslow was responsible for "wicked devices"; that he was "the author of all the confusions, tumults, and noise," and so forth. He also asked about the King, whom he regarded as being as much at fault as Onslow.

Arnold's solicitor with some difficulty did get the peace officer to comment on his assessment of the prisoner's sanity, Allen apparently having described Arnold to others as a lunatic after he had examined him. Pressing further, the solicitor asked "whether the prisoner, at the time that was in the prison, did not desire Mr. Allen to shoot him through the head? And whether Mr. Allen did not declare the same?"[48] Allen replied that Arnold had expressed the willingness and desire to die, wondering why Lord Onslow wouldn't come in to do it or why he couldn't have a gun to kill himself. Nonetheless, although Allen found Arnold "very much out of the common way of men, in the whole course of his life," he did not recall judging him to be insane after examining him in prison.

The witnesses for the defense included Arnold's brothers and sister and in-laws, as well as others who had known him for many years. Nathaniel Arnold declared his brother to be a "madman"; ill-natured toward his father and sisters, beyond governance within the family. William Arnold testified to the same effect, declaring Edward to be "not perfect in his senses"; a man who cursed his father without provocation and who had more recently declared Lord Onslow to be bewitching him: "He plagues me day and night; I can't eat or drink; if I eat anything it comes up: I am, says he, as if they pumped the breath out of my body."[49]

Mary Arnold, Arnold's sister-in-law, then testified that, "I have been in the family eleven years; and to the best of my knowledge I never heard him speak six sensible words together." A month before the crime Arnold entered her house in a great confusion:

He talk'd extremely inwardly; says I, Speak out like a man, if I can answer you I will. He told me he was bewitched; he talk'd to himself; and I heard him curse several times: says I, Who hath bewitched you? He told me, The imps. He told me they danced in his room all night, and he could not lie in his bed for them, and the devil did tempt him, and the imps stood by his bed . . . he said, My lord Onslow, why should I be plagued by him?[50]

Arnold's barber, Wheatly, was sometimes afraid to shave him. "One time, as I was shaving of him, he said, Dammee, cut my throat." Thomas Poulter regarded him as "always out of his mind" during their nine-year association. And there was much more; instances of tearing apart a carpet and stuffing his ears with the pieces; sleeping on roof tops; hurling milk buckets at his own sister; walking the streets mumbling to himself, cursing others. Even

under pressing cross-examination, witnesses denied they were attempting to save Arnold's life or that they had been promised
money for describing him as a madman. After he had summarized
the testimony on both sides and the facts germane to the case, the
time had come for Justice Tracy to explain the law to the jury:

Gentlemen of the Jury, this Edward Arnold, this unhappy
person, is indicted for a great offense. . . . There can't be a
more horrid and wicked thing intended in the design of it,
than maliciously to shoot a man. . . . (T)he shooting of lord
Onslow, which is the fact for which this prisoner is indicted,
is proved beyond all manner of contradiction; but whether
this shooting was malicious, that depends upon the sanity of
the man. That he shot, and that wilfully [is proved]: but
whether maliciously, that is the thing: that is the question;
whether this man hath the use of his reason and sense? If he
was under the visitation of God, and could not distinguish
between good and evil, and did not know what he did,
though he committed the greatest offence, yet he could not
be guilty of any offence against any law whatsoever; for guilt
arises from the mind, and the wicked will and intention of
the man. If a man be deprived of his reason, and consequently
of his intention, he cannot be guilty; and if that be the case,
though he had actually killed my lord Onslow, he is exempted
from punishment: punishment is intended for example, and
to deter other persons from wicked designs; but the punishment of a madman, a person that hath no design, can have
no example. This is on one side. On the other side, we must
be very cautious; it is not every frantic and idle humour of a
man, that will exempt him from justice, and the punishment
of law. When a man is guilty of a great offence, it must be
very plain and clear, before a man is allowed such an exemption; therefore it is not every kind of frantic humour or some-

thing unaccountable in a man's actions, that points him out
to be such a madman as is to be exempted from punishment:
it must be a man that is totally deprived of his understanding
and memory, and doth not know what he is doing, no more
than an infant, than a brute, or a wild beast; such a one is
never the object of punishment. . . . A man that is an ideot,
that is born so, never recovers, but a lunatic may, and hath his
intervals; and they admit he (Arnold) was a lunatic. You are
to consider what he was at this day, when he committed the
fact . . . and if you believe he was sensible, and had the use
of his reason, and understood what he did, then he is not
within the exemptions of the law, but is as subject to punishment as any other person. Gentlemen, I must leave it to you.[51]

Arnold was convicted, was sentenced to be executed, and was
spared through the intercession of his victim. He lived out the
remaining thirty years of his life in the new prison at Southwark.

Tracy's instructions to the jury remain within the ambit established by Roman law and were incorporated into common law
through Bracton, Coke, Hale, and the rest. For the insanity plea to
succeed, the defendant must be insane at the time of the offense,
the degree of insanity extensive enough to preclude any sensible
awareness on the part of the defendant of the gravity of the action.
In juxtaposing infant, brute, and wild beast, Tracy further adumbrated the applicable criterion; not mere immaturity (as is the case
with legal infants of the sort Hale has in mind in referring to a
child of fourteen years), but total mental incapacity. But it is clear
that Tracy reserves the application of this criterion to cases involving "a great offence" than which "there can't be a more horrid
and wicked thing intended." The jury must consider the plea in
the context of the offense itself, weighing the cost to justice of
excusing so grave an offense on less than the most compelling
grounds. If justice is to set an example and deter potential offenders,

trials must be conducted in a way that teaches by example. What one might learn from *Arnold* is that eccentricity, sullenness, distemper, rootlessness, or peevish indignation will not be exculpatory where heinous crimes are involved. The protection of life and property being the law's chief obligation, questions of sanity must be addressed in a "very cautious" way lest life itself become hostage to the "idle humour of a man."

Some decades later, in a trial notable for its socially prominent defendant and for the fact that a medical expert in "lunacy" would be called to testify, Lawrence, the Earl Ferrers, would be found guilty by the House of Lords and executed for the murder of his steward, John Johnson.[52] The summing up by the Solicitor General echoed much of Tracy's reasoning in such cases and also made clear just why medical testimony was not routinely consulted in this otherwise scientifically inclined period. First, it is instructive to follow the questions the defendant put to his expert, Dr. John Monro beginning with the first question where Ferrers refers to himself as deceased:[53]

Ferrers: Did you know the late Earl Ferrers?

Monro: I did. . . I attended him as a physician when he was under the unhappy influence of lunacy. . . .

Ferrers: You are desired to mention what are the usual symptoms of lunacy.

Monro: Uncommon fury, not caused by liquor, but very frequently raised by it; many others there are which tend to violence against other persons or against themselves: I do not know a stronger, a more constant, or a more unerring symptom of lunacy than jealousy, or suspicion without cause or grounds: there are many others too long to enumerate.

Ferrers: Please inform their lordships, whether quarrelling with friends without cause is a symptom of lunacy?

Monro: Very frequently one.

Ferrers: Whether going generally armed where there is no apparent danger is a symptom of lunacy?

Monro: I should think it was.

Ferrers: Whether spitting in the looking-glass, clenching the fist, and making mouths, is a symptom of lunacy?

Monro: I have frequently seen such in lunatic persons.

Ferrers: Whether lunatics are apt to be seized with fits of rage on a sudden?

Monro: Very often.

Ferrers: Without any apparent cause?

Monro: Without any apparent cause.

Ferrers: Is there any other way of discovering whether a man is lunatic or not, but by the irregularity of his behaviour or his pulse;

Monro: I know of no other method; the pulse discovers nothing in general.[54]

The questions were tied to the actual facts of the homicide, Ferrers simply getting Monro to acknowledge that, where such facts obtain, there is the presumption of insanity. But the Solicitor General had no difficulty making clear to the Peers that the doctor's testimony could not possibly excuse the Earl:

The fact of killing Mr. Johnson is admitted as well as proved. The noble lord at the bar only denies the consequence; that the fact is murder. For, he tells your lordships, that, upon considering all the circumstances, he is satisfied, that he was incapable, knowingly, of doing what he did; and therefore insists upon an incapacity and insanity of mind in his defence.

My lords, it is certainly true, that the fact is not murder without malice; so natural justice says; so the law says . . . and malice must depend, in every case, upon the will and understanding of the party. . . . The law of England, which is wisely adapted to punish crimes with severity, for the protection of mankind, and for the honour of government, provides, at the same time, with the greatest equity, for the imbecility and imperfections of human nature. . . .

At this point the Solicitor General applauds and reviews Sir Matthew Hale's writing on this subject, noting that the incapacity must not spare any competent use of reason. But in rehearsing the details of the Earl's offense, the Solicitor General leaves no doubt that the defendant had far more use of his reason than would a child of fourteen—Hale's criterion. And he dismisses Dr. Monro's testimony on lunatics as inconclusive:

> He was brought here to describe, what symptoms he considers as marks of lunacy or insanity. He said, that there were many; and on being asked particularly, as to the several symptoms suggested in this cause, Doctor Monro . . . did not describe any of these things, as absolute marks of lunacy, so as to denote every man a lunatic, who was subject to them. Indeed he could not have said it, consistently with common sense and experience. . . .

> My lords, in some sense, every crime proceeds from insanity. All cruelty, all brutality, all revenge, all injustice, is insanity. There were philosophers, in ancient times, who held this opinion, as a strict maxim of their sect; and, my lords, the opinion is right in philosophy, but dangerous in judicature.[55]

The capstone is: an opinion can be right in philosophy (including natural philosophy; that is, medicine and physiology), but dangerous in judicature because it may be incompatible with the necessary assumptions of judicature itself. What the Solicitor General rejects in his address to the Peers is the power of a philosophical or psychological explanation to constitute an excuse at law. What is explanatory is not thereby exculpatory. Of course acts of violence, cruelty, injustice and the like are evidence of a disturbed mind. But these are precisely the sorts of acts envisaged by criminal statutes. Thus it would be entirely pointless at once to write laws to cover such offenses and then excuse offenders on the grounds that the crime itself established mental incompetence.

Also unmistakable in *Ferrers* is the standard against which medical testimony in such cases is to be weighed: that of common sense. Had Dr. Monro so much as implied that every person possessing the characteristics Ferrers cited was insane, the doctor's testimony could readily be discounted as simply false. There is no suggestion in *Ferrers* that Dr. Monro's judgments had any chance of trumping the balance of testimony and evidence. If Ferrers did not prove, by the very nature of his offense and all other observable aspects of his state of mind at the time, that he was indistinguishable from "infant, brute or wild beast," his conviction would stand. And this was so even if, in some philosophical or medical sense, he was "mad."

The reasoning in this criminal prosecution was matched by the understandings of civil courts at the time as can be seen in tests of testamentary capacity. In *Cartwright v. Cartwright* (1793) Mrs. Armyne Cartwright had left a will in her own hand, leaving her not inconsiderable fortune to her brother's daughters and nothing to the issue of her father's second marriage.[56] Her friend, Lady Macclesfield, stated in her deposition that the deceased considered her blood-brother a "much nearer and dearer relation than her brothers and sisters by the half-blood."[57] But her physician, Dr. Battie, had instructed her nurse and other servants to keep pen and paper away from her and "to prevent her from reading or writing as he gave it as his opinion that reading and writing might disturb and hurt her head." He went even further, informing the deceased that, "whatever she wrote, he must appear as a witness against."[58] Witnesses testified to Armyne Cartwright's difficulty in composing the brief will and spoke of her agitations and past disturbances, which resulted in her treatment by Dr. Battie as an insane person since early in 1775. Months earlier a consultation with Dr. Fothergill produced the diagnosis of a disordered mind, and still other evidence indicated that she had labored under the weight of mental illness since 1759 or thereabouts. On these grounds the will was challenged by her half-siblings.

Sir William Wynne rendered the judgment of the court, leaving no doubt about the grounds of his ruling: "the deceased, by herself writing the will now before the Court, hath most plainly shewn she had a full and complete capacity to understand what was the state of her affairs and her relations. . . . She not only formed the plan, but pursued and carried it into execution with propriety and without assistance. In my apprehension that would have been alone sufficient."[59]

In reviewing other cases germane to *Cartwright,* Sir William observes that in *Coghlan v. Coghlan* probate succeeded even though Dr. Monro and others claimed the testator to be "a person as insane as they had ever seen." Notwithstanding this testimony, the court recognized the will as expressing the intentions of the testator who, like Armyne Cartwright, had his lucid intervals.

Entirely different were the relevant facts in *Clarke v. Lear and Scarwell* (1791). Here the testator, already known to be mentally disordered, made a visit to the seacoast, where he "sees a young woman at the house where he boarded, of whom he had no prior knowledge, and wants to marry her, at a time when he was insane, is brought up to town in a strait waistcoat, and there afterwards writes a paper by way of codicil giving her a legacy. This is delusion."[60] As Sir William Wynne understood the issues, the question was not whether a competent physician regarded the author of a testament to be mentally ill, but whether the instrument itself was clearly and specifically the product of a diseased mind. The Prerogative Court's ruling in *Cartwright* was appealed to the High Court of Delegates in 1795. Two doctors were summoned to support the appeal, but the Prerogative Court's ruling was affirmed.[61]

The years encompassing these cases included momentous world events, many of them presided over by George III, whose own psychological disturbances had entered the public consciousness. Doctors attending or otherwise consulted in connection with the King's illness were at pains to reassure a worried nation that their monarch was competent and his fits episodic and remediable. Dr. William Rowley of Savile Row, taking George III's condition as confirming his own conclusions, distributed his *Truth vindicated: or, the specific differences of mental diseases ascertained . . . with facts extracted from the parliamentary reports, and reasons for declaring the case of a great personage to have been only a feverish or symptomatic delirium* (1790).[62] A world watched as the judgments of medicine and of politics became sporadically interdependent. The regimen imposed by Dr. Willis and others, and sanctioned by that now authoritative treatise of Cullen's, could only cause public concern and alarm. Attitudes began to change quickly when, after George III's illness, "the revelations of his sickroom lifted the veil from professional practice in the mad-business. A feeling of revulsion arose at the idea of the monarch in a strait-waistcoat, and the realization grew that the same fate awaited any gentleman or woman, however high-born, suffering from the same affliction. Finally, concern began to be felt about how the poor and mad fared."[63]

A more humane set of attitudes was now evolving. Medicine, too, was prepared to attach itself more firmly to objective scientific approaches to insanity. The courts, in contexts of revolutionary upheaval and humanitarian reform, moved with the times.

5

THE RISE OF
MEDICAL JURISPRUDENCE

"Truth is simple upon all subjects, but upon those which are essential to the general happiness of mankind, it is obvious to the meanest capacities,"[1] wrote Benjamin Rush, signer of the Declaration of Independence, great American reformer of prisons and insane asylums, founder of an antislavery society, and well-prepared graduate of William Cullen's medical teachings at Edinburgh. Rush was but one of an army of Enlightenment physicians convinced that all diseases were reducible to a mere handful of general laws comprising the soon-to-be systematic science of medicine. A devout Christian, he could protect his faith against the atheistic forms of materialism by insisting that the Supreme Being never "acts without unity and system in all his works."[2]

It should be at least briefly noted that the Scottish contribution to the Enlightenment of the eighteenth century was special and enduring. The "common-sense" philosophy so richly developed by Thomas Reid was no less naturalistic than the Humean system it so relentlessly attacked. In their meetings at the Wise Club, Reid and his fellow Aberdonians developed ideas that were later incorporated into influential treatises on a wide range of subjects. These works were fully compatible with the Darwinian perspective of the next century, with the medical theories being taught at Edinburgh by Cullen and Whytt, and with the liberal dissenting perspective of whole clans of Edinburgh lawyers and divines.[3] If one would attempt to concentrate the energies and tendencies of the period on one case, if only for the purpose of exemplifying them, the trial of James Hadfield would serve especially well.[4] The crime was treason, tried in a year that launched a new century. A most pathetic figure, James Hadfield, had tracked George III to the theater at Drury Lane and fired his pistol at him, causing a great stir but no harm. The appointed counsel for the defense was the greatest trial lawyer in England, Scotland's own Thomas Erskine. The defense was that of insanity; the presiding judge was Chief Justice Lord Kenyon. The main expert testimony was supplied by Henry Cline and by another Scot, Dr. Alexander Crichton. A few words are in order on some of these principals.

Erskine and Kenyon had appeared together before as co-counsels in the notorious trial of Lord George Gordon, whose opposition to the extension of Catholic Relief into his native Scotland culminated in the London riots of 1778. The politically charged climate of the time led to Gordon's standing trial for treason. Kenyon and especially junior counsel Erskine successfully argued that Gordon had never intended to provoke the insurrection, and therefore the charge of treason was jejune. In this they succeeded, though Gordon's troubled life would lead to successful prosecutions for, among other things, libeling the Queen of France—Erskine appearing now as prosecutor—and Gordon would end his years in prison.

Erskine had also accepted the assignment to defend Thomas Paine *in absentia* in the action brought by the Crown against Paine for his seditious writings and speeches. Erskine failed to win the case, but his summoning address in behalf of freedom of the press and the untrammeled movement of ideas was yet another contribution to the Enlightenment's powerful rhetoric of liberation.[5]

Alexander Crichton (who later served as physician to the Tsar of Russia, was Fellow of the Royal Society, and then knighted) had just published *An Inquiry into the Nature and Origins of Mental Derangement*.[6] Though not yet famous in England, Crichton could already claim a celebrated admirer in France. His *Inquiry* greatly impressed Dr. Phillipe Pinel, who, along with his student Esquirol and with Crichton himself, must rank among the founders of modern psychiatry. Pinel would translate and comment on later works by Crichton and would benefit further from Crichton's familiarity with a German medical literature largely inaccessible to Pinel.[7]

Edinburgh-trained, Crichton was a disciple of the Wise Club through the medical writings of Reid's cousin, Dr. John Gregory, as well as the philosophical works of Reid himself and of his most famous student, Dugald Stewart. Reid especially urged upon his contemporaries that approach to science first adumbrated by Francis Bacon and then fully realized by the genius of Isaac Newton.[8] These influences, coupled with his journeys to Leiden and to major German medical centers, committed Crichton to an observational approach (the case-history method) to mental disease and to a fuller appreciation of the integrative functions of the mental faculties. His *Inquiry* devoted particular attention to the effects of emotionality on thought; to the tension between the affective and deliberative faculties; to the pernicious influences of morbid thinking on the whole tone of psychological life; to the continuous interplay of psychological and physiological-neurological processes. Along with Pinel and Esquirol, Crichton was alert to the broad environmental and social forces that shaped character and inclined already vulnerable persons toward mental illnesses of varying degrees of severity. The morbid physiology of the brain as the proximate cause of mental illness reveals the more remote but definite causal influences of the world in which the patient is immersed. In this way, social tumult combines with physiology to produce the full range of macabre results such as those Pinel would so graphically report from the asylums of Salpêtrière and Bicêtre.[9] Dr. Crichton (denominated "Creighton" in the trial transcript) was just the sort of expert Erskine needed, if only briefly, as he set out to change the laws pertaining to criminal insanity.

Early in his address to the jury Erskine explained the special protections that were built in for those charged with treason; protections Hadfield would not have enjoyed "if the same pistol had been maliciously fired by the same prisoner in the same theatre, at the meanest man within its walls."[10] Consequently, "from a prisoner so protected by the benevolence of our institutions, the utmost good faith would, on his part, be due to the public if he had consciousness and reason to reflect upon the obligation."[11]

Erskine then takes the jury, step by step and with an eloquence Cicero would have admired, through the thickets and tares the law must traverse in disposing of cases of this kind. As in all of its branches, the law here strives for precision. With madness, however, "it is extremely difficult to be precise. The general principle is clear, but the application is most difficult."[12] The principle in England "and every other country" is "that it is the REASON OF MAN which makes him accountable for his actions; and that the deprivation of reason acquits him of crime."[13] It is going to be Erskine's burden to modify and clarify and, to some extent, even annul this principle by revealing its defects. The ancient *furiosus,* that durable *exemplum* who survived nearly unchanged till the time of Coke, will be replaced through Erskine's efforts, but not before the rationale is carefully developed. Yes, it is human rationality that renders man fit for the rule of law, but,

> so fearfully and wonderfully are we made, so infinitely subtle is the spiritual part of our being, so difficult is it to trace with accuracy the effect of diseased intellect upon human action, that I may appeal to all who hear me, whether there are any causes more difficult, or which, indeed, so often confound the learning of the judges themselves, as when insanity, or the

effects and consequences of insanity, become the subjects of legal consideration and judgment.[14]

Erskine next reviewed the position taken by Lord Coke, praising his efforts but finding them no longer useful in its taxonomy of mental defects. Lord Hale's illustrious work is next considered as Erskine instructs the jury in the law's regard for insanity in civil matters. A person judged *non compos mentis* has all of his civil transactions nullified—for example, his contractual obligations or the terms of his will—and this is so even when the mental defect takes the form of morbid thoughts themselves not obviously connected to the civil acts in question. In the matter of serious (violent) criminal offenses, however, a different standard has been applied. Referring to Justice Tracy's charge to the jury in *Rex v. Arnold*, Erskine accepts the general proposition that the safety of society cannot be jeopardized by every idle humor. Traditionally, the insanity defense sanctioned by Coke, Hale, and others in cases of serious crime (and which Erskine is committed to replace) has required "a TOTAL *deprivation of memory* . . . to protect a man from punishment, he must be in such a state of prostrated intellect, as not to know his name, nor his condition, nor his relation toward others."[15] To pass such a test, a defendant must be effectively an *idiot;* the sort of defendant who "knows not to tell twenty shillings, nor knows his own age, or who was his father."[16] (Erskine is quoting Fitzherbert and the criteria adopted in his and Bracton's time.)

The problem with this criterion, according to Erskine, is that it is simply not met by the actual insane persons tried in court: persons whose memories have been normal; persons whose knowledge of their relations, their own lives and the nature of their actions has been complete; persons who have, "in general, been remarkable for subtlety and acuteness."[17] Only rarely does one confront the patient whose reason has been so "stormed in its citadel" as to leave all their ideas overwhelmed. In these cases, however, doctors recognize not the maniac but a person overcome by a "delirium from fever": the true if rare *furiosus* who is not, and has never been, juridically problematical. Still other cases involve minds so distracted by the wildest delusions, "which so overpower the faculties, and usurp so firmly the place of realities, as not to be dislodged and shaken by the organs of perception and sense. . . . Here too no judicial difficulties can present themselves."[18]

With the more typical insane criminal defendants, however, we encounter an entirely different condition, seldom involving defects of reasoning or imaginings so terrific as to establish the *furiosus* condition. What marks them off from normal persons? What, indeed, *should* be the proper legal test? "*Delusion,* therefore, where there is no frenzy or raving madness, is the true character of insanity; and where it cannot be predicated of a man standing for life or death for a crime, he ought not in my opinion, be acquitted."[19]

Erskine makes delusion not only a test which, if passed, exonerates, but one which, if failed, results in the defeat of the insanity defense itself. In civil cases, says Erskine, delusion nullifies the civil action even when it is unconnected in any conceptual way with that action. But he would insist on a connection "in a case of such atrocity as this" (that is, attempted regicide): "to deliver a lunatic from responsibility to *criminal* justice . . . the relation between the disease and the act should be apparent. Where the connexion is doubtful, the judgment should certainly be most indulgent, from the great difficulty of diving into the secret sources of a disordered mind; but still, I think, that, as a doctrine of law, the delusion and the act should be connected."

Whereupon Erskine goes on to set ostensibly sharp limits on the application of this criterion, making clear that it would not have spared a defendant like Ferrers:

> I cannot allow the protection of insanity to a man who only exhibits violent passions and malignant resentments, *acting*

upon real circumstances; who is impelled to evil from no morbid delusions; but who proceeds upon the ordinary perceptions of the mind. . . . He alone can be emancipated, whose disease (call it what you will) consists, not merely in seeing with a prejudiced eye, or with odd and absurd particularities, differing, in many respects, from the contemplations of sober sense, upon the actual existences of things; but *he only* whose whole reasoning and corresponding conduct, though governed by the ordinary dictates of reason, proceed upon something which has no foundation or existence.[20]

The details of James Hadfield's life and offense are straightforward, if tragic. A commoner, he served the Duke of York valiantly in Flanders, receiving two severe wounds; one to the head which, on the testimony of the physician-anatomist Henry Cline, may have pushed the skull down into the brain. At the trial Erskine could draw the jury's attention to the still *visible* membranous surface of Hadfield's brain. Another blow nearly severed the head and cut "all the nerves which give sensibility and animation to the body. . . . His head hung down almost disseevered, until by the act of surgery it was placed in the position in which you now see it." But it was not over. Another blow tore off the helmet and cut through the point at which the neck merges with the head; all the while, Hadfield still stood and struggled to perform his duty as a soldier.[21] But after this he would never be the same.

We are not here upon a case of insanity arising from the spiritual part of man, as it may be affected by hereditary taint—by intemperance, or by violent passions, the operations of which are various and uncertain; but we have to deal with a species of insanity more resembling what has been described as idiocy. . . . *There* the disease is, from its very nature, *incurable;* and so where a man *(like the prisoner)* has become insane from *violence to the brain, which permanently affects its structure,* however such a man may appear occasionally to others, his disease is *immovable.*[22]

Two days before his attempt on the life of George III, Hadfield had madly attacked his own eight-month-old son, threatening to beat the child's head against a wall, until his wife and neighbors succeeded in calming him. Not long before, while present at the singing of an indecent lyric against the King, he protested loudly as he then undertook his own patriotic rendition of *God Save the King,* "with all the enthusiasm of an old soldier who had bled in the service of his country." It was Hadfield's delusion that heaven itself wanted him and his baby dead, the result of this being the redeeming of all mankind. He understood the command to require that he be destroyed, but that he could not kill himself. He had visited another lunatic, Bannister Truelock, on the Tuesday before his Thursday attack on the King. Truelock was raving over the second coming of Jesus Christ, spelling the imminent dissolution of everything human. Hadfield was thus reinforced in his own mission to save the world (on another construction, he and Truelock were to be installed as joint monarchs of a new age, with Hadfield as God and Truelock as Satan).

On examination by Erskine, Henry Cline connected insanity to the type of brain injuries sustained by Hadfield, and informed the court that such insanity could be enduring, episodic, and not at the expense of all rational powers. Next to testify was Dr. Crichton, examined by Sergeant Best. Crichton regarded the head wounds as very likely to reflect the cause of Hadfield's insanity, "many instances of this kind of madness having been occasioned by such injuries done to the brain."[23] Moreover, claimed Crichton, it was quite usual in such cases for victims of such brain injuries to conduct themselves rationally on any number of counts, but to reveal their insanity on a particular subject; in Hadfield's case, religious subjects. Although there can be seasonal variations in the symptoms, it is the sufferer's overall health that may alleviate or aggravate them. Still, hot weather "is a very common cause of the augmentation." (The offense was committed on May 15th.)

Other testimony from associates and family members further established James Hadfield as a deluded and deeply disturbed person. Erskine had another twenty witnesses lined up at the time Lord Kenyon interrupted to ask whether the prosecution had rebuttal witnesses. The attorney general, conceding Hadfield's insanity, agreed with Lord Kenyon that the defendant was too dangerous to be released and asked only that the jury acknowledge insanity in their verdict, which they did. In the immediate wake of *Hadfield,* statutory provision was made for keeping such acquitted parties in custody for the safety of themselves and the public.[24]

For some time the complexities of the human mind had begun to be considered outside the traditional philosophical categories. Leading scientists and clinicians were classifying not only recurring symptoms of mental disease but the many and various predisposing and disposing causes of which, of course, brain pathology was primary. As the causes increased in number and subtlety, it became obvious to many ranking scholars that even the ordinary medical practitioner lacked the scientific and clinical resources needed for precise diagnosis. Dr. John Gregory had made this clear as early as 1765 in his widely read *A Comparative View of the State and Faculties of Man with Those of the Animal World.* Although he was Reid's cousin, a charter member of the Wise Club, and a devout Baconian scientist, Gregory nonetheless found the intricate nature of mental life and mental illness to require more than the "assiduous and accurate Observation, and a good Understanding" sufficient for "the practical part of Medicine." If one would "cure the diseases of the Mind, there is required that intimate knowledge of the Human Heart, which must be drawn from life itself, and which books can never teach; of the various disguises, under which vice recommends herself to the Imagination; of the artful association of Ideas, which she forms there; and of the many nameless circumstances that soften the Heart and render it accessible."[25]

Long before *Hadfield,* then, physicians and jurists and the larger public had liberated their thinking on the matter of insanity and no longer expected it to confine itself within the stark person of the *furiosus.* For these and related reasons Nigel Walker sternly warns against attaching too much importance to *Hadfield,* going so far as to credit Erskine's success to the physical spectacle of the defendant rather than to the power of his arguments.[26] It is true of course that *Hadfield* was not the first case in which acquittal was won in an English court without the defendant qualifying as a "wild beast" or establishing that he could not distinguish between right and wrong. Nonetheless, looking back over the history of the subject in 1876, Henry Maudsley would state matter-of-factly that "It was at the trial of Hadfield, in 1800, for shooting at the King in Drury Lane Theatre, that Lord Hale's doctrine was first discredited, and a step forward made for the time."[27]

The case offered by Nigel Walker as a relevant anticipation of *Hadfield* was the trial in 1795 of Miss Broadric for the murder of John Errington.[28] Indeed, Erskine too refers to this trial but underscores what he takes to be the important differences between *Broadric* and *Hadfield.* Miss Broadric had, in the words of Erskine, murdered a man "who had seduced and abandoned her and the children she had borne to him." She went to Errington's house to kill him because of "a resentment long rankling in her bosom, bottomed on an existing foundation."[29] Granting that she was insane and that she deserved acquittal, her actions were *not* like those of James Hadfield, and her trial, as Erskine would argue, was not to be understood in the same terms. Miss Broadric was not deluded as to the nature of the wrongs she had suffered at the hands of her victim. Hadfield was.

In the end, the importance of *Hadfield* is that the case made explicit, and widely broadcast, an already general if largely implicit understanding among leading jurists and physicians. No longer could courts sit comfortably, needing to decide only whether a defendant was a raving madman at the time of the offense. No longer could the ordinary perceptions of the man in the street provide conclusive evidence of an actor's sanity. Erskine made it clear to the jury that the complexities of mental illness being what they are, the meaning of an action cannot be confidently inferred from the action itself.

An otherwise (seemingly) reasonable person, deluded on but one subject, might comport himself in a perfectly normal way until an occasion arises wherein the delusion can fully express itself. Hence a man may regard a neighbor as a wild animal or as a potter's vessel and proceed to destroy him on that unquestioned assumption. Suppose further that he has enmity toward this very person when in his right mind, though when he is under the controlling influence of the delusion, he somehow perceives the other as an inanimate object. He knows, therefore, that the perceived "potter's vessel" belongs to a person he loathes and he shatters the vessel as a result of this malice. Although "he had full knowledge of all the principles of good and evil; yet would it be possible to convict such a person of murder, if, from the influence of his disease, he was ignorant of the relation he stood in to the man he had destroyed, and was utterly *unconscious* that he had struck at the life of a human being?"[30] But from the mere physical actions, how could a juror, uninstructed in the subtle and knotted progress of the disordered mind, distinguish between criminal intent and delusional behavior?

In some respects the argument developed by Erskine was rather more conservative than it is sometimes portrayed. "I do not stand here to disturb the order of society," he insisted, as he informed the jury of the three assumptions available to them.[31] They could conclude that Hadfield, insane or not, acted out of malice toward the King, intending to kill him. If the jury should reach this conclusion, "LET THE MAN DIE. The law demands his death for the public safety."[32] Or the jury may judge the act to have arisen from a mixture of malice and insanity. In that case, "I leave him in the hands of the court, to say how he is to be dealt with: it is a question too difficult for me."[33] But if the jury finds that the act was wholly the product of Hadfield's insane delusion, then acquittal would be required. The focus from first to last was on *delusion* and the actions proceeding from it. Medical testimony was sought and was cited from other cases to show the jury how clever one must be to find the delusional elements in defendants whose general demeanor was otherwise unremarkable.

Some of the difficulties arising from *Hadfield* would soon make their way into both criminal and civil cases. In May of 1812 John Bellingham was tried and convicted of the murder of Prime Minister Spencer Perceval, previously Chancellor of the Exchequer. The victim was a popular head of government, the crime was heinous, and the public was outraged. Only a matter of four days separated arrest and trial; Bellingham's counsel did not have sufficient time even to summon relevant witnesses from distant locations. Medical testimony played no part, except to establish that the victim's death had been caused by the shot fired by the defendant. Bellingham's motive was a groundless claim that the Crown owed him money for time he had served in a Russian prison while Perceval had been Chancellor of the Exchequer. Failing to secure compensation from the Treasury, he hunted down Perceval and fired a fatal bullet at him in the lobby of the Commons House of Parliament. A plea of insanity was filed, though contested by Bellingham himself.

In his charge Lord Chief Justice Mansfield instructed the jury as to the criminal law in relation to insanity. Focusing on *Arnold* and *Ferrers,* and not even considering *Hadfield,* Mansfield simply reiterated the traditional understanding, but in rephrasing it, he expanded the meaning.[34] To be relieved of the burden of one's crime, a defendant pleading insanity must prove "by the most distinct and unquestionable evidence" that at the precise time of the offense he could not tell right from wrong, and did not consider that murder is "a crime against the laws of God and nature." This goes beyond the "wild beast" standard in that it leaves room for the successful defense of one who is assuredly not *furiosus* but is nonetheless so bereft of moral judgment and conscience as not to comprehend the gravity of his offense. As Maudsley would contend a half-century later, reflecting on Mansfield's instructions, "The law had changed considerably without ever acknowledging that it had changed."[35] And it had done so in a trial marked by a nearly "lynch-law" animus against the defendant.

Mansfield was not unaware of *Hadfield*, even if he didn't cite it. James Hadfield had suffered from morbid delusions which linked his attack on the King to what he took to be the will of his Lord and Savior. Had this belief not been deluded but grounded in fact, Hadfield could not have been punished in a Christian country. But is there no limit to the exculpatory reach of morbid delusions? Bellingham judged himself wronged by the Crown which had refused to compensate him for his time in jail. Is this an excuse worthy of the law's regard? Mansfield left no room for doubt on this point: "If a man fancied he was right, and in consequence conceived that if that fancy was not gratified, he had a right to obtain justice by any means which his physical strength gave him, there is no knowing where so pernicious a doctrine might end."[36]

By a strained species of juridical logic, *Hadfield* fostered the conclusion that actions arising from morbid delusion should be judged according to what the law would require or permit *were the contents of the delusion true.* If, indeed, it could be known that James Hadfield had been commanded by God to rid the world of himself, but not by taking his own life, and if he sought to obey this command by seeking to have the King's defenders kill him, no English court would have found him guilty of a crime. But supposing John Bellingham's grievance to be valid, his lethal assault on Spencer Perceval would still have resulted in the law's maximum penalty. What was at issue here was the ability of those already judged as insane in virtue of a controlling delusion thereupon to conduct themselves in such a manner as would a normal persons in whom the same ideas happened to coincide with the actual facts.

The standing secured for the criterion of delusion would be revealed in other cases, both civil and criminal. In the civil arena, it is instructive to compare *Cartwright v. Cartwright,* disposed of in the context of the "wild beast" standard, with *Dew v. Clark and Clark* settled in the Prerogative Court in 1826. Both cases involved challenges to testamentary capacity. *Cartwright* was decided in favor of the will, the capacity of the testatrix established to the court's satisfaction by the instrument itself. But in *Dew* one sees that times had changed. In his decision to overturn the will in this case, Sir John Nicholl would discourse at length on the complexities of the mind, citing Locke and quoting from Erskine's spirited defense of Hadfield. As for the criterion the Court would adopt, Sir John left no room for doubt:

> The true criterion—the true test—of the absence of presence of insanity I take to be, the absence of presence of what, used in a certain sense of it, is comprisable in a single term, namely—delusion . . . I look upon delusion . . . and insanity to be almost, if not altogether, convertible terms. . . . In the absence of any such delusion, with whatever extravagances a supposed lunatic may be justly chargeable . . . the supposed lunatic is, in my judgment, not properly or essentially insane.[37]

He reached this conclusion, he says, from "writers, as well medical as other, best qualified to discuss" such matters.

It was claimed that Mr. Stott had entertained hostile feelings toward his only child by a previous marriage almost from the time of her birth. In all of the several instruments produced in Court, a large part of Stott's substantial estate (some £40,000) not reserved to his wife would go to Stott's nephews, Thomas and Valentine Clark; a much smaller part was left to his daughter. This effective disinheritance was taken by the Court to be "the direct unqualified offspring of that morbid delusion" which produced such enmity toward his daughter. Accordingly, "that will itself is null and void in law."[38]

Without considering the degree or nature of such mental illness as Ely Stott, the testator, may have suffered at the time he executed the contested will, progressive thinking on such subjects could only lead to confusion and ambiguity. The considerations entering into the disposal of property are many and various. People routinely make bequests to mere acquaintances, to religious organizations, to clubs and schools, to charities, to total strangers, and to their pets! A close examination of the rationale behind such offerings would no doubt turn up any number of assumptions that might well qualify as delusional, or at least suspect. There is a difference between requiring rational competence on the part of those whose testaments will have the force of law, and requiring that the terms of such testaments also be "rational." The first of these requirements is grounded in a respect for the rights of ownership and a commitment to ensure that property will not be disposed of in ways that the owner, when competent, would oppose. But the second requirement creates something of a receivership when the terms of a will fall too far from what courts are prepared to accept as "reasonable."

In the patrimony of the *furiosus* standard, courts (as in *Cartwright*) tended to accept the validity of contractual and testamentary provisions as long as the provisions were reasonably set forth and accurate in their relevant details. The profusion of medical theories of insanity early in the nineteenth century drew the courts into ever more subtle considerations and into an increasing dependence on technical literatures and persons with specialized training. Commenting on the birth of mental asylums in the Enlightenment,

Michel Foucault would find something that was "peculiar to the world of the asylum . . . at the end of the eighteenth century: this is the apotheosis of the *medical personage.*"[39]

The revolutions in France and America, though different in many and significant ways, shared a nearly innocent confidence in science and in systematic knowledge in all its forms. Pinel, in his famous *Treatise,* paused to tally the several causes leading men and women to such dreadful places as Salpêtrière and Bicêtre. Social conditions and the disruptions and upheavals of revolution were high on the list. Pinel also noted a phenomenon he called *manie sans delire,* which would evolve into the theory of moral insanity; a type of insanity that spares the intellect and most outward signs of rationality in a person who, nonetheless, has greatly diminished powers of self-control. Soon theories abounded to the effect that progress itself was cause of insanity, and that the most progressive nations—England, France, the United States—were especially vulnerable. In 1845, a New York doctor studying some 550 mental patients was able to discern 43 distinct causes, of which bad health was the most common (104), followed by "religious anxiety" (77), unrequited ambition (41), loss of property (28), studiousness (25), blows to the head (8), political agitation (5), and immersion in cold water (1). The famous York retreat established by and for Quakers (though coming to serve non-Quakers in equal numbers) would show among its first admissions between 1796 and 1843 patients suffering from mania (36.1%), melancholy (32.1%), and dementia (7.5%), with moral insanity accounting only for 0.6%.[40] The doctors did not quite agree on the particulars and made clear how very difficult it was to make such diagnoses, but the nosologies became authoritative nevertheless, and ever larger numbers in the general population seemed to fit them. In that climate of inchoate romanticism, and with Rousseau's echo still reverberating, even a progressive reformer of the stature of Dorothea Dix could conclude that the calamitous decline in mental health was the direct result of

"the habits, the customs, the temptations of civilized life and society." A widely read textbook of the period traced some forms of
insanity to overworking the brain, a classmate of the author's having
become insane "from too severe application to study. He has subsequently died in a lunatic asylum." This became a commonplace.
"Cases of insanity among gentlemen of the several professions, particularly those of law and divinity, resulting from overtaxing the
brain, are familiar to all."[41]

The French Revolution, America's War of Independence, and
Britain's own reform movements imparted to the early decades of
the nineteenth century a tone of heightened solicitude toward all
victims of injustice, warfare, illness, poverty, and prejudice. Antislavery movements, utopian projects, Reform acts, universal suf-
frage, anticolonialism, publicly funded houses for the poor, new
and more humanely managed asylums for the mentally ill were
springing up daily. Leading reformers of the age, such as England's
Anthony Ashley, Seventh Earl of Shaftesbury, and America's Benjamin Rush and Dorothea Dix, paid special attention to the plight
of the insane. Britain's Lunacy commissions would guide Parliament to the Lunacy acts of 1828 and 1845, with Shaftesbury's moral
outlook very much the animating spirit.

The abortive and often pathetic assaults perpetrated by individuals who were clearly deranged, combined with the growing concern for their proper care and for the safety of society, established
the context for the asylum movement and its enabling legislation.
When Margaret Nicholson made an attempt on the life of George
III (1776) or John Frith hurled a stone at the royal carriage (1800),
acquittals simply restored offenders again to the public byways
where they were encouraged to repeat the same or similar outrages.
The trials of such figures, not to mention Hadfield, perhaps the
most tragic of all, alerted a now sensitive and more caring public
to the need for proper places in which to maintain decent custody
of those who were simply unable to keep up with the pace of a

world in transition. Dorothea Dix was not entirely excessive in her appraisal, therefore, for the social dislocations taking place in this period certainly must have overburdened the sensibilities of many. Texts began to appear in numbers on the causes and treatments of moral insanity as professionals became convinced of its validity. The leading writer on the subject in the English-speaking world was James Cowles Prichard, who described the disease as one preventing the sufferer from "conducting himself with decency and propriety in the business of life." As Anne Digby has observed, this very definition was an open invitation to assign mental disorders to such a category, the "mad-doctors [pronouncing] on the 'disease' with a surprising self-confidence."[42] Still other texts appeared devoted to the subject of medical jurisprudence, for by now the medical community was regarded as an integral part of the overall program of human and social improvement, and was expected to work together with lawyers and the courts toward this end.

Reflecting on the state of affairs before passage of the Insane Offenders' Bill of 1800, W. Charles Hood, Superintendent of Bethlem Hospital in the 1850s, would observe that the law "was so defective, that the Attorney-General stated to the House of Commons, that it had been found that persons who had committed the most shocking acts, and had been acquitted on the ground of being deranged in their intellects, had been again allowed to go at large, and again committed similar atrocities."[43] He argues for facilities set up in response to the degree and nature of criminally insane acts, but not entirely separate facilities. For this would leave prisoner-patients "to prey mutually upon their morbid associations." The housing of insane inmates should be governed by the degree and quality of the disorders and their likelihood of cure, not by simplistic notions of whether or not the disorders yield criminal conduct. Through what Hood calls moral treatment, the patient recovers within an asylum which serves as a bridge to normal life. Country asylums house mostly paupers, and "as the feelings of this class of lunatics are by no means so acute and sensitive . . . as to render the society of Criminal Lunatics any infliction upon them," it is enough to keep the criminal away from middle-class lunatics![44]

Turning his attention to the 1851 census figures, Hood offers four quite interesting and revealing generalizations. First, insanity seems to be on the increase, rising from 1 in 7,000 to 1 in 500; it is more common in rural than in town settings (owing, following Prichard, to "hard labor and low diet," which explains why children suffer higher incidence; more common among paupers than among the middle and upper classes; more common among women than men.[45] Why paupers? Because the predispositions to pauperism include "irregular habits, intemperance, love of excitement, libertinism, general self-indulgence, and giving way to the impulses of the passions."[46]

Hood nonetheless eschews the "brainular" theory of insanity on solid Cartesian grounds, and with an admixture of Christian ethics: "If all our actions, virtuous as well as vicious, resulted from this presumed condition of the brain, man would possess no more control over his actions, than the paddle-wheels of a steam-boat over the engine by which they are set in motion."[47] Quoting the pessimistic Baron Alderson, who had testified before the House of Lords that "I believe crime to be a chronic disease, and not curable by a short process, if indeed curable at all," Hood would acquit all whose crimes arise from "irresistible impulses." On these and related grounds, he dismisses the reasoning in *Hadfield,* noting that the insane may have full rational comprehension of their actions. Even so, the insane murderer warrants incarceration for life:

> It may appear very severe to doom a man to perpetual confinement; but in cases where murder has been committed, or malicious attempts to murder have been made, how otherwise can society be protected?. . . . It should also be remembered . . . that if it had not been for the reformation which has

recently taken place in the Criminal Laws of this country, [men such as Hadfield] . . . would, unquestionably, have expiated their offenses on the scaffold—a circumstance which would disarm the hyper-criticism of those professed champions of humanity.[48]

In his *Statistics of Insanity* Hood reports that criminality is five times higher among men than women, but that insanity itself is higher among the latter—even if criminality is to some extent an expression of insanity.[49] He pauses to observe the relative purity of the "unmixed Celtic race of Cornishmen" as part of the explanation of the incidence of insanity in various counties. But he also concerns himself with occupational factors, recidivism rates (high among criminals), and the different pressures on rich and poor. The epidemiology of insanity has gained a clear voice.

One of the contemporary authorities was the same James Prichard of "moral insanity" repute. His *A Treatise on Insanity and Other Disorders of the Mind* (1835) and *On the Different Forms of Insanity in Relation to Jurisprudence* (1842) became classics in their own time.[50] Edinburgh-educated (1808 degree), a Fellow of the Royal Society, and internationally recognized, Prichard put moral insanity on the map of medical psychology, though not at the expense of medical expertise. To declare a disorder to be one of *moral* insanity was not to remove it from the medical and scientific contexts of study and explanation, and certainly not to turn it over to the clergy. Rather, it was left to the highly experienced clinical investigator to gauge the subtle failures of the disordered mind.

The line of argument was carried forth in Prichard's 1842 book, which gives a measure of the most authoritative and progressive thinking of the age regarding insanity in relation to jurisprudence. This work moved discussions of insanity away from considerations of defective *understanding* and toward the "moral" and affective side of mental life. For with regard to insanity, "almost every case, not only involves a disordered exercise of the intellectual faculties, but . . . implicates more remarkably the moral affections, the temper, the feelings and propensities so that it affects in reality the moral character even more decidedly than the understanding."[51] Moral insanity is "a disorder which affects only the feelings and affections, or what are termed the moral powers of the mind."[52] "In this disorder, the will is occasionally under the influence of an impulse, which suddenly drives the person affected to the perpetration of acts of the most revolting kind, to the commission of which he has no motive. The impulse is accompanied by consciousness; but it is in some instances irresistible."[53]

But just how is one to distinguish murders from insane homicides? Prichard offers the relevant criteria, all variously qualified, but all signaling the need for medical sophistication in comprehending the nature of the disordered mind. There will generally be a history of moroseness or such diseases as epilepsy; the act is often devoid of motive; there may be several victims; there are no accomplices, usually no plan of escape, typically no remorse; the victim is often a family relation.[54] Prichard's principal focus, however, is on the absence of a rational motive. In addition, he insists that the partially insane have as great a claim to acquittals as the raving lunatics, and thus rejects out of hand Hale's dicta and the entire "wild beast" tradition.

The nineteenth century was perhaps the original century of "the brain sciences," laying the foundation and setting the agenda for the large projects of the twentieth century. Franz Gall (1758–1828), sometimes trivialized for his founding of phrenology, was one of the premier neuroanatomists of his age. His detailed studies of fetuses aborted at different gestational ages were foundational for developmental neuroanatomy, as were his studies of the brains of different species for comparative neuroanatomy.

His observations of the brains of deceased geniuses, insane persons, criminals, and the mentally deficient led to the major conclusions appearing in his influential works: that the mental and moral faculties are innate; they are controlled by centers in the brain; their relative richness and impoverishment is a direct result of the mass of brain devoted to them. Virtues and vices, criminality, sexuality, deviancies of all sorts, not to mention affection, social affiliation, and benevolence can all be traced to regulative centers in the brain which, when diseased, result in every form of mental and moral degradation. Of course the environment and education count for much, for it is these that exercise and enrich the brain and enlarge its functions. But limits to these influences are natively established. Brain pathology yields social pathology, and the latter can in turn make the former even worse. Forbidden by the Viennese authorities in 1802 to lecture further on "craniology"—on the grounds of endangering religion—Gall thus came to have an even greater reputation than his scientific work alone might have gained for him.[55]

In the English-speaking world, Spurzheim and the Combe brothers in Edinburgh would advance phrenology, tying it to the faculty of psychology of Reid and Stewart, and extending its applications into any number of social, artistic, and educational domains. A nearly serene confidence characterized the leading writers in this tradition, as exemplified by George Combe's explanation of the causes of religious and political fanaticism: "The phrenologist in contemplating these organs operating in excess, or in a state of disease, obtains light on this subject which other persons cannot reach. Mere excess in size and activity leads to fanaticism and to a persuasion of inspiration, such as occurred in Bunyan, Swedenborg, and the late Edward Erving. . . . Diseased activity produces belief in actual communication with Heaven."[56]

Gall and his phrenological disciples were not alone, of course. By the first decades of the nineteenth century there was little doubt among medical persons as to the proximate causes of insanity. William Battie had published *A Treatise of Madness* in 1758, fortified in his arguments by his experiences as a Governor of Bethlem Hospital. These were sufficient to convince him that "the one immediate necessary and sufficient cause of the praeternatural and false perception of objects . . . must be some disorder of that substance which is medullary and strictly nervous."[57] Dr. Battie would appear or be cited in any number of cases involving questions of criminal liability or testamentary capacity.

Such theoretical conformity so firmly in place by the nineteenth century was not at the expense of respect and concern for the impact of social conditions on that most frail entity, the human mind. Yet the greater the concern and respect for the influence of such conditions, the more complex the relationship seemed to be, and the greater the need for the courts to be properly advised by the growing cadre of medical authorities. The welter of attitudes, theories, and concerns abounding in this period became crystallized, as often is the case, by a celebrated trial producing an unpopular outcome. This was the trial of Daniel McNaughtan in 1843.[58]

So much has been written about the actual trial of McNaughtan and the "rules" regarding the insanity defense allegedly propounded in the case that the broader political context tends to be ignored.[59] The intended target of McNaughtan's assassination plot was Prime Minister Robert Peel, a founder of the Conservative Party and a man with a somewhat protean political philosophy. He had vigorously opposed the Reform Act of the 1830s and became an active supporter of Catholic emancipation some years later. He was resolved to preserve the protectionist laws (the Corn laws) favoring the agricultural aristocracy, even as these led to higher food prices that were increasingly hard on the laboring classes. Pressed by public opinion to take corrective action, Peel defended the Corn Laws but promised adjustments which, on the whole, seemed intended more to gull the unsuspecting than to provide any significant relief. Anti-Corn-Law factions became large, vocal and occasionally threatening. Sentiment against the Peel government in Scotland was especially virulent, not to mention organized, and Daniel Mc-Naughtan was active within one such group.

In this climate of unrest several attempts had been made on the life of young Queen Victoria. Edward Oxford, an eighteen-year-old who probably had no real intention of harming the Queen, entered her carriage and fired two pistols, though it's not clear that there was a ball in either.[60] His acquittal on the grounds of insanity upset the Queen and much of the nation. The general attitude at the time can be gleaned from an article covering the case in *Blackwood's.*

> But there came five doctors on the scene, and at their approach the light of reason darkened. These astute personages—mysterious in their means of knowledge, and confident in their powers of extinguishing the common sense of both judges and jury—came to demonstrate that the unfortunate young gentleman at the bar was no more the object of punishment than . . . is the torch with which a hay-stack is fired, or the bullet, cannon-ball, or dagger with which life is taken away! But let them speak for themselves—these wise men of Gotham—these confident disciples of the *"couldn't help it"* school![61]

The article goes on to quote from the expert testimony of doctors, one of whom identified the precise form of Oxford's insanity as "a lesion of the will."

The Queen's attitude was no different. Writing to Peel after McNaughtan's acquittal she would complain, "We have seen the trials of Oxford and MacNaughten *(sic)* conducted by the ablest lawyers of the day—and they *allow* and *advise* the Jury to pronounce the verdict of not guilty on account of insanity, whilst *everybody* is morally convinced that both malefactors were perfectly conscious and aware of what they did."[62] And in her diary she recorded a letter received from Robert Peel which included printed matter found in McNaughtan's lodgings: "Had a letter from Sir Robert Peel, with very curious enclosures, relative to MacNaughten who is clearly not in the least mad."[63] Some of the attempts on the Royal person were serious, some frivolous, but all of them together created an atmosphere of fear and impatience toward pleas of insanity or mental deficiency, and increased vigilance of the authorities in this time of political and economic turmoil.

Mistaking his victim for the Prime Minister, McNaughtan had stalked and then fatally wounded Robert Peel's secretary, Edward Drummond, on Friday afternoon, January 20, 1843. The victim of this attack languished for days, dying on January 25th. Many quickly concluded that the assassination rhetoric of the Anti-Corn Law League had finally been put into lethal practice. The actual facts were different.[64]

Daniel McNaughtan had tried his hand at acting, had worked for his family in Glasgow, and finally began his own woodworking business. He was keenly interested in political and social issues, because an avid reader of such egoistic philosophers as La Rochefoucauld, and was an active participant in Glasgow's Athenaeum Debating Society. His affiliation with the Mechanics' Institution brought him into contact with other political radicals, including large number of Chartists and Socialists, all of them quite sympathetic with McNaughtan's own outspoken hostility to the policies of the Peel government. For its part, the government kept watch on such societies and radical groups and may well have provided good reason for McNaughtan to consider himself, as he said, "driven to desperation by persecution."

The Queen against Daniel M'Naughton (sic) was heard before Lord Chief Justice Tindal and Justices Williams and Coleridge.[65] The prosecution was led by Sir William Webb-Follett, the Solicitor General, who reviewed for the benefit of the jury the law as it pertains to the defense of insanity. McNaughtan's counsel was the future Lord Chief Justice, Alexander Cockburn, whose principal medical expert in court was another of the famous Monros, Edward Thomas Monro. The expert *in absentia* was a young American doctor, Isaac Ray.

The Solicitor General drew the jury's attention to the law as it had been set down by Hale and amplified by Tracy in *Rex v. Arnold,* by Mansfield in *Rex v. Bellingham,* and by Erskine in *Rex v. Hadfield,* "who made one of the most eloquent and able speeches, probably, that was ever delivered at the bar."[66] What Webb-Follett wanted the jury to learn from Erskine's address is that, in matters of this kind, it is not sufficient to show that the defendant suffered from delusion, but that "he committed the act in consequence of that delusion."[67] Moreover, the jury was not to be led all the way by Erskine's thesis, for it was at once too narrow and too broad. Surely an individual may have so defective a state of mind as not to be able to distinguish between right and wrong and still not be suffering from insane delusions. More to the point at hand, one who is deluded but nonetheless knows the difference between right and wrong, and knows further the nature of the act he is committing, is not to be acquitted merely because of some delusion. The corrective for Erskine's generalizations was, by Webb-Follett's lights, ably supplied by Mansfield in *Bellingham,* and this is what Webb-Follett would have control the verdict in the trial of McNaughtan.

In his opening speech for the defense on the next day, and fully aware of the sensitive nature of his mission, Cockburn made it a point to say that he was "addressing a British jury, a tribunal to which truth has seldom been a suppliant in vain."[68] He then reminded the jury that English law, like that of all civilized nations, takes special cognizance of those whom "Providence . . . thinks fit to lay upon a human being the heaviest and most appalling of all calamities . . . the deprivation of that reason, which is man's only light and guide."[69] A person who suffers a mental disease that leads to frantic imagination and ungovernable fury is exempt from legal responsibility, and "to hold otherwise would be to violate every principle of justice and humanity."

The question, then, will be whether McNaughtan is the victim of such a disease, and whether his actions were the product of it. To answer this question, it will not help to consult fair-minded but dated authorities. "It must not be forgotten that the knowledge of this disease in all its various forms is a matter of very recent growth." Consequently, "I feel that I may appeal to the many medical gentlemen I see around me, whether the knowledge and pathology of this disease has not within a few recent years first acquired the character of a science?"[70]

Cockburn then read a lengthy passage from Isaac Ray's *A Treatise of Medical Jurisprudence* (1838), calling it "perhaps the most scientific treatise the age has produced upon the subject of insanity in relation to jurisprudence."[71] In this work Ray summarized the insanity provisions of the laws of different countries, pausing to comment critically on famous dicta. He made clear that Hale's classification and understanding of the forms of insanity were the product of limited knowledge and experience, and that no competent and contemporary medical person would find much merit in them. His impatience with attempts to tie insanity to one or another characteristic feature is most economically expressed in a later work, but still fully in agreement with the position expounded in the *Treatise*:

The existence of insanity in any form is not always proved by the presence of any particular symptom, or even group of symptoms, but rather by changes of mind or character, which can be explained on no other hypothesis than that of disease. In other words, the party must be compared with himself, not with any imaginary standard of sanity or insanity . . . I have no wish to conceal any difficulty which the subject may present. Science is full of difficulties, and the pleasure and dignity of its pursuit consist mainly in triumphing over them. . . . If the difficulty of distinguishing between moral depravity and moral insanity is a sufficient reason for ignoring the latter altogether, the argument would be equally strong against admitting any kind of insanity in defence of crime. Was there ever a case on trial entirely free from doubt?[72]

With the latest scientific authority behind him, Cockburn then referred to other cases, noting with confidence that "most scientific men" would agree that "Bellingham was a madman"; that others executed out of ignorance in the past would be spared today; most importantly—and following Ray's position—that each case must be understood in its own terms lest adherence to mere generalities lead "into disastrous results." Nonetheless, science and medicine do provide principles now admitted by all competent persons. To wit:

> Whatever and wherever may be the seat of the immaterial man, one thing appears perfectly clear to human observation, namely—that the point which connects the immaterial and the material man—is the brain; and, furthermore, it is clear that all defects in the cerebral organization . . . have the effect of impairing and deranging the faculties and functions of the immaterial mind. . . .
>
> Modern science has incontrovertibly established that any one of these intellectual and moral functions of the mind may be subject to separate disease, and thereby man may be rendered the victim of the most fearful delusions, the slave of uncontrollable impulses.[73]

All of Cockburn's address indicated how thoroughly he had absorbed the socio-medical perspective on deviant behavior. McNaughtan's mother had died when he was young and he was raised by a stepmother who did not show him "that full measure of kindness which is usually shown to legitimate offspring." He spent much time alone, living "without friend or associate, without recreation or amusement, save that which was found in turning from severe toil to severer study." Inevitably there were physical consequences, McNaughtan's headaches compelling him on occasion to "throw himself into the waters of the Clyde in order to seek some relief from the torturing fever by which his brain was consumed."[74]

The defendant had been examined by several physicians. Dr. E. T. Monro, claiming for himself "an experience of thirty years" with insane patients, expressed no doubt at all but that McNaughtan was insane. McNaughtan had told him of plots against his person and his good name; that he was a man tossed like a cork on the sea and beyond the reach of even "a ton of drugs." Wherever he went he found people watching him; watching him in Glasgow, in Edinburgh, in Liverpool, even in France. Only when confronting his victim at Charing Cross did he realize that he would gain peace by killing him.

Solicitor General: Do you mean to say, Dr. Monro, that you could satisfy yourself as to a person's state of mind by merely going into a cell and putting questions to him?

Dr. Monro: In many instances I can.

Solicitor General: May insanity exist with a moral perception of right and wrong?

Dr. Monro: Yes; it is very common.

Gradually but inexorably the authority of Coke, Hale, Tracy, and Mansfield was not so much subverted as understood to be the pardonable result of philosophies and folk-sciences of the mind, now clearly overcome by the new medicine. The final testimony was given by the leading British figure of the time in medical jurisprudence, Dr. Forbes Winslow, whose *Plea of Insanity in Criminal Cases* had just been published.

Mr. Clarkson: (co-counsel): Mr. Winslow, you are a surgeon residing in Guildford Street?

Dr. Winslow: I am.

Mr. Clarkson: You are the author of "Plea of Insanity in Criminal Cases," and other works on the subject of insanity?

Dr. Winslow: Yes.

Mr. Clarkson: I think, Mr. Winslow, that you have been in Court during the whole of the trial and have not been summoned on either side, and have heard all the evidence on the part of the Crown and for the defence?

Dr. Winslow: I have.

Mr. Clarkson: Judging from the evidence which you have heard, what is your opinion as to the prisoner's state of mind?

Dr. Winslow: I have not the slightest hesitation in saying that he is insane, and that he committed the offence in question whilst afflicted with a delusion, under which he appears to have been labouring for a considerable length of time.[75]

With this Lord Chief Justice Tindal informed the Solicitor General that unless rebuttal testimony was offered to challenge the statements of the experts, he would have to stop the case. As there was no medical evidence on the other side, the Solicitor General informed the jury that he would not be discharging his duty properly to ask for a verdict against the defendant. The learned judges had decided "that the evidence on the part of the defendant, and more particularly the evidence of the medical witnesses, is sufficient to show that this unfortunate man at the time he committed the act was labouring under insanity."[76] In remarkably summary fashion, Tindal then informed the jury that the medical evidence in favor of the defense was so preponderant that "no part of it . . . leaves any doubt on the mind. It seems almost unnecessary that I should go through the evidence." The jury required no more, and found

McNaughtan not guilty on the ground of insanity. As a result of the verdict and the outpouring of resentment that followed, the House of Lords agreed to put five questions to the judges in order to clarify the law as it is to be understood in cases such as *Mc-Naughtan*. Tindal and Maule met with the Peers on June 19 to answer the questions and to supply posterity with that elusive guide, the so-called McNaughtan Rules. The questions and the judges' replies are still worth considering, even apart from their relevance to the history of the insanity defense:[77]

"1st.—What is the law respecting alleged crimes committed by persons afflicted with insane delusion in respect of one or more particular subjects or persons; as, for instance, where, at the time of the commission of the alleged crime, the accused knew he was acting contrary to law, but did the act complained of with a view, under the influence of insane delusion, of redressing or revenging some supposed grievance or injury, or of producing some supposed public benefit?"

This question is obviously connected to the entire web of conceptual difficulties arising from the abandonment of the "wild beast" standard in the form of it as bequeathed by Coke and Hale and as applied by Tracy, Mansfield, and others. The defendant Hadfield arguably knew he was acting contrary to law, but insisted that nothing less than the redemption of the human race hung in the balance. Bellingham's crime was committed for the express purpose of redressing a (delusional) grievance, and McNaughtan represented a veritable *league* of disaffected and indignant countrymen convinced that the death of Robert Peel could only have salutary consequences.

Both Chief Judge Maule and the Lord Chief Justice Tindal expressed reservations about answering so general a question in the absence of specific facts. Still, Maule was prepared to take the position that persons "circumstanced as stated in the question" would *not* be acquitted, for the settled law only exonerates those whose mental defects prevent them from "knowing right from wrong." In any case, whether the mental illness envisaged by the question would actually constitute grounds for acquittal "is not a matter of law, but of physiology, and not of that obvious and familiar kind as to be inferred without proof." Maule here seems to want it both ways, at once preserving Mansfield's "knowing-right-from-wrong" test, while still having expert medical testimony supply the necessary proofs.

Tindal's response to the first question was even more traditional. A partially insane individual, deluded with respect to one or more subjects or persons, is nonetheless punishable for his crimes "if he knew at the time of committing such crime, that he was acting contrary to law, by which expression we understand your Lordships to mean the law of the land." But McNaughtan surely knew that his attack on Edward Drummond was contrary to English law so, again, it is not obvious that Tindal's answer to the first question is compatible with the position he took toward the close of the trial itself.

"2nd.—What are the proper questions to be submitted to the jury when a person, alleged to be afflicted with insane delusion respecting one or more particular subjects or persons, is charged with the commission of a crime (murder, for example), and insanity is set up as a defence?"

Maule took the burden of this question quite literally, replying that the point is simply to determine whether the accused is guilty or not. To assist the jury, the judge may have to review the standards or criteria of insanity, in which case Maule would rehearse what he had stated in answering the first question. Tindal's answer provided what would come to be known as the McNaughtan Rule (or Rules): jurors are to be instructed in such cases that every defendant is presumed to be sane until the contrary is proven, and what must be proved to the satisfaction of the jury is that "at the time of the committing of the act, the party accused was labouring under such a defect of reason, from disease of the mind, as not to know the nature and quality of the act he was doing, or, if he did know it, that he did not know he was doing what was wrong."

Tindal went on to explain that this wording is preferable to versions that cite or suggest a knowledge of the law of the land, or a general knowledge of right and wrong. The important consideration is the defendant's mental capacity as regards the specific act with which he has been charged. One senses the influence of Isaac Ray in this, too, for Ray had noted the failure of the criminally insane to regard their own acts as wrong, even though displaying a robust sense of right and wrong in general.

"3rd.—In what terms ought the question to be left to the jury as to the prisoner's state of mind at the time when the act was committed?"

Maule crisply replied that this is at the judge's discretion, constrained only by established law in such cases and by the need to help the jury reach a right verdict. And Tindal's answer to the second question was taken by him as answering this one as well.

"4th.—If a person under an insane delusion as to existing facts commits an offence in consequence thereof, is he thereby excused?"

This question looks back to *Hadfield* and to Erskine's example of the potter's vessel. Maule refers to his answer to the first question, presumably still content that such a question is to be settled by "physiology" (that is, medicine). Clearly following Erskine's rationale and thereby reconciling the outcomes in *Hadfield* and *Bellingham,* Tindal was prepared to offer a general principle to cover such cases:

We think he must be considered in the same situation as to responsibility as if the facts with respect to which the delusion exists were real. For example, if, under the influence of his delusion, he supposes another man to be in the act of attempting to take away his life, and he kills that man, as he supposes, in self-defence, he would be exempt from punishment. If his delusion was that the deceased had inflicted a serious injury to his character and fortune, and he killed him in revenge for such supposed injury, he would be liable to punishment.

Some years later, New Hampshire's Justice William Spencer Ladd, in *Smith v. Jones* (1871), would encapsulate the perilous logic already long recognized in Tindal's position:

It is, in effect, saying to the jury, the prisoner was mad when he committed the act, but he did not use sufficient reason in his madness. He killed a man because, under an insane delusion, he falsely believed the man had done him a great wrong. . . . If he had killed a man only because, under an insane delusion, he falsely believed the man would kill him . . . that would have been giving the rein to an instinct of self preservation, and would not be a crime.[78]

The fifth question posed by the Lords was partly responsive to the criticisms arising from Forbes Winslow's comments, so confidently expressed without Winslow's ever having examined McNaughtan:

"5th.—Can a medical man, conversant with the disease of insanity, who never saw the prisoner previously to the trial, but who was present during the whole trial, and the examination of all the witnesses, be asked his opinion as to the state of the prisoner's mind?"

Maule's truncated answer to this question reduced finally to the proposition that if three eminent judges such as those presiding over the trial of McNaughtan had seen fit to admit such testimony, then the answer to the question is simply "yes." Judges decide on the admissibility of evidence, the standing of witnesses, and other issues. Tindal, who was in fact the sitting judge when just such an opinion was admitted, answered the question more directly, concluding that such a specialist could not "in strictness" offer evidence as to the state of mind of a person he had never examined; but where the facts (of insanity) are not disputed, and the general question is a *scientific* one, it may be simply convenient to have the benefit of such expert opinion.

Even before learning the details of *McNaughtan,* Chief Justice Shaw of Massachusetts—also influenced by Isaac Ray—had instructed the jury in the landmark trial of Abner Rogers (1843) in such a way as to avoid the sorts of problems inherent in the McNaughtan Rule.[79] Rogers had stabbed to death a Mr. Lincoln, the warden of the Massachusetts State Prison at Belchertown. Ample evidence attesting to the insanity of the defendant was marshaled at trial. What was special about the case, however, was Shaw's instructions to the jury, which contained a particle of great novelty. There was little doubt but that Rogers was deluded and, under the weight of delusion, regarded the warden as a threat upon his own life. Thus Shaw could have stopped at *Hadfield* in his charge to the jury, leaving them only to decide whether the homicidal act was the product of this specific delusional fear. But Shaw went beyond this in listing the criteria the jury must apply. Rogers was to be acquitted if the jury found that his actions were "the result of disease." Reflecting on this precedential utterance a year later, Ray would observe, "Had he discarded every other condition of irresponsibility, and planted himself firmly upon this . . . he would have achieved the honor of making a signal advance in the criminal law of insanity."[80]

Ray had argued tellingly for just such a position. Indeed, the year before McNaughtan was tried, Prichard's *On the Different Forms of Insanity in Relation to Jurisprudence* had been published in England and, as previously noted, had reached conclusions of a similar nature. An insane person may be "otherwise in possession of the full and undisturbed use of his mental faculties," for the disease often "affects in reality the moral character even more decidedly than the understanding."[81] Again, Prichard's focus on moral insanity, his attention to the emotional over the rational-intellectual defects of the insane, and his coherent thesis that the disordered mind is—like the mind of the idiot—not fit for the punishments of law would stand as the central elements of enlightened thought on the whole subject. Thus, far from appeasing the new view, *McNaughtan* could only arouse the impatience of those at the forefront of medical jurisprudence.

The momentum that had been imparted as early as *Hadfield* increased significantly by mid-century and would reach its peak in American cases. Writing in the 1870s, Henry Maudsley remarked that, although initially docilely following the lead of British jurists, recent decisions in the United States constituted a marked advance on anything that been settled to date in England.[82] The three cases leading him to this conclusion were all decided in the Supreme Judicial Court of New Hampshire, and the judges—William Spencer Ladd, J. Everett Sargent, Charles Doe, and Ira Perley— were uncommonly familiar with the leading texts of the day in the field of medical jurisprudence.

In *Boardman v. Woodman,* a complex testamentary case involving challenges to the competence of the testatrix, Margaret Blydenburgh, the Court, through Justice Sargent, laid down the principle that the court alone shall determine the competence of those presenting themselves as expert witnesses, but that qualified persons are entitled to offer evaluations based on hypothetical cases they take to be relevant to the instant case. The jury must decide whether the actual and hypothetical instances are relevantly similar. Further, the opinion of witnesses who are not experts is not admissible as evidence regarding the mental state of others. Citing *Dew* and the opinion of Sir John Nicholl, as well as the writings of

Drs. Battie and Willis, Sargent is prepared to apply the criterion of delusion to determine whether there is "active insanity" in such cases. But absent proof of delusion, the Court would be disinclined to "disturb those numerous testamentary dispositions of property which are made by those whose moral sense be none of the keenest, or whose affections may not run in the same channel with those of their neighbors."[83] Dissenting on several technical points, Justice Doe added a revealing comment on Coke and Hale, who "unfortunately copied the opinions of the medical authorities of their day on the subject of insanity, and their successors were slow to question anything endorsed by so great names."[84] Doe went on to express concern lest books written by doctors be taken as proofs on question of fact. This was Nicholl's mistake, and it led to the arbitrary adoption of delusion as the sole criterion. But "that cannot be a fact in law, which is not a fact in science," and the last word is surely not in on the question of the essential nature of insanity. Doe, seeing the future more clearly, would settle cases such as *Boardman* by adhering to the principle that no crime can be committed and no will expressed "by any form of mental disease, and that the indications and tests of mental disease are matters of fact."[85]

In *State v. Pike,* a murder case, the Court considered Pike's defense in the lower court, which was that his homicidal act was the product of a mental disease called "dipsomania."[86] Writing for the Court, Justice Doe presented an extraordinary analysis of the modern history of juridical understandings of insanity and what he took to be the mistaken views only recently corrected. One of these, just set aside by this same New Hampshire court in *State v. Bartlett,* is the "great error" according to which it is a defendant's burden to prove insanity.[87] But "the presumption of sanity is not an artificial or legal presumption, but a natural inference of fact to be made by a jury from the absence of evidence to show that the party did not enjoy that soundness which experience proves to be the general condition of the human mind. . . . The state has no more need of a legal presumption of sanity, than the defendant has of a presumption of innocence."[88]

On the question of whether a jury is to regard "dipsomania" as a mental disease, Doe is equally impatient with the past. Hale, he recalls, had instructed a jury that witches no doubt existed. Any number of pathological conditions were obscured in "theological clouds that . . . were appalling." This encumbrance now gone, it is still the case that very few persons recognize insanity to be a disease. England's Lord Chancellor is quoted as protesting before the House of Lords as recently as March 1862 that medical specialists were proceeding "upon the vicious principle of considering insanity as a disease."[89] What the long history of the subject teaches, according to Doe, is that it has been far too easy to install tentative and untried medical theories as legal doctrines, thus prejudging the progress of science while saddling courts for decades with pronouncements long abandoned by the scientific community. The now hegemonous "right-wrong" standard is illustrative: "It is the common practice for experts, under the oath of a witness, to inform the jury, in substance, that knowledge is not the test, and for the judge, not under the oath of a witness, to inform the jury that knowledge is the test. And the situation is still more impressive, when the judge is forced by an impulse of humanity, as he often is, to substantially advise the jury to acquit the accused on the testimony of experts, in violation of the test asserted by himself."[90]

On questions of the sort raised by, say, "dipsomania," one either recognizes this as a technical, scientific question to be settled factually by relevant experts, or one should regard it as a question of law and forego the judgments of the doctors. Clearly, such questions are questions of *fact,* and judges should either remain silent or present themselves as experts, take the oath and testify![91] Justice Ladd, in *State v. Jones,* made the point in his own and equally forceful way as he considered Tindal and Maule in their attempt to inform the House of Lords:

It is entirely obvious that a court of law undertaking to lay down an abstract general proposition, which may be given to the jury in all cases, by which they are to determine whether the prisoner had capacity to entertain criminal intent, stands in exactly the same position as that occupied by the English judges in attempting to answer the questions propounded to them by the House of Lords in [McNaughtan]; and whenever such an attempt is made, I think it must always be attended with failure, because it is an attempt to find what does not exist, namely, a rule of law wherewith to solve a question of fact. . . . No formal rule can be applied in settling questions which have relation to liberty and life, merely because it will lessen the labor of the court or jury. . . . In a matter where we must inevitably rely to a great extent upon the facts of science, we have consented to receive those facts as developed and ascertained by the researchers and observations of our own day, instead of adhering blindly to dogmas which were accepted as facts of science and erroneously promulgated as principles of law fifty or a hundred years ago.[92]

As this understanding made inevitable progress in other jurisdictions and beyond the United States, the effect was to place ever greater weight on the testimony of doctors, in the absence of a general principle or universally applicable standard which courts might convey to jurors. The state of affairs was an open invitation to "trial by medicine," and to what often has become the spectacle of "experts" of well-known but often rather eccentric views being chosen by each side.[93]

Toward the end of his distinguished career Isaac Ray too addressed this problem, but could offer little more than the hope that those who administer the laws would have "broader views and a firmer spirit," and that doctors and lawyers would rise to a "higher sense of professional honor."[94] Such hopes have not been redeemed, and attempts by judges ever since to assist jurors in making sense of the competing claims have sometimes sunk to the level of low comedy.[95] Nor has there been wide recognition of the gulf between the traditional legal notion of a fact and what the psychiatric specialists would be inclined to call by that name.[96]

Considered abstractly, the progressive orientation of courts such as New Hampshire's in the second half of the nineteenth century might seem to have provided an improved alternative to the less pliant reasoning grounded in the "wild beast" standard. By the lights of Ray, Prichard, Hood, Bucknill, Guy, and other specialists and judges influenced by them, even the more relaxed rationale applied in *McNaughtan* was in keeping with what was then known—or thought to be known—about insanity. Though quick to identify the ignorance and hopeless confusions of the past, the progressive doctors and judges of the previous century were less able to regard their own orientations under a comparably historical light. Well into the 1880s and beyond, it remained customary for medical specialists to include epileptics in the category of the insane or latently insane. With the further liberalization of standards of insanity, and the increasing ease with which those meeting such standards could be committed, large numbers of persons who would never have been deprived of their liberties in earlier centuries were consigned to asylums for life in the "progressive" nineteenth century; sometimes out of misplaced philanthropy, sometimes as a result of a simply ignorant diagnosis, and sometimes for the financial benefit of those who had secured the court order.

Even referring to trends in this area as "progressive" is risking to discover novelty where the pendulum has simply moved to another position. The American experience with the mentally disturbed is alone sufficient to illustrate the trial-and-error approach of the courts and the larger society. In colonial times the insane were entrusted to the care of immediate family or of those in the community willing to bear the civic burden. The solicitude required of good Christians was fortified by the belief that God had supplied the impoverished and defective as a test and trial, as opportunities for good works. In the decades surrounding the American Revolution the rhetoric shifted, the causes of crime and insanity now located in bad laws and evil regimes. Prisons and almshouses and fledgling asylums were organized to provide moral instruction and sound discipline. The understanding was widespread that criminality and defective personalities would be transformed by nurturing and orderly communities that would be models of the good and free community, the good republic itself.

The Age of Jackson, which presided over a thoroughgoing democratization of society, seemed to compound the problems of the less fortunate. By the 1830s and 1840s these tendencies—the tendency to regard maladaptive behavior as socially caused, and the tendency to regard special environments as essential for dealing with problem-citizens—resulted in what David Rothman has called "the discovery of the asylum."[97] But it was only a matter of decades before hope collided with reality. Psychopathology and criminality were not significantly touched by the theories on which these asylums were based and operated. Predictably, as the environmental hypotheses failed of evidence, physiological theories were asserted more vigorously. By the 1850s most "experts" regarded insanity as an expression of brain pathology, requiring (therefore) a medical rather than a moral approach.

The nineteenth century hosted the great reform movements of modern times; for that matter, of *all* times. The cruelties and exploitations of earlier ages tended to be traced to the past's relatively primitive levels of scientific understanding, tied of course to superstitions and fanaticisms of one sort or another. The corrective, then, was to be found in the positive knowledge contributed by science itself. The courts, as society's principal source of justice and equity, found common cause with a medical community now liberated from ageless superstitions and clerical impertinences. The attempt to invigorate legal thought with the findings and general outlook of the new medical and social sciences was sincere and in some respects successful and worthy. But the adaptability of law is not limitless, and the challenges the new perspective would bring to any number of foundational jural assumptions created a number of problems and dilemmas embracing far more than the relatively isolated province of the insanity defense.

6

JURAL SCIENCE
& SOCIAL SCIENCE

The actual or perceived "rules" developed during and in the immediate wake of *McNaughtan* satisfied few and were often breached. Within two years of the verdict, W. Griesinger's authoritative *Mental Pathology and Therapeutics* came to challenge all of the comforting generalizations nonspecialists had adopted in the matter of insanity.[1] Griesinger, on the basis of extensive clinical experience, rejected the proposition that insanity invariably includes the element of delusion; that the insane cannot distinguish between right and wrong; that there are always irresistible motives behind the productions of madness. The one generalization he did endorse, and this on the very first page of the book, concerns the origin of the symptoms of insanity: "What organ must necessarily and invariably be diseased where there is madness?. . . . Physiological and pathological facts show us that this organ can only be the brain."[2] But certitudes stop here. Only the clinic, with its wealth of varied and often surprising material, can supply the facts and principles on which any responsible diagnosis must depend, and the clinic already defeats the sorts of criteria that have been invoked by courts.

Nonetheless, well into the twentieth century in the United States and elsewhere, the controlling criminal statutes commonly asserted or strongly implied a "right-wrong" test as the test of insanity, though remaining vexingly delphic on the nature of the knowledge embraced by the standard. Also acknowledged were "irresistible impulses"—Erskine's "motives irresistible"—as courts attempted to make room for those whose knowledge of right and wrong was nonetheless incapable of overcoming their mad will and desire. Then, too, there were defendants who well knew that their actions violated statutory law, but nonetheless claimed to serve some higher moral or divine law. The courts were inclined to bend the *McNaughtan* rules in these cases as well. Thus in *Schmidt v. New York,* Judge Cardozo held that "there are times and circumstances in which the word 'wrong' as used in the statutory test of responsibility ought not to be limited to legal wrong."[3]

Burden of Proof and Expert Testimony

Always a source of confusion and of struggle between competing perspectives, the insanity defense late in the nineteenth century raised any number of criterial problems. On the surface, both British and American courts subscribed unreservedly to the proposition that all defendants are presumed sane; the burden of proof is therefore on them if they wish to raise the defense of insanity. However, it remained unclear as to how heavy this burden is. As far back as the trial of Abner Rogers, presided over by Lemuel Shaw, a close follower of Isaac Ray's medical jurisprudence, jurors expressed confusion as to how persuaded they must be of a defendant's claimed insanity. Shaw had made clear to the jury that

> the ordinary presumption is, that a person is of sound mind, until the contrary appears; and in order to shield one from criminal responsibility, the presumption must be rebutted by proof of the contrary, satisfactory to the jury. Such proof may arise, either out of the evidence offered by the prosecutor to establish the case against the accused, or from distinct evidence offered on his part; in either case it must be sufficient to establish the fact of insanity; otherwise the presumption

will stand. (*Commonwealth v. Rogers,* 7 Met. [Mass.] 500 [1844])

Nonetheless, after several hours of deliberation, the jury returned to ask Shaw whether proof of insanity had to be "beyond a doubt." Shaw then informed them that in such cases the standard of proof is a *preponderance of the evidence.* But within a year, in the same state, another murder charge answered by the defense of insanity would find jurors instructed to consider proof *beyond a reasonable doubt* (*Commonwealth v. York,* 9 Met. [Mass.] [1845] 93, 116). In his dissenting opinion, however, Justice Wilde insisted that a jury must acquit if they merely have "a reasonable doubt" (p. 134).

The U.S. Supreme Court first took up the question of the burden of proof (of insanity) in 1895 in *Davis v. U.S.* The *Davis* Court was greatly moved by the reasoning of Chief Justice Nicholson in an earlier case, where he had written:

Malice is presumed from certain facts and persons are held responsible for the consequences of their acts upon the principle of presumption. These presumptions are fixed rules established by public policy and not by the reasoning upon each particular case. . . . It has been said that statistics show that a majority of the persons acquitted on the ground of insanity were not insane, and this even in England, where the strongest rule against the defendant prevails. The probability of a jury finding an insane man guilty, under the rule that insanity must be established to their reasonable satisfaction, is very slight as compared with the evil that results to society from the application of the doctrine that a reasonable doubt as to whether the defendant is sane or insane must be followed by acquittal. *Dove v. State* (3 Heiskell, 366, 374)

The "public policy" to which Nicholson referred is perhaps better understood as the basic set of presuppositions on which a rule of law achieves its broad intelligibility. It is better, thought Nicholson, to rely on a jury's inclination in capital cases to give defendants the benefit of the doubt, than to require them through a questionable legal doctrine to acquit just in case they have some reservations about the defendant's sanity.

Dennis Davis had been indicted in 1894 for the murder of Sol Blackwell in western Arkansas. He was found guilty and his motion for a new trial had been denied. He was thereupon sentenced to be hanged. In the original trial, evidence was offered to suggest that at the time of the crime Davis was of unsound mind. A physician and other witnesses who knew him well spoke of Davis as "weak minded" and "half crazy." The instructions to the jury made clear that the presumption in such cases is that of sanity, and that the performance of an act clearly arising from hostile motives and executed according to a plan constitutes proof of intent and of competence. The judge noted, however, that for a person to be relieved of criminal responsibility it was not necessary that he be "a raving maniac," but that something more than "mere eccentricity" was required. The echo of "idle humours" was audible here. A failure (owing to mental disease) to understand the nature of the act, or to be able to control one's will to the point of refraining from the act, would constitute grounds of exculpation. But in this, instructed the judge, insanity must be established by the evidence "to the reasonable satisfaction of a jury, and the burden of proof of the insanity rests with the defendant."

In examining this case and its precedents in *Davis,* Justice Harlan noted that the controlling dicta had been laid down in *McNaughtan* and repeated often in British and American cases. But what had not been settled was whether the test to be met was one of *preponderance of evidence* or the sterner test of proof *beyond reasonable doubt.* The influential Massachusetts Supreme Court tended to impose the heavier burden on the government. And Harlan's Court now moved in the same direction:

We are unable to assent to the doctrine that in a prosecution for murder, the defence being insanity, and the fact of the killing with a deadly weapon being clearly established, it is the duty of the jury to convict where the evidence is equally balanced on the issue as to the sanity of the accused at the time of the killing. On the contrary, he is entitled to an acquittal of the specific crime charged if upon all the evidence there is reasonable doubt whether he was capable in law of committing crime. . . . Upon whom then must rest the burden of proving that the accused, whose life it is sought to take under the forms of law, belongs to a class capable of committing crime? On principle, it must rest upon those who affirm that he has committed the crime for which he is indicted. That burden is not fully discharged, nor is there any legal right to take the life of the accused, until guilt is made to appear from all the evidence in the case. . . . Strictly speaking, the burden of proof, as those words are understood in criminal law, is never upon the accused to establish his innocence or to disprove the facts necessary to establish the crime for which he is indicted. It is on the prosecution from the beginning to the end of the trial and applies to every element necessary to constitute the crime.   (160 U.S. 469; 40 L. Ed. 499; 16 S. Ct. 353)

Harlan's understanding here is that the successful insanity defense is tantamount to a finding of not guilty, whereas the failure of that defense yields a guilty verdict. As it is not a defendant's burden to prove his or her innocence, it should not be a defendant's burden to establish insanity. Rather, as the state must establish the defendant's guilt, so too it must be the state's burden to show that the defendant possessed the requisite mental capacities. Nor was Harlan moved by that older understanding according to which the very nature and fact of the offense made clear that the defendant really possessed the requisite powers.

From 1895 until quite recently, Harlan's reasoning guided Federal courts and imposed on the state the burden of adducing positive proof of sanity where the insanity defense was successfully raised. Only after nearly a century of reflection did it become clearer that "proof of sanity" must be will-o-the-wisp and is surely not drawn from the domain of proofs which prosecutors should be expected to navigate. Harlan's laudable concern was that the notoriety of cases such as *Rogers* and *McNaughtan* would erode juridical principles of unsurpassed value; principles that confer special protection on the isolated citizen facing the otherwise unopposable power of the state. He concluded his opinion in that spirit:

> It seems to us that undue stress is placed in some of the cases upon the fact that, in prosecutions for murder the defence of insanity is frequently resorted to and is sustained by the evidence of ingenious experts whose theories are difficult to be met and overcome. Thus, it is said, crimes of the most atrocious character often go unpunished, and the public safety is thereby endangered. But the possibility of such results must always attend any system devised to ascertain and punish crime, and ought not to induce the courts to depart from principles fundamental in criminal law, and the recognition and enforcement of which are demanded by every consideration of humanity and justice. No man should be deprived of his life under the forms of law unless the jurors who try him are able, upon their consciences, to say that the evidence before them, by whomsoever adduced, is sufficient to show beyond a reasonable doubt the existence of every fact necessary to constitute the crime charged.

A century later, in the wake of the trial of John Hinckley, who was acquitted of all charges connected with his assault on President Reagan and members of the President's entourage, Congress proceeded to revamp the Federal laws pertaining to the insanity defense. In the process, the conclusions of the Harlan Court were set aside. The Insanity Defense Reform Act (IDRA) of 1984 established insanity as an affirmative defense to be proved by the defendant *by clear and convincing evidence*. To be sure, it was not the trial of Hinckley alone that promoted these changes, for they had been in the wind for decades. In *Leland v. Oregon* (343 U.S. 790; 72 S. Ct. 1002; 1952 U.S), for example, the Court expressly denied that the burden of proving insanity violated Leland's Fourteenth Amendment rights, and insisted further that *Davis* had not established a constitutional doctrine. At the time some twenty states had requirements as stringent as Oregon's. But the Hinckley verdict did solidify these long-developing tendencies, and afterward seventeen states shifted the burden of proof from prosecution to defense.

It should not be assumed that shifting the burden one way or another significantly alters the outcomes of trials involving the insanity defense. The defense itself is rare, its success rate spotty. And in such matters the fallacy of *post hoc ergo propter hoc* stalks the statistically minded. Nonetheless, studies of acquittals before and after the adoption of *Durham* (discussed below) do show a measure of effect. Studies comparing outcomes under different standards of burden-of-proof have been more equivocal. If a relatively safe generalization can be made, it is that the locus and weight of the burden does not seem to have any pronounced effect in actual or in experimentally simulated trials.[4] This, however, is not germane to the conceptual and juridical issues surrounding the question of burden of proof. Presumably, there is a principled argument favoring one distribution of burden over another. The force of that argument should not be augmented or diminished by empirical findings showing that little of practical consequence hangs in the balance. The pendulum carrying the burden has swung back and forth, perhaps with little effect on verdicts. With each such swing, however, the conundrum merely shifted locations. The question now must be to determine just what exactly counts as *clear and convincing evidence* of insanity, whether the mental state is to be proved by the defense or refuted by the prosecution. But neither psychiatric expertise as now constituted nor recent technical advances (like those in the brain sciences) can be expected to present such evidence beyond what the details of the offense already suggest.

If courts struggled in the late nineteenth century to find the valid marks of insanity in criminal trials and to allocate the right distribution of burdens in the matter of proof, they were rather less scrupulous about committing citizens to asylums. In progressive Massachusetts, for example, the statutory language permitted "any judge authorized under this chapter to commit lunatics . . . not furiously mad . . . to the county receptacle . . . and they shall be governed or employed in such manner as the county commissioners may in the exercise of their discretion deem best." In Dakota, the term "insanity" for purposes of commitment covered "any species of insanity or mental derangement," and in Delaware, "the words 'insane person' shall be construed to include every idiot, non-compos and lunatic person." The man who studied the statutes and practices of every state and of a number of European countries in the 1880s offered this picture of the life of those consigned to asylums under existing laws:

> The insane in hospitals exist in such unmitigated seclusion that the eyes of the community never rest upon them to any appreciable extent. . . . This indifference not unfrequently extends itself even to those who are set over these unhappy beings, from the chief to the lowest attendant of the hospital. Rarely or never can injuries be so exposed as to come to the public eye, and are never considered, much less believed, upon the testimony of the suffering patient; who in a large majority of cases is quite capable of clearly and truthfully presenting the facts. It is unnecessary to say . . . that brutality even to the extent of causing death may obtain immunity in a court of justice.[5]

Actually, the same reformist solicitude that influenced legal approaches to criminal insanity was at work in this area as well, even if the actual conditions of asylums were often deplorable. The impulse in both statutory domains was paternalistic and progressive, drawing strength and confidence from ostensibly scientific discoveries in psychology and psychiatry.

By 1945, in *Holloway v. United States,* the progress of these disciplines, as proclaimed by the specialists themselves, impressed jurists sufficiently to mount a frontal attack on the very presumption of the *McNaughtan* Court. "The modern science of psychology," declared the Court, has no place for "a separate little man in the top of one's head called reason whose function it is to guide another unruly little man called instinct, emotion or impulse in the way he should go."[6]

It is not without relevance that 1945 also marked the end of World War II; this was in many respects the historical event that put "the modern science of psychology" on the map. Psychological tests and related methods of assessment had been used to select persons for service, to assign them to various pools of specialists, to train them under adverse and hurried conditions, and to determine their capacity for continued service. The record compiled by these psychologists overall—in the areas of selection and training, rehabilitation, human factors, information-processing—was widely judged to be outstanding. Moreover, two world wars had produced a veritable army of mentally unsettled veterans, some of whom could never again adjust to civilian life, and many of whom would bring claims for various combat-related residual disorders. Again, psychiatrists and psychologists were called upon to make the necessary diagnoses and to propose and provide therapies. In that insensible way that the popular enthusiasm shifts toward or away from ideological candidates for moral or social or scientific authority, the war years found "the modern science of psychology" enjoying widespread favor.

But the twentieth century in these respects was not to be a mere or reinforced echo of the nineteenth, or the redeeming of promises confidently made by Ray, Griesinger, Maudsley, and the other defenders of what their critics called "brainiology." The two dominant schools of psychological thought throughout most of the twentieth century and until quite recently have been the behavioristic and the psychoanalytic. Neither placed an especially high premium on neurological modes of inquiry and explanation. The most influential version of behaviorism had been long and explicitly opposed to them.[7] Accordingly, the concept of insanity as courts would have to engage it in the present century became increasingly separated from the basic sciences in medicine (such as biochemistry or neurophysiology) and from one of the more developed of the clinical sciences, neurology. As a result, assumptions or theories (or even unadulterated opinions) about the brains of defendants that were routinely offered by doctors in the nineteenth century have been less common in the present century.

Psychiatry and clinical psychology in the postwar years became specialties unto themselves, attached perhaps more hopefully than actually to those basic sciences which their supporters might claim as foundations. The behaviorism advanced by B. F. Skinner was to be a "purely descriptive" science, concerned with the relationship between behavior and environmental events. Though taken to be consistent with an overarching evolutionary theory, behaviorism tended to hold itself aloof from the biological sciences and "physiologized" approaches to explaining behavior.

Psychiatry, largely in the patrimony of Freud and the psychoanalytic school, developed its own theoretical apparatus and methods of validation. In general, psychiatric practice has been confined to the treatment of patients sufficiently accessible to interviews, testing, and discourse as to be distinguishable from the fabled "wild beast." Although prepared to administer psychoactive medications and electroconvulsive therapy for severely disturbed patients, psychiatrists at large have worked less within the context of medical science than within one of their own making.

Lacking widely accepted and tangible evidence of mental disease, and remaining at some distance from medical or physiological training, the mental health experts of the twentieth century have tended to create their own classifications and terminology, grounding claims of expertise not on a body of established facts but on mastery of these very creations. The courts followed either reluctantly or dutifully, sometimes abandoning older and even recent criteria once the weight of expert judgment told against them. In the circumstances, the ratio of assumption to established scientific fact has been higher in psychiatric testimony than what courts have permitted elsewhere by way of dispensations to experts.

Expertise and Daubert

It is worth noting at this point that the highest courts have moved not insensibly but quite deliberately in the direction of liberalizing the criteria to be applied to expert opinion testimony. This is evident in such recent Supreme Court rulings as *Daubert v. Merrell Dow Pharmaceuticals* decided in June of 1993 (113 S. Ct. 2786, 1993). The petitioners in this case were two minor children and their parents, the children suffering serious birth defects allegedly caused by the mother's prenatal ingestion of Bendectin, marketed by Dow Pharmaceuticals. The details of the case are not relevant here, except for the conflict in expert testimony that arose in the lower courts. The principal defense mounted by Dow Pharmaceuticals was that published epidemiological studies had failed to support the claimed teratogenic effects of Bendectin. Although the petitioners did not challenge summaries of the published findings, they did present conflicting expert testimony based on unpublished studies involving tissue cultures and laboratory animals, and even reinterpretations of the published data. Thus two different bodies of allegedly expert opinion were presented; one drawn from the traditional peer-reviewed and published scientific literature, and another drawn from reports by properly credentialed scientists whose methods were not epidemiological and whose principal claims had not appeared in the established peer-review journals.

The Court of Appeals agreed to apply the *Frye* standard, articulated in the 1923 case of *Frye v. United States* (54 App. D.C. 46, 47, 293 F. 1013, 1014), according to which scientific techniques or practices must be "generally accepted" within the relevant scientific community. By the *Frye* standard, the expert testimony supporting the petitioners simply fell outside the "generally accepted" methods of investigation and reporting within the relevant scientific community. But in *Daubert* the Court noted that the Federal Rules of Evidence had changed since *Frye* and had not incorporated the *Frye* standard. In the *Syllabus* of *Daubert* the Court noted that the application of *Frye* "would be at odds with the Rules' liberal thrust and their general approach of relaxing the traditional barriers to 'opinion' testimony" (pp. 4–8).

The relaxation of traditional barriers, needless to say, has long since opened a path for mental health experts who would have been hard pressed to point to anything "generally accepted" within the ambit of *Frye*. This becomes clear under Rule 702 of the Federal Rules of Evidence. By this rule trial judges have the responsibility to ensure that expert testimony is grounded in reliable "scientific . . . knowledge," so that the testimony will "assist the trier of fact to understand the evidence or to determine a fact in issue." Indeed, the Court in *Daubert* does consider it to be relevant whether a given theory or technique has been tested, has been subjected to peer review and publication, and has been assessed for its known or potential error rate. But in the end the Rules cover what must be "flexible. . . . Focus must be solely on principles and methodology, not on the conclusions that they generate" (pp. 12ff.). There cannot be the "wholesale exclusion under an uncompromising 'general acceptance' standard."

The Court was unanimous in *Daubert,* Justice Blackmun writing in the opinion that Rule 402 of the Federal Rules of Evidence provides the baseline: "All relevant evidence is admissible, except as otherwise provided by the Constitution of the United States, by Act of Congress, by these rules, or by other rules prescribed by the Supreme Court pursuant to statutory authority. Evidence which is not relevant is not admissible." Blackmun, citing the language in the Rules, explained that " 'Relevant evidence' is defined as that which has 'any tendency to make the existence of any fact that is of consequence to the determination of the action more probable or less probable than it would be without the evidence'. . . . The Rule's basic standard of relevance thus is a liberal one."

Recall that in *Rex v. Arnold* Justice Tracy had noted in passing that the lucid intervals of an insane person are thought to be related to the phases of the moon, here disclosing an enlightened eighteenth-century jurist's awareness of what "experts" of a sort had concluded. The question arises, in light of *Daubert,* whether relationships of this kind, if accepted by properly credentialed practitioners, would fall under the current Federal Rules of Evidence. Justice Blackmun answers the question by way of exemplifying the Court's reasoning in this case:

> The study of the phases of the moon, for example, may provide valid scientific knowledge about whether a certain night was dark, and if darkness is a fact in issue, the knowledge will assist the trier of fact. However (absent creditable grounds supporting such a link), evidence that the moon was full on a certain night will not assist the trier of fact in determining whether an individual was unusually likely to have behaved irrationally on that night. (p. 22)

The phrase "absent creditable grounds," however, actually begs the question rather than answers it, for it is just the property of *being creditable* that is often controversial when psychiatric or psy-

chological expertise is claimed. The clinician who insists that "long
clinical experience" has established a link of some sort is offering
this clinical experience (which Blackmun now discredits) as creditable evidence. But if such experience is not creditable, then just
what would be? The problem, to say the least, is that comparable
records of experience in these fields routinely generate irreconcil-
able differences in diagnosis and prognosis. Such recent rulings,
then (as Chief Justice Rehnquist himself observed in *Daubert*), have
not clarified let alone settled the criterion problem in the matter
of psychiatric expertise. Rather, the problem has become exacer-
bated precisely because of the unwillingness to impose a "wholesale
exclusion under an uncompromising 'general acceptance' standard."

As Justice Blackmun explained, *certiorari* was granted in *Daubert*
owing to the "sharp divisions among the courts regarding the
proper standard for the admission of expert testimony." He noted
further that since the formulation of the "general acceptance" test,
Frye had been widely relied on in determining whether novel scientific evidence will be admitted at trial. Yet the test itself had a
rather inauspicious birth. It arose in a case involving the use of a
precursor of modern lie-detection devices, here a device for mea-
suring systolic blood pressure. Addressing the question of whether
evidence gleaned from such a novel procedure might be admitted
at trial, the Court of Appeals for the District of Columbia observed
that,

> Just when a scientific principle or discovery crosses the line
> between the experimental and demonstrable stages is difficult
> to define. Somewhere in this twilight zone the evidential
> force of the principle must be recognized, and while courts
> will go a long way in admitting expert testimony deduced
> from a well-recognized scientific principle or discovery, the
> thing from which the deduction is made must be sufficiently

established to have gained general acceptance in the particular field in which it belongs. (54 App. D.C., at 47, 293 F., at 1014)

Clearly this was a judgment destined to have controversial effects and to spawn no end of consultations with "experts" in various fields of medical and scientific work. Merely to determine if an approach has gained general acceptance requires evidence from those allegedly informed about such matters. "Indeed," wrote Blackmun, "the debates over *Frye* are such a well-established part of the academic landscape that a distinct term—'Frye-ologist'— has been advanced to describe those who take part." Apart from this, there is something of a Catch-22 in the test, for it would tend to disallow as evidence any number of state-of-the-art procedures and findings, including those judged most promising (but not yet generally used) by experts.

In *Daubert,* however, it was less a question of the aptness of the *Frye* test than of the very standing of that test in light of the Federal Rules of Evidence developed over the decades since *Frye.* The petitioners' primary claim in *Daubert,* Blackmun noted, was not that *Frye* was defective but that it was no longer dispositive; that is, that it was overtaken by the Federal Rules of Evidence, and in this the *Daubert* Court concurred. Referring to Rule 402, the Court acknowledged that the "basic standard of relevance thus is a liberal one." Moving then to a consideration of Rule 702, the Court found a principle that addressed the central issue in *Daubert:* "If scientific, technical, or other specialized knowledge will assist the trier of fact to understand the evidence or to determine a fact in issue, a witness qualified as an expert by knowledge, skill, experience, training, or education, may testify thereto in the form of an opinion or otherwise." There is no requirement here for a "general acceptance" test which, in any case, would defeat the evolving relaxation of what the Court called the "traditional barriers to 'opinion' testimony."

But the *Daubert* Court also warned that the displacement of *Frye* did not create room for arbitrary or capricious testimony or evidence. Nor, said the Court, are trial judges "disabled from screening such evidence." The Federal Rules themselves require judges to screen any and all scientific testimony or evidence for relevance and reliability; what Chief Justice Rehnquist called "gatekeeping responsibility."

But how is this responsibility to be met? Rule 702 calls for the expert's testimony to be a matter of "scientific knowledge," prompting the Court in *Daubert* to observe that "scientific" implies "a grounding in the methods and procedures of science," and that " 'knowledge' connotes more than subjective belief or unsupported speculation." Within the domain of mental disturbances and deficits it is not at all clear that either of the terms can be honored in practice; but that is not because—in the words of Justice Blackmun—"arguably, there are no certainties in science." Rather, the very nature of the case will encourage theories and opinions to range widely over the imaginable possibilities, and they will surely strike disinterested observers as being very much on the order of "subjective belief and unsupported speculation." Then, too, rules 701–703 grant to experts far wider latitude than to the general public in the matter of opinions, even where the expert lacks first-hand observations. The rationale here is that an expert can draw upon scientific resources of a general nature and apply them to the case in point in ways that the lay population cannot. In this, wrote Blackmun, "the expert's opinion will have a reliable basis in the knowledge and experience of his discipline." This, of course, begs the very question at issue, which is whether the discipline itself possesses sufficiently incontrovertible knowledge and experience.

Daubert is directly relevant to the matter of expertise in cases of insanity because it sets guidelines for Federal courts on such central issues as who is qualified and what counts as relevant and reliable data. Credentials of an academic and a professional nature are taken to be signs of expertise, but it should be clear that they may be neither necessary nor sufficient to the purpose. Surely a practitioner, once at the leading edge of his or her specialty, might at some point be rendered incompetent by age or disease. The fact that advanced degrees were once earned does not confer continuing expertise. But beyond this, credentials of one sort or another are earned in any number of pursuits (and awarded by any number of institutions) in which the very possibility of expertise for evidentiary purposes would seem to be less than credible. The judge as "gatekeeper" is, in the end, a member of the lay community needing guidance from those who can distinguish between authentic and counterfeit knowledge bases. But no phrenologist, for example, will declare phrenology to be a counterfeit, and no one outside of phrenology will be regarded as an expert by phrenologists. This is a convenient example to draw upon, if only because phrenology was promoted by Dr. Gall as a new science of the mind, and Gall himself was one of the leading neuroanatomists of his age. Moreover, there were many widely read journals of phrenology from early in the nineteenth century, and articles appearing in them received some form of "peer review." The wording of Rule 702 might now be considered in relation to opinions and evidence that might have been provided by the trained phrenologist of the previous century: "If scientific, technical, or other specialized knowledge will assist the trier of fact to understand the evidence or to determine a fact in issue, a witness qualified as an expert by knowledge, skill, experience, training, or education, may testify thereto in the form of an opinion or otherwise" (28 USCS Appx F. Rules of Ev. R 702 [1994]).

One may ask in this connection whether the phrenologists of old would be excluded. Rule 702 continues:

> The rule is broadly phrased. The fields of knowledge which may be drawn upon are not limited merely to the "scientific" and "technical" but extend to all "specialized" knowledge. Similarly, the expert is viewed, not in a narrow sense, but as

a person qualified by "knowledge, skill, experience, training or education." Thus within the scope of the rule are not only experts in the strictest sense of the word, e.g., physicians, physicists, and architects, but also the large group sometimes called "skilled" witnesses, such as bankers or landowners testifying to land values.   (Ibid.)

It is too early to tell how the *Daubert* decision will influence attitudes and the admission of expert evidence in the matter of mental competence. The spring 1995 issue of *Behavioral Sciences and the Law* was devoted entirely to the decision but with uncertain results. One of the articles, by Judge Alan Gless, concluded that the problem all along has been less with the experts than with the judges, whose lack of scientific knowledge has left them handicapped in the matter of admissibility. It is not at all clear, however, that the study of the psychological or behavioral sciences would solve any of the problems in evaluating insanity. The "expertise" at issue, it is to be recalled, is based on just such studies. Still others contributing to the volume urged clinicians (1) to confine their testimony to "descriptive and explanatory issues," including, for instance, prognosis and prediction of violence (Schopp and Quattrocchi); (2) to expect greater scrutiny by the courts (Goodman-Delahunty and Foote, p. 202); (3) to contribute, by way of empirical findings, to such specific issues as the reliability of eyewitness identification and memory (Penrod et al.). What was not considered in any sustained fashion is the possibility that *Daubert*-level expertise and the vagaries of human mental life are simply incompatible; that expertise in this context must finally be quite different from what is properly expected from the developed sciences.

The Criterion Problem

If expertise remains elusive, so much more so do the criteria of mitigating mental states or conditions. Some forty years ago, great attention was given to the opinion Judge Bazelon delivered in *Durham*. Following the precepts of Isaac Ray, the judge underscored the "fallacious" nature of the right-wrong test and duly recognized current legal notions of insanity as having "little relation to the truths of mental life."[8]

The facts in *Durham* were these: between his discharge from the Navy in 1945 for psychiatric reasons until his appeal before the Bazelon Court, Monte Durham had been in and out of prisons and mental hospitals for a variety of offenses; fraud, breaking-and-entering, and so on. It was decided in *Durham* that diagnostic categories such as "psychopath" and "sociopath" were acceptable for the defense of insanity, and that the traditional tests were no longer binding. In words similar to those Justice Shaw had used in instructing the jury in *Rogers,* the Court in *Durham* found that "an accused is not criminally responsible if his unlawful act was the product of mental disease or mental defect."[9]

Durham, as all of the famous insanity cases, was influenced considerably by a professional literature in which claims of great progress were made but not rigorously substantiated. The *Durham* Court cited Isaac Ray's century-old criticism of the faulty science used by the courts of his own day. As a more recent authority, Harvard's Sheldon Glueck was cited approvingly for his comments on that "outworn era of psychiatry" which attached itself to the right-wrong test; an era that refused to acknowledge how fully intact the knowledge of right and wrong can be in a defendant who is "otherwise demonstrably of disordered mind."[10]

A year before *Durham,* Britain's Royal Commission on Capital Punishment had issued its own influential report. On the basis of statements from recognized authorities in many countries, the commission concluded that "the gravamen of the charge against the M'Naghten Rules is that they are not in harmony with modern medical science, which, as we have seen, is reluctant to divide the mind into separate compartments."[11] The *Durham* case thus took one more step in law away from the *furiosus* standard of old, and for reasons not unlike those affirmed by Erskine, reinforced and developed further by Isaac Ray and others, and now rendered consistent with "the best scientific opinion." That such opinion is challenged from time to time was seen as no obstacle to adopting the core principle in *Durham*. After all, declared the *Durham* Court, "the questions of fact under the test we now lay down are as capable of determination by the jury as, for example, the questions juries must determine upon a claim of total disability under a policy of insurance where the state of medical knowledge concerning the disease involved, and its effects, is obscure or in conflict."[12]

The wide latitude this created for defendants led predictably not only to a marked increase in the number of experts appearing at trials, but to significant if less public reconsideration by various segments of the mental health community. St. Elizabeth's Hospital, for example, recognizing that the decision in *Durham* could lead to a dramatic increase in the number of defendants successfully pleading insanity, altered its classification of sociopaths to include the qualification, "without mental disorder." On this understanding, it became possible to label an evaluated defendant a "sociopath," but to return him to the courts as competent to stand trial if he is "without mental disorder." No serious inquiry was made into the sense in which a sociopathic personality was, nevertheless, untroubled by a mental disorder. The designation allowed psychiatry to preserve the background assumption that crimes of violence proceed from pathological conditions, but spared hospitals the duty to treat the perpetrators.

Required by the courts to evaluate prisoners scheduled to stand trial, the psychiatric staff of the hospital rather routinely identified sociopaths as mentally competent for purposes of law.[13] For instance, after Comer Blocker killed his common law wife and pleaded insanity, he was found to be sociopathic (but without a disabling mental disease), and his conviction was secured. But then, as is often the case, psychiatric opinion quite suddenly shifted, and the medical administration of St. Elizabeth's restored the policy of classifying sociopathic personalities as mentally diseased. Although such a flip-flop, as it was called, may have been warranted within the context of psychological theory and practice, it introduces arbitrary and capricious elements into the juridical context. Accordingly, once St. Elizabeth's policy shifted, Comer Blocker appealed his conviction. It was with controlled frustration that Appeals Court Judge Warren Burger addressed the matter of these shifting views within psychiatry: "No rule of law can possibly be sound or workable which is dependent upon the terms of another discipline whose members are in profound disagreement about what those terms mean."[14]

The understanding reached in *Durham* clearly could not be sustained, but for reasons that the ancient courts merely took for granted and that Hale, Tracy, and Mansfield had made explicit. Every alcoholic, drug addict, compulsive gambler, bigot, political radical, and prostitute might credibly claim that his or her foibles and offenses were based upon a "mental defect" of one sort or another. As stated in *Durham,* the test was simply too close to that "idle humour" Tracy warned jurors to ignore.

The remedies for *Durham* were to be found, it was hoped, in *Brawner,* a case argued in that same Federal Appeals Court that had heard *Holloway, Durham,* and *Blocker,* for the Court had resolved by then to adopt in such cases standards that had been developed by the American Law Institute (ALI) in its Model Penal Code: "A person is not responsible for criminal conduct if at the time of such conduct as a result of mental disease or defect he lacks substantial capacity either to appreciate the criminality (wrongfulness) of his conduct or to conform his conduct to the requirements of law."[15]

The appellant, Archie Brawner, had been drinking with his uncle all afternoon and then went to an evening party where fights broke out. Brawner had been struck in the jaw and his mouth was bleeding when he left the party. Complaining that he had been "jumped," he got into a rage, punching a mailbox and threatening that he would return to the scene where "someone is going to die tonight." He did return to the party, fired five shots through the closed metal door, and killed one of the partygoers. After being charged, Brawner was required to undergo psychiatric and neurological tests and was diagnosed variously by experts for both sides as having a "psychologic brain syndrome," a "personality disorder associated with epilepsy," and "an explosive personality."

The government's experts insisted that Brawner's assault was not the result of disease but of anger. Experts for the defense disagreed, contending that the criminal offense was directly (causally) prompted by Brawner's psychological disturbance. In permitting the government's expert to state that, in his opinion, said causal relationship did not exist, the trial court erred, according to *Brawner*. The authority cited was *Washington v. United States*,[16] one of several cases in which the Court had sought to preclude undue influence by psychiatric experts, specifically in light of the fact that "there is no generally accepted understanding, either in the jury or the community it represents, of the concept requiring that the crime be the 'product' of the mental disease."[17]

It was on just this point that the Court now resolved to depart from *Durham,* wherein the term "product" was used as "a legal reciprocal" for a term common in civil cases, "proximate cause." Laymen could not be expected to understand the several and even conflicting senses that attach to the notion of "product." And so the wording of the ALI standard was adopted as the now famous *Brawner* rule, according to which the conduct in question must be *the result* of disease or defect if the crime is to be attributed to it. In the same opinion, the Court acknowledged the growing general enthusiasm for abolishing the insanity defense altogether, going on to explain why such proposals nevertheless should be shunned:

The defense focuses on the kind of impairment that warrants exculpation, and necessarily assigns to the prison walls many men who have serious mental impairments and difficulties. The needs of society—rooted not only in humanity but in practical need for attempting to break the recidivist cycles, and halt the spread of deviant behavior—call for the provision of psychiatrists, psychologists and counselors to help men with these mental afflictions and difficulties, as part of a total effort toward a readjustment that will permit re-integration in society.[18]

The ALI Model Penal Code also contained what has come to be called the "caveat paragraph" in Section 401, stipulating that "the terms 'mental disease or defect' do not include an abnormality manifested only by repeated criminal or otherwise anti-social conduct." This wording is intended to avoid a persistent complaint brought against versions of the insanity defense that have the crime stand as the *evidence* of insanity rather than as one of its consequences.

Nineteenth-century specialists were not oblivious to the possibly vicious circularity of any theory of insanity that is only confirmable by the very offenses it would then be deployed to excuse. Griesinger, for example, acknowledged that criminal offenses may often present "the only ground for the assertion that insanity exists," but in most cases this sequence is inadmissible; physicians must, instead, "endeavor to establish before, exclusively and quite independently of the deed itself, the marks of insanity."[19]

The question lingers, of course, as to just how the terms "mental disease or defect" used in the ALI "caveat paragraph" might be instructively used in a criminal defense without making any reference to the antisocial conduct of the defendant. Monte Durham had been habitually in trouble with the authorities. Had it not been for his "repeated criminal or otherwise antisocial conduct," it is unlikely he would have suffered a medical discharge from the Navy in the first place, or that he would have ever been the subject of psychiatric assessments. To cut the feared tautologous knot, the Court in *Brawner* would have had to find a way (a) to protect the proceedings against excessive influence by experts, and (b) to find yet another way, consistent with (a), of distinguishing between those who (for whatever reason) engage repeatedly in antisocial behavior, and those who do so because of a mental defect. But how can (b) be established, except on the authority of those whose influence is to be limited via (a)?

Autonomy and Causality

A more general conundrum, within which others are nested, is disclosed by the seemingly innocent conjunction *"because."* The confusions and vexations of *Durham* and *Brawner* arise from the variety of meanings that might be attached to this word. Is violent behavior a "product" of mental disturbance? Does that mean the violence occurred *because* of it, or did mental disturbance make the subject simply more disposed toward violence? Was the behavior the *result* of the mental defect so that whenever this defect appears, the behavior nearly invariably occurs? Just what sort of connection must obtain between a mental defect or disorder on the one hand, and specific actions on the other, such that the actor is to be regarded as not responsible?

Throughout its history, the insanity defense specifically, and the more general concept of mental defect or incompetence generally, have been grounded in the assumption that those fit for the rule of law are able to give and to comprehend reasons for their actions. They are able to defend their actions by supplying reasons which are, after all, within the purview of law, to be justified or penalized by it. The concept of *mens rea* is but the technical term for one of the core and common-sense assumptions of legal responsibility and liability. Even when a legal system is silent on the particular psychological or mental powers on which such responsibility depends, the very efficacy of law arises from the possession of such powers by the public at large. Otherwise, as H. L. A. Hart noted, "no legal system could come into existence or continue to exist."[20] But the relevance of being able to give and comprehend reasons must itself be grounded in some understanding of the relationship between reasons for acting and actions. To say that Smith did what he did "for the following reason" appears to invest in the word "for" some special power or potentiality without which the action would not have occurred or, if it had occurred, would not be explicable in the same terms.

Moreover, terms such as "for" and "because" not only imply a power to bring about events of a certain kind, but point to a unique or defining power that makes what follows seem conceptually required by the act itself. It would make no sense and would, therefore, not be an explication—even less a justification—to say that John drove his car quickly because he wished to be late; or spent money profligately because of his tendency toward moderation; or proposed to Mary as a result of his great love for Jane. At a common-sense level, then, the *because* conjunction explicates the action by some intended or desired state of affairs.

A moment's reflection, however, reveals that, thus understood, the notion that an action takes place *because of* some state of affairs that it might *subsequently* bring about is mired in difficulty. It seems to require that a future event serve as the cause of an earlier one, thus reversing time's arrow. It suggests, too, that given such a reason for action, the conceptually tethered behavior must take place and is therefore in some sense caused by the reason. However, (1) everyone has had the experience of having a reason for acting and yet, in a given circumstance, finally withholding the action; and (2) a given goal or objective generally can be realized by more than one course of action such that for the given goal A, any one of the actions A, B, C . . . K may be efficacious. Separately and jointly, (1) and (2) are not characteristic of those causal sequences that bring about or are features of purely physical events. But then why would one assume that an agent, having a good (or, for that matter, bad) reason for acting, was in some sense thereby caused to act? Why not accept, therefore, the common-sense or "folk psychology" assumption whereby the cause of an action is the will of the actor, and the cause of the will is the actor himself?

These and related quandaries enter into any understanding of legal insanity and need to be examined. They have taken an especially complex turn in recent decades, owing in large measure to developments in philosophy of law in the twentieth century, and to a more widespread scientific positivism that has informed and influenced jurisprudence. It is useful briefly to consider these developments as a prologue to further discussion of the legal understandings of insanity and of the concept of actions as occurring because of mental states (reasons, desires, motives).

Jurisprudence and Positivism

The most significant additions to philosophy of law in modern times have been the various renderings of the movement called legal positivism. While its philosophical foundations were laid by Hume and by Bentham in the eighteenth century, legal positivism enjoyed its first systematic exposition in John Austin's lectures and writings.[21] Austin had been more or less handpicked by Bentham for the jurisprudence lectures to be given at the new University of London, where middle-class and working-class students would enjoy the benefits of higher education. In full sympathy with the reformist atmosphere of the 1830s, Austin set out to demystify law by extricating it from those dense moral philosophies alleged to be its very essence, and from transcendent religious principles long regarded as the source of the law's validity and authority.

As Austin understood the law, it was reducible to a command issued by a superior to those whose compliance could be forced by punishment if necessary. The "command" theory of positive law—law as enacted and promulgated by authority—conferred on law a validity entirely independent of any judgments that might be made about its moral content or its compatibility with the divine will. On this theory, positive law is a production, something made for a purpose and thus intelligible in terms of the real ends it would serve. The way to understand "law," therefore, is by studying laws as social or historical creations, and not by attempting to deduce it from some other body of principle or theory.

Later and more developed versions of legal positivism retained the Austinian respect for the social origins of positive law and for the resulting imperative that laws be understood contextually. As such, the concept of law came to refer to observable items; to actual entities having empirical properties such as dates and modes of authorship, ranges of application, stated penalties for violations. Law on this account does not refer to moral *desiderata* or rational abstractions, nor is it validated by moral precepts or universal propositions immanent in the very concept of law. In the works of such American legal realists as John Chipman Gray, the state is seen to exist for the protection of real human interests, and the laws of a jurisdiction are to be understood accordingly. Or, as Justice Holmes would insist, "the law" is but a collection of rules that courts follow; a set of statements that permit one to predict what judges and juries will do in a given cause.[22] If anything more fundamental is required to elucidate the ultimate foundations of positive law, it will be found, to use Austin's remarkable phrase, "bottomed in the common nature of man."[23] How a given law is to be understood, then, and whether or not a specific action constitutes a violation of it are matters inextricably bound up with questions of policy and social goals, with the status of scientific understandings of "the common nature of man," and with any number of factors unique to the given case. Presumably, all of these considerations can be undertaken in a factual manner, stripped of eternal verities, moral truths, or metaphysical canons.

Outside the specific domain of law, but having an unmistakable influence on it, was the scientific outlook that guided so much of intellectual and social life in the Enlightenment and the nineteenth century. This perspective found its most developed expression in the competing positivisms of the early decades of the present century. As understood by the leaders of the Vienna Circle, the primary requirement of valid explanation is that it conform to the facts of experience.[24] It is the method of verification that either appeals directly to experience (and is, therefore, literally *sensible*) or it does not, in which case the proposition at issue is literally *nonsense*. This is the basis on which to differentiate scientific and merely philosophical or "metaphysical" utterances.

The pedigree of positivism reached back to David Hume and included the leading writers in the tradition of philosophical empiricism, notably J. S. Mill, but the spiritual father of the movement was Ernst Mach. His lectures at the University of Vienna and his writings on physics and philosophy of science influenced a wide ranging audience that would include artists, scientists, philosophers and, alas, students of law, salient among whom was Hans Kelsen.[25] In *The Analysis of Sensations* Mach developed a coherent picture of scientific theory as systematic description of experience, and the task of science as the elaboration of precise and reliable means by which experience may be reduced to order.[26] Indebted to the theory of causality crafted by Hume and Mill, Mach took the causal laws of science to be redactions and condensations of replicable experiences in which a given class of antecedent events was regularly followed by another identifiable class of events. To explain an occurrence, then, is to identify its reliable experiential antecedent conditions. No philosophical excursus on the nature of causality is necessary, nor is there any need to invoke invisible or occult causal powers or forces.

The logical positivism growing out of this tradition, though itself varied and rife with disputes, projected an economical and confident approach to any number of traditionally vexing problems in science, and particularly in the social and psychological disciplines. The task of explanation was reducible to a set of statements, all of them "empirical" and containing only a summary of the events to be explained and the identification of those antecedent events which, under comparable conditions, regularly culminate in events of the sort under investigation. Thus to explain any phenomenon is no more than to identify the general law of which it is an instance. And the general law itself is but the empirically established statistical regularity with which events of type A are followed by events of type B.[27] According to this view, there are no special mysteries associated with the social and psychological dimensions of reality. To the extent that these admit of order and coherence, it must be because they are based on underlying general laws and are therefore candidates for scientific explanation.

In this light, how is one to understand the "because" in the statement "Smith killed Jones *because* he was deluded in regarding Jones as his enemy"? On first inspection, two different answers recommend themselves; one that might with qualification be called traditional, and the other positivistic. On the traditional understanding, we would be inclined to regard Smith as unique, and his behavior in this case as traceable to any number of problems and difficulties that affected his character and judgment. They inclined Smith's thinking in a certain way, making him suspicious beyond warrant of other persons and particularly of Jones. Owing to his great if delusional suspicions, Smith framed a rationale according to which his own safety would be more secure if Jones were killed. He then acted on this reasoning, and now stands accused of murder.

But then, did the delusion cause Smith to commit a crime in the way that, for example, gravitational forces cause objects to fall toward the center of the earth? If so, might it not then be the case that Smith's behavior was so thoroughly determined as to leave no room for that moral responsibility *(mens rea)* required by the very concept of guilt? The traditional reply to questions of this sort is that having a reason or a motive or a desire is not like being over-come by the coercive powers of physical causes. After all, one is also responsible for developing a rationale for action, for harboring desires of one kind or another, and for "giving in" to motives. On the traditional view (Erskine's "motives irresistible"), if this term accurately described the state Hadfield was in, it would be excul-patory in the sense that the motives really did cause the behavior. But this is not the way motives generally work; if they did, adju-dication would be pointless. To regard persons as powerless in the face of strong motives or desires—to regard their conduct as caused by such states—is to regard them not in a jural or moral light but solely as natural objects subject to the causally determinative laws that govern the whole realm of purely natural objects. As this is fully incompatible with the very possibility of a rule of law, the traditional outlook takes a skeptical position in the face of such a thesis and places the burden of proof on those who would adduce it in support of, say, an insanity defense. Indeed, more than one scholar arguing for the traditional view has concluded that for the purpose of explaining consequential human actions, causal ac-counts are "wholly irrelevant."

The Case for Folk Psychology

In this connection, Stephen Morse has acknowledged that expla-nations of human action remain "mysterious" even in the face of "the herculean efforts of the metaphysicians," and argues that the perspective of folk psychology remains the most compelling, and is precisely the perspective presupposed by criminal law. Before rejecting physiological "reductionist" theories now so common, Morse first tests their aptness. Some imaginable form of crime-control system might simply ignore all considerations of moral blameworthiness and autonomy:

Instead, the criminal law might treat persons as part of the biophysical flotsam and jetsam of the universe and respond solely on the basis of the type and degree of dangerousness people threaten, without regard to moral responsibility. In such a world, practices such as blame and punishment would have primarily instrumental value, useful for controlling the harm-producing behavior of homo sapiens, much like antibiotics are useful for controlling the dangerous propensities of bacteria. In the Anglo-American world, however, virtually no criminal law theorist or lawyer adheres to the purely consequentialist dystopia just sketched . . . the necessity for just deserts presupposes a view of persons as potentially morally responsible, that is, as rational, uncompelled agents, rather than as merely bodies moving in space.[28]

But if causal explanations are rejected, what sense can be made of the "because" in the example given or in the myriad cases in which questions of motivation are central? As Donald Davidson insisted in a widely cited essay, absent such a causal account there is no way to analyze the meaning of the conjunction when followed by the alleged reason for acting.[29] For to say that Smith acted as he did "because" of a delusion that made him fearful of Jones is to say that the state of fear brought about the action. Thus if Smith was in a state of fearfulness owing to the deluded belief that Jones was plotting against him, this belief must be the cause of the fear. And the desire to get rid of Jones (if this is the reason for Smith's action) must then work as a reason only insofar as it was causally efficacious in bringing about Smith's behavior.

From this it is but a short and, it may be argued, inevitable step to the related thesis (which Davidson, however, would reject) that if such states are causal in their operation, it can only be because they operate as states and events in the brain, the dynamics of which constitute the proximate cause of all human actions. How else can a "reason" function as a cause, except by way of the mediating or representational operations of the brain? There can be no disembodied reasons on this account; if there were, it would not be possible for them to influence bodies such as Smith's. If, indeed, Smith acts on a reason, in the sense of a reason as causally determining a course of action, then it becomes necessary to understand the reason in such a way as to admit of causal efficacy. The chain of positivistic argument must conclude, then, as Erskine did in *Hadfield,* as Ray and Maudsley and Griesinger did in their influential texts, and as the experts did who found the defendant in *Brawner* to have a "psychologic brain syndrome."

There is another position between the traditional and the positivistic; it has been burdened by the designation "teleological" and is thus believed to suffer the special defects commonly ascribed to such explanations.[30] According to the teleological approach, actions realize ends; ends (which are later in time) obviously do not cause the actions that bring them about. Homeostatic mechanisms are illustrative.[31] The body perspires on hot days as a way of maintaining a constant core temperature. One can say properly that perspiration occurs because of the need to maintain a constant core temperature, without suggesting that the constant body temperature thereby brought about or caused the very perspiration that preserves the constancy. (Note that time's arrow is not reversed by properly framed teleological explanations.) Clearly, causal and teleological explanations are different, and one can be in hand while the other remains elusive. Darwin thus explained the plumage of the male bird of a species teleologically when he traced it to the principles of sexual selection. The explanation is grounded in the delineation of conditions favoring the preservation of the species. The "cause" of such variations in plumage, however, is at the level of genetic and microphysiological processes of which Darwin was utterly ignorant.

The example of a simple mechanical tool further illustrates the point. The temperature of a room can be regulated by a device, a kind of thermostat, composed of a strip of two different but fused metals having different coefficients of expansion. When the room is heated, one metal expands more quickly than the other, and the strip bends away from electrical contacts which, when "closed," turn on the furnace. By bending away from the contacts, the metal strip "opens" the circuit and the furnace is turned off. As the room cools, the strip bends in the opposite direction, closes the contacts, and turns the furnace on once again.

Several explanations are available in answer to the question, "Why is the furnace going on and off?" One can say it is because a thermostat is controlling it. Or one can say it is because of a desire to keep the room at constant temperature. Or one can undertake an analysis of the molecular and atomic and subatomic events by which the mean kinetic energy of the gases in the room causally alters the configuration of the elements of which the bimetallic strip is composed. The last of these is a *causal* explanation. The first is a kind of *instrumental* explanation. The second is a *teleological* explanation, where the behavior of the thermostat is just one of a large number of ways the goal of maintaining a constant temperature in the room is realized; in this case through the design and installation of a thermostatically regulated heating system.

People who may fail to understand the physics of heat would have no difficulty with the second explanation. Indeed, the future might disprove the thermodynamics laws on which the third explanation is based, without at all affecting the explanatory power and validity of the teleological explanation. It is worth noting that in circumstances in which significant human interests are achieved or strived for, the intuitive appeal and intelligibility of teleological explanations survive the fate of any scientific law offered as being more fundamental. Refutation of the latter leaves the former unscathed.

There are good grounds on which to defend the proposition

that in these contexts the teleological explanation is in fact the most fundamental. Why did Smith attack Jones? To say that Smith had a reason for doing this is, on the teleological account of reasons, not to say that something called a "reason" (or desire or motive) caused Smith to do what he did. Rather, it is to say that through a chosen course of action Smith realized a goal that he had come to regard as desirable. There is nothing mysterious in this, for a teleological explanation can also encompass actions that realize the desires of others: "Smith did what he did *because* he was persuaded that his friend desired it." No one would argue that the desires of another person are "causal" in the received sense, though positivistic models of explanation seem to require as much. To complain that all this leaves Smith's behavior unexplained is to repeat the demand for a causal account and for the conversion of reasons into some palpable event in the brain. Those who demand this of reasons-explanations mistakenly judge teleological accounts not as wrong but as incomplete, insisting that the outcome still must be explained in terms of how it was brought about. An example from Collins is useful in seeing what is demanded by positivistic modes of explanation.

He gives the causal explanation for how a heavy engine was moved: it got moved because someone put a jack under it. This is paradigmatic of accounts sought within the positivistic framework. So if someone switches on a light, the paradigm then would have it that his behavior was caused by, let us say, the desire to have the light come on. Thus for any action teleologically explained, the positivist's reply is: "That was the outcome, but how did he get something with that outcome to come about?" Referring to desires and the like as "pro attitudes," Collins then goes on to say,

> If this were a feasible interpretation for the role of pro attitudes, then, "He wanted to turn on the light," would parallel, "He put a jack under it." They would be offered as causes of

the motion of the engine and the switch-flipping. . . . Where an understanding of causes is involved, an agent can say, "If I could put a jack under that I could get it up on the bench." If pro attitude reasons were offered as causal illumination, they would also generate "I could have the switch flipped in no time if only I had a cause like wanting the light on."[32]

It should not be thought that the adoption of teleological modes of explanation reduces or dissolves the complexities of *mens rea*. The point of discussing these explanations was to give a somewhat more precise expression to what has been more or less traditional in juridical contexts in the pre-positivist era, and to make clear that the adoption of such an approach invites no mystery into the law's reasoning. The problem with teleological explanations is not that they are mysterious; as explications of ordinary behavior they are far less mysterious than causal explanations based on actual or assumed events in regions of the brain few laymen could name or recognize. The problem is that such explanations are no longer accepted as juridically discriminating where the issue is one of legal responsibility. John Hinckley claimed to have fired a pistol at President Reagan and others in order to bring himself more fully to the attention of a young woman who was the object of his obsession.[33] Whether one accepts the account as the folk version of a description of the defendant's brain states, or as a teleological explanation of the factors prompting the offense, nothing is settled as regards current understandings of mental competence. One might argue (as it was successfully argued in *Hinckley*) that the offense was the product of schizophrenia, thus providing an allegedly causal explanation of the behavior; or one might make a teleological argument (as it was unsuccessfully argued in *Rex v. Arnold*) that the defendant was convinced his victim had sent imps to disturb his sleep. But as Barbara Wootton concluded many years ago, and with an obvious air of resignation, the advent of the term "kleptomania" gave sociological standing to what once had been the thief without a motive: "No longer compelled to plead that he 'doesn't know what made him do it,' he can now at least explain his own conduct: 'I did it,' he says, 'because I am a kleptomaniac'; and 'I did it,' says the poor man, 'because I was hungry.' The analogy is complete."[34]

It might be assumed wrongly, in behalf of the teleological mode of explanation, that an allegedly insane defendant, in giving an account of his actions, will admit to palpably delusional elements establishing the actions as products of mental illness. Though well-known disagreements surround any number of diagnostic terms in psychiatry, at least with delusions there would seem to be a less will-o-the-wisp epistemic standard. In such matters it is widely believed that there is a fact test that can be applied to classify cognitive contents as delusional or real. But as William Fulford has made clear, even this assumption is only serviceable for purposes of law when the discovered "delusion" is coupled with at least an implied defect of reason.[35] Dictionary definitions of delusion, which would count as delusional any firmly held belief that is clearly false and not imparted by one's education or culture, offer a standard that will not of itself establish pathology on the part of those who hold such beliefs. In testamentary cases, for example, where a testator's attitudes toward potential beneficiaries are regarded as delusional, denial of probate would, presumably, have to be based upon something more substantial than evidence to the effect that the testator's beliefs happened to be false. Thus in testamentary challenges such as *Graham v. Darnell,* it was not enough to prove that the deceased misjudged his estranged daughters' affection for him; a further requirement was that the misjudgment itself was the product of a mental disorder.[36] It is worth noting, too, that delusional beliefs are not found by clinicians to be invariably false, particularly in cases in which what may have been an initially false belief leads to actions that then realize the content of the delusion; for example, the "Othello" syndrome.[37]

The *Brawner* Court was wary of the "product" test for want of a "generally accepted understanding . . . of the concept requiring that the crime be the 'product' of the mental disease." This signaled a move away from one version of the causal theory of mitigation, but only to move toward yet another version of the theory implicit in the ALI statement. To describe an offense as being "the result of" some condition is, after all, to say that it was caused by it. Modern psychology and psychiatry, still unable to forge the durable causal links that would render such understandings juridically satisfying, can only present the courts with dubious generalizations based on "clinical experience," which in some unspecified and unspecifiable way supports the opinion that a defendant's actions either were or were not "the result of" a mental illness. But the experience taken to be relevant in such cases is itself bound up with the very subjectivity, cultural biases, theory-laden perceptions, and prevailing professional and social norms so evident in actual trial records. It is far from clear that prolonged engagements of this sort actually enhance the "expertise" of those identified as experts at trial. No wonder, then, that still other standards have come to modify or replace *Brawner.* The 1984 Comprehensive Crime Control Act recovered the very "right-wrong" test so roundly condemned by the experts of a century ago. Utah, Idaho, and Montana eliminated the insanity defense altogether, the balance of the states being roughly divided in adopting either *Brawner* or *McNaughtan.*

Other proposals have sought to suspend the search for precision in specific cases and to adopt a form of categorical exemption from punishment. H. L. A. Hart concluded from the well-known failures to identify mental disorders with precision that it might be best to adopt a "coarser-grained technique" similar to that which creates the class of legal infants. Hart took this to be sanctioned by understandings long at work in English law, whereby "in the case of very young children it has made no attempt to determine, as a condition of liability, the question whether on account of their immaturity they could have understood what the law required."[38] But this strategy, too, is a veiled appeal to a causal theory, somewhat surprising when advanced by one who wrote with such insight on the limitations of this form of causal explanation in adjudicative contexts.[39] The appeal to a causal theory consists in treating the concept of diminished capacity for adult defendants as akin to the diminished capacity of the very young, in whom the lack of capacity (relative to their ultimate adult powers) is presumably attributable to overall neuropsychological immaturity. In the case of the juvenile defendant there may be grounds for a teleological account of the offending actions; what is missing is the presumption of full responsibility in the framing and implementation of the course of action. So, too, with defendants such as Arnold, Ferrers, Hadfield, Bellingham, McNaughtan, Hinckley and the others.

To invoke "diminished responsibility" for classes of defendants each of whom individually has been judged by experts to suffer from one or another mental disorder is not to settle but to beg the question at hand. What nearly all eight-year-old children have in common is that state of childhood which all members of the adult community who would judge them have experienced. It is plausible then that adults, in self-referential and introspective fashion, should waive the particulars presented by a specific child and establish childhood itself as a mitigating state of affairs. The intellectual and emotional aspects of childhood being what they are, and being part of the intimate knowledge of adult citizens, a prosecutor's burden would be to call for proof that a specific child defendant was so precocious in relevant cognitive and affective respects as to be worthy of the law's punishments.

The mentally disordered are not properly equated with children for purposes of law, for their disorders are not part of the universal human experience, nor is there wide agreement on the specific defects or impoverishment they suffer relative to the larger population. The failure to produce a valid fine-grained technique does not sanction the use of a coarser-grained one, for the entire issue of responsibility rests on the question of precisely which mental powers were or were not available to the defendant at the time of the crime. Surely it would be irrelevant to report that at the time he committed arson, a defendant was suffering from the common cold. Intuitively, it would seem that not just any disorder, including any "mental" disorder, must have exculpatory force, whatever the nature of the action. One would not be inclined to invalidate a will on the grounds that the testator had a morbid fear of heights. In these cases the exculpatory condition ought to bear directly on the matter at hand. Erskine was of this mind in *Hadfield*. However, it was precisely this rationale that excited such penetrating criticism from leaders in psychiatry and medical jurisprudence. To accept as a fact that a defendant suffers from a mental disease, and then to require of that defendant that the disease express itself with specificity and aptness is Pickwickian.

Reasons, Causes, and Mens Rea

Is it *mens rea* itself that plagues legal reasoning in such cases, and might it best be allowed, as Barbara Wootton opined, to "wither away"? Or, following Hart, should the question of *mens rea* be raised only after conviction, to determine whether punishment or treatment is the proper course of action?[40] Is there finally more to be said for the "guilty but insane" provision in a number of jurisdictions in the United States; more than that the provision is oxymoronic? These questions are likely to remain unsettled, for they are jural questions and are largely beyond the range of scientific or technical solutions. It seems to be part of the mixed bequest of a century of positivistic thought that jurists continue to look for illumination from just those quarters that unwittingly spread the long shadows in the first place.

Mens rea, far from being a concept one would choose to have "wither away," is at the very foundation of all criminal law as well as much of the law of torts. Those who are participants in the very rule of law are qualified for this participation in virtue of psychological capacities distilled in such terms as "rationality," "judgment," "intelligence," "stability." But the terms themselves, having been exposed to centuries of philosophical, scientific, and medical scrutiny, have long been disengaged from the common sense understandings and modes of verification adopted by courts over many centuries. Part of the problem of *mens rea* is that the concept is an outgrowth of juridical and moral thought that has been largely unaffected by scientific and philosophical refinements developed in other contexts for entirely different purposes, and in ages remote from those in which the concept of *mens rea* was first applied. The presumption was that if you did the foul deed, this means that you had the capacity for doing it. The burden was theirs to prove otherwise, and this burden became unsupportable once the courts established a functional or conceptual connection between the act itself and the aims plausibly imputed to the actor. With exceptions duly recorded, the prevailing standard was that of the "wild beast," the *furiosus* for whom the punishments of law would be all but meaningless.

In the ages when these understandings were unchallenged, it was further assumed that laws had a definite civic and moral mission. Threats of punishment not only were assumed to have an arresting effect on the passions but were also deemed to express the values of the community. Pressures toward conformity were great in these ages. Contemporary expressions of individualism would have been regarded as hubristic and much in need of the law's own chastening influences. And while philosophers and doctors pursued studies of life and mind, the judges and juries of antiquity were satisfied that common sense and the standards of the community were enough to guide courts toward just verdicts. The features of the actions themselves sufficed to disclose the quality of mind that produced them, especially when supplemented by information concerning the balance of the defendant's life.

Attempts to reconcile the *mens rea* concept implicit in the folk psychology of the distant past with that same concept as filtered through the theoretical machinery of the recent ages of science must founder. Such efforts are not unlike attempts to understand the atomism of Democritus or Epicurus, including the ethical implications to be drawn from it, by consulting a twentieth-century treatise on quantum physics! But this analogy is too critical of ancient jurists and too complimentary of modern psychology. The former included persons whose comprehension of the nature of law and of its moral foundations is at least on a par with the understanding of most modern students of these subjects. But modern psychology is scarcely on a par with quantum physics.

As originally developed, the concept of *mens rea* was to serve as a threshold test of the mental state of defendants, which is why references to "wild beasts" are so commonly found in ancient sources discussing insane actions. A defendant was either guilty or not guilty, simply in the sense that someone has either done something or has not. The laws pertained then (as now) to specific and completed actions whose consequences were amenable to redress. But *mens rea* under more modern lights, as views of both "guilt" and "mind" have unfolded, has been modified and refashioned into a more elastic or protean concept.

Plato was able to present a complete ethics, a moral and political philosophy, and a robust human psychology by distinguishing among only three powers or dispositions of the psyche; the rational, the volitional, and the passionate. Modern psychologists and philosophers offer veritable tables of mental faculties or "modules," as numerous as those proposed by Gall and Spurzheim when phrenology commanded wide allegiance. This atomizing of the mind, whatever value it may prove to have for theoretical psychology, has had predictably disorganizing effects on juridical and moral thought. The traditional narrative of a crime begins with the wishes and plans of a person, proceeds to a series of clearly intended steps—some of them separated by days or even years—and culminates in events for which the actor-agent is now held responsible. In the nineteenth century this narrative began to be radically transformed. It has been apostrophized by reference to actual or hypothetical states of the brain or the body, to distinct compartments of perception or passion or motivation, to diurnal or seasonal or genetic or lunar variations in one or another propensity—all of this then having to be integrated into the concept of the *mens* in *mens rea*.

The current literature abounds in examples designed to tax the imagination and analytical resources of judge and jury. Jack and Jill have insurance policies, Jack's covering the passengers on flight A, and Jill's covering the airplane to be used on flight B. Both are prepared to place bombs on their designated planes. Note that Jack intends to kill the passengers, for his fortune can only be obtained through their deaths. Jill directly intends to destroy only the plane, though she knows full well that the passengers must die in the process.[41] Supposing now that each executes the chosen plan. How are the intentions to be understood in such cases? It was not part of Jill's desire to kill the passengers, even if she knew this was inevitable. Nor was Jack's intention to destroy property. Should one, therefore, hold them both responsible for the same offense?

To complicate matters, let it be assumed that Jack's action was predicated on the desire (the "mental state" of desire) to bequeath his fortune to a nonexistent party, and that Jill's intention is to bomb the plane to avenge a loss for which she (insanely) blames the airline. And, to add one more complication, it turns out that neither plane crashes, because the bombs are found in time. How is *mens rea* to be applied in such cases? By contemporary lights one would have to distinguish first the intention to destroy property from the intention to kill actual persons. But this distinction would be nugatory once one realizes that the former intention could only and knowingly be accomplished by simultaneously killing those on board. Yet this inference must itself be of no consequence if the defendant suffers from an insane delusion. Still, even if deluded, Jill certainly knows that the law would not permit the taking of innocent lives as a form of compensation for injuries she imagines she has suffered at the hands of the airline. Indeed, in her deposition she acknowledges as much. But what confidence is one to have in the deposition of a defendant found to be suffering from a mental disease?

Clearly, it is not the concept of *mens rea* that is causing the problems here. Rather it is the willingness of courts to understand this concept in a quasi-scientific or ostensibly medical way. Similar plots are available in challenges to testamentary capacity, in hearings to determine competence to stand trial, in commitment proceedings that might result in prolonged confinement. Moreover, as clinical and experimental research unfolds, the range of allegedly causative factors becomes broader and the burdens of judgment heavier.

In recent years, any number of medical or biological or genetic correlates of criminal behavior have been adduced in support of pleas of diminished capacity. Deborah Denno offers this concise review:

> Criminal defendants have introduced biological and medical evidence in a number of celebrated cases over the last years. Jack Ruby, who was televised killing alleged presidential assassin Lee Harvey Oswald, was diagnosed as a temporal lobe epileptic . . . Oswald himself had a long history of uncontrolled and assaultive behavior. Both Charles Whitman, who shot forty-one people and killed seventeen in the Texas tower tragedy, and Richard Speck, who murdered eight nurses in Chicago, had evidence of brain disease. . . . Physicians introduced considerable medical and psychiatric data in the trial of John Hinckley, including CAT scans of Hinckley's brain, that they claimed provided organic evidence that Hinckley

was schizophrenic. . . . More recently, lobbyist and former White House aide Michael Dever attempted to demonstrate that his alcoholism and sedation created a state of amnesia that led him to lie inadvertently to a grand jury and to Congress about details concerning his client relationship. . . . Dan White, the former San Francisco supervisor who was accused of murdering Mayor George Moscone and Supervisor Harvey Milk, successfully pleaded diminished responsibility to avoid a first degree murder conviction. He was held unable to tell right from wrong due to a major "mood disturbance," said to be caused in part by junk food and extreme stress prior to the killings. . . More recently, Ann Green, after admitting that she had killed her first two children, was found not guilty by reason of insanity in the attempted murder of her third child. Her case was one of several in this country to use a defense of postpartum illness.[42]

Deborah Denno recommends that conditions such as these be considered only in that "less than 1%" of the cases in which the defense of insanity is successfully raised, but the reasoning behind the recommendation raises basic questions. Denno does not doubt that biological conditions have a determinative power, but social and medical sciences have yet to yield sufficiently reliable correlations. While rejecting the exculpatory effect of such conditions now, she would still urge replacing what she calls the "free will fiction" with the scientifically more realistic principle of "degree determinism." Significant human actions, on this account, are after all determined, but the ultimate question at law has to do with the degree of determination. Clearly, however, if there are degrees of determinism, then there must be degrees of nondeterminism, and it would seem that within these degrees one might plausibly defend free will as something more substantial than a "fiction." Addressing this general issue, Stephen Morse has asked the right question and drawn the right inference:

What reason is there to believe . . . that degrees of causation are a metaphysical feature of the universe, rather than a feature of our current level of knowledge, and lack of it, about causation?. . . . Moreover, why is causation the equivalent of compulsion, even if it is true that the universe metaphysically admits of degrees of causation? Each year when I politely ask my criminal law students with brown hair to raise their hands to aid a classroom demonstration, all the brunettes do so. The unanimous hand-raising is not a random event; it is fully caused by obvious variables, but there is not a scintilla of lack of control among the students.[43]

The complexity of "because" clauses is increased further when the actor's own behavior or negligence creates a condition (a biological state) known to have a great influence on behavior. What is to be done about the noncompliant offender, for example, previously excused of an offense on the grounds of insanity but now committing further offenses in part because of a refusal to take the essential medicines?[44] One might insist that the psychiatric state is self-induced and thus cannot be grounds of exculpation, but it might well be countered that persons already judged to be "insane" cannot be expected to behave rationally and to conform to a therapeutic regimen. Or it may be contended that there was no insanity in the first place, and that the rebelliousness displayed in the initial offense is now repeated in the form of noncompliance. Note that this is a theoretical ball that can be served and returned endlessly.

Mental Competence and Punishment

Further complications arise from the delicate balance to be struck between the foundational principles of law and the unavoidably shifting theories and methods adopted by the psychological disciplines wrestling with conceptions of intentionality and competence. In two rulings separated by less than three years, the Supreme

Court considered whether constitutional safeguards preclude the execution of mentally defective prisoners. In the first, *Ford v. Wainwright* (477 U.S. 399; 106 S. Ct. 2595; 1986), the Court acknowledged a long-held common law principle forbidding the execution of the insane, as well as the uniform adoption of this principle by the separate states. The question, however, was whether this consistent history incorporated a constitutionally binding understanding. In *Ford,* the Court found just such an understanding.

The petitioner in this case had been convicted of murder in Florida and sentenced to death. His competence to stand trial had not been challenged. After imprisonment, however, he displayed signs of a disordered mind. He referred to himself as Pope John, saw himself as the target of conspiracies involving the Ku Klux Klan, and undertook to write letters to prominent persons. He had no idea of why he was scheduled for execution and reasoned that, as he owned the prison and could control the warden by mindwaves, the execution would not take place. One psychiatrist examined him and declared him unfit for execution. The state ordered three additional evaluations and these reached conflicting conclusions, but the governor signed the death order and lower courts refused repeated appeals. The Supreme Court reversed the judgment of the lower court on the ground that the Eighth Amendment prohibits the state from inflicting the death penalty upon a prisoner who is insane. Writing for the majority, Justice Marshall explained that "The reasons at common law for not condoning the execution of the insane—that such an execution has questionable retributive value, presents no example to others and thus has no deterrence value, and simply offends humanity—have no less logical, moral, and practical force at present."

Speaking against "the barbarity of exacting mindless vengeance," the Court found the petitioner entitled to an evidentiary hearing on the question of competence to be executed. The Court found little room to doubt that the Eighth Amendment's ban on cruel and unusual punishment covers any form of punishment thus regarded when the Bill of Rights was adopted. Although history reveals one exception to the common law precepts on this matter, namely Henry VIII's enactment of a law requiring the execution of traitors even if they became mad (33 Hen. VIII, ch. 20), that law was uniformly condemned at the time.

Yet the Court would later reach quite different understandings in *Penry v. Lynaugh* (492 U.S. 302; 109 S. Ct. 2934; 1989). Penry had been charged with capital murder in Texas and had pleaded insanity as a defense, claiming organic brain damage and retardation. His victim had been raped, beaten, and stabbed; before she died, however, she had time to describe her assailant to the authorities. Assessments of Penry's mental abilities supported the claimed retardation, as he was found to have the mental age of a 6.5-year-old child. Penry's mother had testified that her son had been unable to complete the first grade. His sister testified that their mother had frequently beaten him on the head and locked him away from extended periods. His youth was spent in and out of institutions. Nonetheless, he was judged competent to stand trial and his insanity defense was rejected by the jury. The state's psychiatrists testified that Penry was not suffering from mental illness at the time of the crime, and that he knew the difference between right and wrong.

Interestingly, the Court was less influenced by psychometric evidence of mental retardation than by psychiatric evidence of relevant mental powers. It was specifically suspicious of "mental age" as establishing something akin to legal infancy, and it worried that acceptance of the measure could work against the Eighth Amendment interests of the retarded in other areas of life. Beyond this, the retardation claimed by Penry was seen as "a two-edged sword," reducing his moral blameworthiness while at the same time raising the specter of dangerous behavior in the future. The dilemma courts face in such cases is that the same mental disposition that diminishes the moral powers of the defendant renders him unfit for life beyond the prison walls. Hence, reasoned the Court, "Even if a juror concluded that Penry's mental retardation and arrested emotional development rendered him less culpable for his crime than a normal adult, that would not necessarily diminish the 'unreasonableness' of his conduct in response to 'the provocation,' if any, by the deceased."

As the Court noted, the common law prohibition against punishing "idiots" and "lunatics" for their crimes was the precursor of the insanity defense. One might think that rationale in *Ford v. Wainwright* would then be applied here too. But that was reserved to those so severely disabled as to be the "infants, brutes, and wild beasts" envisaged in Tracy's address in *Rex v. Arnold,* and Penry was not found to be in this category. The insanity of Ford seemed to offer a degree of mitigation not provided by the retardation of Penry, though clearly in both cases the moral powers presupposed by the rule of law were patently diminished. If Penry had sufficient cognitive power to kill his victim lest he be found out, so too did Ford have sufficient cognitive power to envisage controlling the warden and the prison in his own cause. Ford was "insane" in this, for he lacked the powers his troubled mind had invented. But Penry, too, could not have reasoned right or well in the circumstance, or when he confessed all to the authorities. Can there be right answers to problems arising from such cases?

Other Minds and Their Contents

Though tortuous and open-ended, the analysis of legal responsibility and the powers of those fit for the rule of law cannot be abandoned. In Stephen Morse's words, "To reject the relevance of action theory, to fail to wrestle with the mystery of action, is both implicitly to do it anyhow and explicitly to abandon the quest for deeper understanding."[45]

The quest for deeper understanding of actions is ancient. In this century it has been taken to a different level, at least in philosophy, by Ludwig Wittgenstein's elucidation of the problem of mental states and their alleged privacy. Wittgenstein raised the intriguing possibility that long-embraced conceptions of mental states and the private screen on which they are viewed are essentially linguistic constructs clouded in ambiguity and protected by discursive conventions. He referred to mentalistic concepts as a species of "grammatical fiction" which, to him, had the effect of making internal and private what must in fact be irreducibly public and social creations. Wittgenstein asked in his *Philosophical Investigations* just what is, as it were, "left over" when we subtract from the statement "one's arm was raised" the statement "he is raising his arm."[46] The point of the question is that the primary datum available to an observing world is the movement of an arm. It is an event that can brought under one of two descriptions: behavioristic or intentionalistic. So the question that arises has to do with what differentiates the descriptions, since there is nothing to differentiate the event from itself. As Robert Audi suggests, this "subtraction problem" will admit of solution only by positing volitions, for it is these that permit a distinction between actions proper and mere bodily movements.[47]

But plumbing the volitional recesses of another's mind, without presupposing the contents from the nature of the act itself, is no easy matter. It is not surprising, in light of the difficulty, that modern sensibilities turn toward experts on the assumption that psychiatry and psychology have gained some sort of privileged access to the workings of the mind. In the end, what this approach has produced are interesting and clinically informed narratives which, however, can assist jurors only to the extent that they can enlist the empathic resources of the jurors themselves. It is ironic that when the accounts are not unlike those that would come from folk psychology, they assist jurors who actually need no such assistance. When the accounts are drawn instead from the arcana of the mental and brain sciences, it is not at all clear how a jury could be informed by them.

An illustration of this difficulty may be drawn from the legal defense of *automatism*. Under certain conditions persons are known to perform complex acts over a period of time, displaying design and clear intent, but subsequently and credibly claiming to have been in something of a "sleep-walking" state throughout. At the level of observable behavior, the performances have all the marks of rationality, intentionality, and volition. Norval Morris has reviewed a number of such cases and the complexities surrounding their adjudication.[48] In *Bratty v. Attorney General* (1963 A.C. 386, 408–415; 1961), for example, the defendant in a murder trial claimed that he had strangled his victim while in the throes of a psychomotor epilepsy which controlled his actions unconsciously. The defense failed, but the trial did establish two different forms of automatism, sane and insane. Courts are required by the rationale in *Bratty* to establish whether acts performed in such states arise from a "disease of the mind," thus triggering the *McNaughtan* rules.

It is quite obvious that if the defense includes a claimed neurological disease such as epilepsy, expert testimony is at once needed and available. Presumably the question of whether or not Bratty suffered from this disease could be established by various neurological tests and assessments of the anatomy and functioning of his brain; it could be verified in much the same way as would a claimed cancer or bacterial infection or fracture of a bone. But the tests administered to determine whether Bratty suffered from psychomotor epilepsy could not, in and by themselves, constitute grounds of exculpation. Rather, an entirely different class of evidence would have to be consulted for this determination; namely, the connection (if any) and the nature of the connection between the disease and the defendant's conduct.

Even supposing that psychomotor epilepsy in some percentage of the cases gives rise to or is reliably correlated with aggressive, assaultive behavior, there are further questions that must be settled in each case that cannot be settled merely by producing the medical findings. If, for example, those suffering from the disease, when they do behave violently, attack victims indifferently—whereas this defendant murdered someone he declared he would kill—a jury must consider whether *mens rea* might persist even through periods of ostensible or relative unconsciousness. (No one can perpetrate a crime while "unconscious," so a better term is nonconscious or maybe unaware). Moreover, from the fact (if it is a fact) that the defendant suffers from psychomotor epilepsy and that others with this disease have been known to be nonconscious assailants, it remains to be established whether this defendant's behavior is to be thus understood. The point is perhaps obvious: even when relevant expertise can be found within the psychological-neurological community, the evidence it supplies must still be absorbed into that larger "folk psychology" wherein questions of motivation, intent, and capacity are settled.

Students of the mind/brain sciences have argued cogently that the most current developments in these areas could soundly inform juridical outcomes; by continuing to ignore these developments, the courts are little removed from the innocence and ignorance of bygone ages. In his "Unpacking the Myths," Michael Perlin laments the "persistent ambivalence" of the legal system toward developments in dynamic psychiatry and neurodiagnostics. He traces some of the ambivalence to what he calls "a 'culture of punishment' flowing from the medievalist conceptions of sin and evil" and locates the source of the "procedural shrinkage of the insanity defense" in nothing less than a "societal fear of and ambivalence toward dynamic psychiatry."

Although the standard of "reasonable scientific certainty" has now been reached by recently developed psychiatric assessment tools, the law has remained aloof. "Similarly, while the development of 'hard science' diagnostic tools, such as Computerized Axial

Tomography (CAT), Magnetic Resonance Imaging (MRI), and Positron Emission Tomography (PET), have helped determine the presence of certain neurological illnesses, they have had little impact on the development of insanity defense jurisprudence." Even the refinements of moral philosophy, which have clarified the concepts of responsibility, causation, and rationality, "have had little impact on the basic debate. Thus, the public continues to endorse a substantive test for insanity that approximates the 'wild beast' test of 1724."[49]

How should the law's refractoriness in the face of scientific progress be understood? Surely not as a residual of medieval conceptions of sin. It seems more likely to arise from the very logic of moral accountability on which developed legal systems depend. The "dynamic psychiatry" Michael Perlin defends can do no more than unearth some of the conditions or factors in the life and thought of a defendant that entered into a chain of reasoning and sentiments culminating in an unlawful act. Nothing in the psychiatric narrative, however, can serve to exculpate the deed merely by elucidating these thoughts and feelings. The very act of legislation in the criminal domain is predicated on the thesis that life's burdens conspire with individual eccentricities to incline persons toward antisocial behavior. Psychiatric accounts of these burdens and eccentricities can rise no higher than a gloss on the main argument.

The reply to those who would have adjudication conform itself to the state of the art in psychiatry and the brain sciences is at once obvious and unsettling, at least at first blush. It does not include the adoption of a "guilty but insane" verdict, for the extension of the term "guilty" includes the concept of relevant capacity. For the same reason it surely does not call for the abolition of the defense of insanity or the refusal to consider it in civil cases. Courts and legislatures do not wish to create a new category of marginal citizenship, like that of "infants," membership in which sooner or later must invite the macabre abuses of the past. The remedy begins with the acknowledgment that, for purposes of adjudication, evidence as to mental states is never public but always inferential. There is simply no way a mental state can be known with any certainty; it can be known introspectively, but only by the person who experiences that state. Brain scans, magnetic resonance imaging, EEG recordings, and other devices for visualizing activity within the nervous system cannot disclose mental states or independently establish mental diseases. The diseases are sometimes the result of identifiable lesions in the brain, but the devices that identify such damage are used to confirm the suspicion of a mental defect. The initial problem is spotted by observing the patient in a variety of contexts and by recognizing that ordinary patterns of perception, behavior, and emotionality have been significantly disrupted; that rudimentary psychological attributes and abilities commonly found within any large sample of untroubled and competent citizens are lacking in this patient. The standard, by whatever name, is the gift of folk psychology, and in its absence literally nothing can be said about the relevance of neuropathologies to mental life.

In his close examination of the *mens rea* concept Richard Bonnie has argued that the insanity defense must be retained as part of the very "moral integrity" of the criminal law.[50] Bonnie resists the temptation to count on jurors to ignore technicalities and reach verdicts based on their own common sense: "The cause of rational criminal law reform, however, is not well served by designing rules of law in the expectation that they will be ignored or nullified when they appear unjust in individual cases." As he makes clear, there really is something special about the insanity defense when both the question of burden of proof and that of *mens rea* are considered. It is a juridically sound maxim that requires the prosecution to take on the full burden of proof of guilt. It is also a sound maxim that a defendant claiming duress or self-defense must adduce convincing evidence in support of the claim. In these contexts, as Bonnie notes, jurors can set such claims against ordinary experience and connect them to "external realities." Testing the claims against commonly accessible standards reduces what Bonnie refers to as "the likelihood of successful fabrication or jury confusion." On the other hand, however, "A defendant's claim that he had a mental disorder that disabled him from functioning as a normal person . . . is not linked to the external world and by definition cannot be tested against ordinary experience."

Standing behind a modified version of the McNaughtan Rules (now widely abandoned in the United States though still dispositive in England), Bonnie offers his own version of the principles that should guide juries in such cases:

> A person charged with a criminal offense shall be found [not guilty by reason of insanity] [not guilty only by reason of insanity] [not responsible due to mental disease] [guilty of a criminal act but not responsible due to mental disease] if he proves, by the greater weight of the evidence, that, as a result of mental disease or mental retardation, he was unable to appreciate the wrongfulness of his conduct at the time of the offense.[50]

What Bonnie seeks to avoid is that *mens rea* approach that will find guilt where there is intent, notwithstanding the presence of severe mental disturbance. The proper standard, he argues, considers the overall mental capacities of the actor and not merely the volitional elements of the act. He acknowledges that there are "risks of fabrication and 'moral mistakes' . . . greatest when the experts and the jury are asked to speculate whether the defendant had the capacity to 'control' himself." Thus Bonnie would narrow the defense by simply eliminating the "volitional" component because, on his account, there is no scientific method for assessing one's capacity for self-restraint.

Bonnie's influential analysis has much merit, but one quite specific objection can be raised against his premise that only scientifically established measurements are credible in the circumstance. What is questionable are the very sources of such measurements and the basis on which they could ever be validated. Indeed, their validation presupposes the validity of the very personal and "subjective" judgments they would strive to replace. Furthermore, the entire history of adjudication, not to mention its foundational rationale, has assumed that judgment must always be based on an insufficiency of objective facts. It is this that calls for judgment in the first place. Were adjudication suspended until every aspect of the proceeding enjoyed the support of scientific findings, there may well be no trials at all.

Once it is appreciated that all evidence of mental states is inferential and that neither neurology nor psychiatry has any magic lantern to light up the concealed corners of a defendant's mind, the question for the courts becomes the more tractable one of determining the grounds of valid inference. If it is to be the nature of the offense itself, then, contrary to the ALI's caveat, the insanity defense will not invariably succeed whenever a defendant has a record of persistent and bizarre criminal behavior. The success of the defense will depend on how the courts instruct jurors in the matter of insanity itself. Tracy's instructions in *Rex v. Arnold* set quite a high threshold; Shaw's in *Rogers* a lower one. Determining where the threshold is to be set is not a medical but at once a legal and a social question, not unlike questions pertaining to libel, fraud, breach of contract, negligence, dereliction of duty, and other offenses in which judgments must be made as to a defendant's state of mind or powers of comprehension.

In these respects the needed remedy awaits fuller adoption of the proposition that the concept of insanity need not and should not be the same in medicine and law, and that attempts to merge the two were doomed from the start. To disentangle the separate senses of insanity, however, it becomes necessary to free juridical reasoning and procedures from what one court has called "the

modern science of psychology." To accomplish this requires that
the courts reconsider the part to be played by expert testimony and
opt for a far more sparing use of such testimony, even an outright
rejection of it as irrelevant or inadmissible in most instances. Previous attempts failed to regulate the influences of such experts on
the authority of the court and the deliberation of jurors. Hence the
wiser course of action could be to work to restore the earlier confidence in juries to reach just verdicts on the basis of less contested
information. In the process of reducing and even excluding such
influences, the courts would affect not only those relatively infre-
quent proceedings in which testamentary challenges and criminal
defenses invoke the concept of insanity. They would bring about a
radical transformation of the juridical perspective on the very nature of responsibility, which would further clarify the civic purposes
of law.

Jural Science and Social Science

Jural science is not a species of natural science, nor for that matter
(*pace* legal positivism) is it a "social science" in the current accep-
tation of the term. Whether a court is convened to determine
criminal guilt or the settlement of property or the validity of con-
tracts or the propriety of preserving a citizen in his liberties, it is
the specific individual who is the subject of the judicial process.
The question at law is not whether this defendant is, in some psychological or social or ethnic respect, "like" other defendants who
were found guilty; or whether the testator was genetically related
to persons who were certified to be insane; or whether others
whose psychological profiles matched the prisoner's thereupon returned to a life of crime when paroled.

These, however, are just the sort of questions that social scientists
address for entirely valid theoretical purposes. The ambitions of the
social scientist include the discovery of reliable statistical laws permitting better-than-chance predictions of complex social phe-

nomena. For such purposes it may be quite useful to know, for example, that criminal behavior displays significant coefficients of heritability, or that there is a higher incidence of sexual deviancy among those who were abused in childhood.

It is simply a mistake, however, to think that it would be of comparable value to the court to know that a particular defendant had been abused, or that this particular will had been composed by a testatrix whose grandmother had been diagnosed as manic-depressive. To use such facts as evidence would be to subscribe to a theory of (partial or complete) causal determinism incompatible with that presumption of autonomy in which concepts of justice are grounded. The problem here is not that correlations discovered by psychologists and other investigators are not high enough. The problem would endure if the correlations were as high as $+1.0$. Consider the empirical probability that, if a victim is robbed in Harlem between 2:00 A.M. and 4:00 A.M., the assailant is Afro-American. Presumably the probability would approach moral certainty. Suppose, now, that a robbery takes place, that a dozen suspects are rounded up by the police, and that eleven of them are ethnic Chinese and citizens of China visiting New York for the first time. The twelfth is a young Afro-American male. Once one reasons through to the conclusion that a trial is still necessary, the irrelevance of the social scientist's "predictive efficiency" in such matters becomes all too obvious.

In matters of mental life the term "expert" likewise involves something akin to claims of predictive efficiency. Yet whether the expertise arises from extensive clinical experience or epidemiological studies or studies of families, it can be of juridical import only to the extent that it bears directly on the case at hand. To bear upon the instant case, however, the knowledge must be unarguably generalizable across cases—across persons. But this obtains only when the unique and identifying features of the given life are largely irrelevant, and when the correct explanation of the event is the scientifically causal explanation.

There are, to be sure, instances in which this is the right, the best, and the only plausible explanation; instances in which profound retardation precludes the possibility of *mens rea,* or where the recorded life of the defendant or the deceased is so filled with the indisputable signs of derangement as to turn his or her actions into mere reactions or undeliberated responses. In a word, *furiosi* exist, and it takes no expert to identify them, for there is no narrative into which their conduct can be coherently inserted. And, after all, jurors and judges are guided by narrative. The explanation they seek is in fact the narrative that succeeds in integrating the otherwise fragmented collection of persons, facts, motives, and actions. What is required for purposes of adjudication is not a causal explanation of the violent act—"because the bullet struck a vital organ"—but a narrative explanation: he committed the act "because, in his hatred for the victim, he resolved to track him down and to fire what became the fatal shot." If the quest for suspects fails, then a search for (physical, material) causes is most likely to produce answers; lacking both forms of explanation, the event tends to be regarded as accident. Instead of weighing or testing the claim that a defendant or testator was insane, courts might more properly determine whether the offenses and actions can be integrated into a coherent account which is rendered neither more coherent nor explicative by assuming mental disorder on the part of the actor. Note, then, that scientific or medical or "expert" evidence—if, in matters of the mind, there is such—comes to be needed only when all else fails. Even then, however, caution is needed. As Judge David Bazelon, one of psychiatry's most loyal defenders, observed, "Psychiatry . . . is the ultimate wizardry. My experience has shown that in no case is it more difficult to elicit productive and reliable expert testimony than in cases that call on the knowledge and practice of psychiatry."[51]

This is not to say that the courts in general, or the Supreme Court specifically, are reserved in their enthusiasm for such assistance as psychiatry and psychology might be prepared to extend. In *Ake v. Oklahoma* (470 U.S. 68, 1985) the Supreme Court has held that the due process clause of the Constitution actually requires the government to provide competent psychiatric services—to be something of a psychiatric advocate—in cases in which an indigent defendant's sanity may be at issue. Indeed, the courts continue to ingnore facts that speak decisively against the very concept of expertise in these matters. Pretrial hearings as well as civil commitment and parole proceedings continue to rely on predictions offered by experts as to whether the party at issue is likely to engage in antisocial, violent, or self-destructive behavior. Yet study after study has made abundantly clear that the predictive efficiency of mental health specialists is embarrassingly poor in just such cases.[52] Yet the outcomes of such decisions determine periods and places of confinement and constraint of liberty; issues associated with the most precious of civil rights. And the numbers are not small. A NIMH study completed in 1980 indicated that there were then on record more than 300,000 involuntary commitments to mental facilities of one sort or another. Another unsettling fact is that periods of confinement endured by offenders acquitted on grounds of insanity generally reflect the severity of the offense of which they have been acquitted, and not the severity of the mental disturbance diagnosed at the time of admission.[53] All told, the system that would strive for due care and consideration of the mentally troubled tends toward the punitive and away from the therapeutic even where the law's punishments have been suspended.

The courts have not only continued to rely on experts; they have prodded them in the direction of ever firmer positions. *Foucha v. Louisiana* (112 S. Ct. 1780; 1992) is instructive. Terry Foucha, aged seventeen, had entered the home of an elderly couple and, with a loaded pistol, intimidated them and forced them outside. When the police arrived, Foucha attempted to escape and shot at the officers. His trial resulted in a verdict of not guilty by reason of insanity, whereupon he was committed to a Louisiana psychiatric facility for four years. Psychiatric evaluations found Foucha to be no longer insane, but the psychiatrists went on record as being unwilling to judge him no longer dangerous. When Louisiana courts failed to support his appeal against continued hospitalization, Foucha appealed to the Supreme Court, which reversed the lower courts. After all, the psychiatrists, though convinced that Foucha still might prove to be dangerous, had cleared him of insanity. The perplexities arise from the very rationale on which confinement was initially justified. If the only judicially acceptable reason for confinement is the insanity of the defendant, then a subsequent finding of sanity would appear to require release. Dangerousness in itself—as some sort of psychiatric hypothesis or prediction—failed to sustain the burden in *Foucha*. Clearly, psychiatric statements need to be less equivocal; that is, less equivocal in equivocal cases!

At one extreme, the courts have been hostage to speculations traded within a therapeutic community that is properly more concerned with the welfare of patients than with sorting out the various problems and conundrums implicit in what used to be called jural science. At the other extreme, the courts have taken the very reliance on such expertise as constitutive of a reversible error. The position of the California Supreme Court in *People v. Murtishaw* (29 Cal. 3d 733, 631 P.2d 446, 175 Cal. Rptr. 738; 1981) is illustrative. California law separates trial and sentencing procedures where the death penalty might be imposed. In *Murtishaw* psychiatric evaluations declared the defendant to be dangerous and predicted he would engage in harmful conduct. On appeal, the Court noted that such psychiatric predictions are at once utterly unreliable and prejudicial to the defendant, and thus constitute a reversible error. Nonetheless, the grounds on which psychiatric conclusions were reached in *Murtishaw* are the same as those on which diagnoses of insanity, mental incompetence, diminished capacity, and the like are based. Current reliance on psychiatric opinions leaves room for the possibility of having "expertise" accepted by a trial court determining fitness to stand trial, only to be rejected by an appeals court as being prejudicial.

To be sure, not all students of the intersections of law and psychiatry are equally concerned with consistency or with the articulation of jurally sound principles, at least not if the latter must be won at the cost of what some take to be "common sense." In his review of Carol Warren's *The Court of Last Resort: Mental Illness and the Law,* Andrew Scull refers to those "Periodic moral panics over the issue of the improper commitment of the sane to asylums . . . endemic in the nineteenth century in both England and the United States." He gently rebukes jurists like Sir Frederick Pollock, who would "limit the criteria justifying involuntary commitment to the narrowest possible compass," charging Pollock with "spasms of anxiety."[54]

It will be fruitful to consider Scull's reasoning on this subject, for it represents what is probably a widespread view among contemporary medical sociologists and historians of psychiatry. As a group (with notable exceptions), scholars in this field in recent years have adopted something of a dramatic idiom with which to present historical main characters fighting each other over diametricallty opposed alternatives and depicted as blinded by conviction to a degree that arouses the disinterested reader's suspicions. Perhaps Samuel Walker put his finger on what is most troubling in this now influential field in his thoughtful and otherwise positive review of David Rothman's *Conscience and Convenience:*

Rothman's *The Discovery of the Asylum* is one of the better examples of the genre. One finds a common dramatic structure in these works. They open with a description of the old order; the rising action involves the mobilization of the reform effort; the dramatic climax is the creation of the new institution; finally the falling action traces the failure of the institution to fulfill the hopes and dreams of its creators. A number of problems are associated with this approach to history. . . . Methodologically, these histories tend to rely primarily on the writings of the reformers, and we are generally asked to accept their view of things at face value. . . . *The Discovery of the Asylum* relies heavily on the 'pamphlet wars' between the advocates of different approaches to prison design.(Thus, the 'war' is really a skirmish between rival groups of reformers.) The point here is not that *The Discovery of the Asylum* is a bad book; rather, because it is one of the best in the field, it illustrates the limitations of the approach it takes.[55]

According to Andrew Scull, Pollock's efforts in the last century were impelled by a suspicion of psychiatry and doubts about the competence of psychiatrists as regards the business of a court. Scull believes that Pollock's position was more or less overtaken by history and had but a marginal effect on the evolution of mental health law. But in this Scull's historicism fails to comprehend that essentially continuing culture of law of which Pollock was a most serious student and practitioner. Pollock's position—which has been defended and proclaimed in Western courts by one jurist or another for more than two millennia—is informed by a recognition of the necessary presuppositions for a rule of law in the first instance; one of these being an essentially "agentic" theory of human action which takes the powers of the person to be sufficient unto the purposes of law. Bound up with this, of course, are concepts of guilt and innocence, and just and unjust penalties. Constraint of liberty being a punishment, it must be justly meted out.

Over the past several centuries the culture of law (not an ideal, as Scull suggests, but the work of actual assemblies of jurists and legislators) has systematically developed safeguards against arbitrary and capricious actions against the liberty of citizens, at least in those nations that take freedom seriously. These safeguards (classified as the rights of the defendant and the duties of the state) are most clearly defined in the constitutional protections available to those charged with serious crimes. It was the advent of psychiatry's participation within the adjudicative domain that came to introduce the very arbitrary and capricious elements that jural science had sought to expunge. Initially taken to be a source of needed evidence and scientific judgment, the psychiatric expert witness over a course of decades came to be regarded instead as a source of confusion and distraction. The problems arising from this were not exhausted by the occasional celebrated case in which a defendant escaped punishment. Rather, an overarching psychological perspective was guiding civil commitment proceedings, parole hearings, pre-trial, and sentencing deliberations.

Scull points to the late 1960s as a period of "a virtual explosion of law and litigation in the United States relating to the mental health system." It is with some impatience that he notes how this ushered in "a marked trend away from traditional commitment codes, with their typically loose standards and protections and broad grants of discretionary authority."[56] But of course the "commitment codes" Scull refers to were of a rather recent "tradition," and the "tradition" that had dealt with defendants' rights "loosely" had been subjected to serious moral and constitutional scrutiny.

It was California's Lanterman-Petris-Short Act (LPS) that signaled the sea-change, requiring courts to pronounce defendants actually dangerous (rather than simply "in need of care") before committing them to psychiatric facilities. Carol Warren's *The Court of Last Resort* is an important analysis of the manner in which the new protections embodied in LPS were circumvented in practice by a court system in which judges and attorneys on both sides entered into a kind of "insider" understanding of what was best for the defendant and society overall. A counsel for the defendant who innocently undertook to secure the rights of his client within the ambit of LPS soon "would learn the ropes, and would become socialized to the way things are done."[57] Needless to say, this was not the purpose of the LPS Act. What it aimed to achieve was the preservation of liberty absent clear evidence of imminent danger or of defendants' utter inability to care for themselves. The understanding behind LPS is that citizens are not to be stripped of their standing as citizens except under extraordinary and relevant conditions illuminated and tested within a properly adversarial proceeding.

In his *Museums of Madness* Andrew Scull had already reflected critically on just such an understanding, obtaining from early in the nineteenth century to the present, according to which "it made some sort of sense to hold the lunatic responsible for his actions, and that by doing so his behaviour could be manipulated."[58] In that book and in his review of Warren's he has taken to task advocates of that strong voluntarist theory of human action who would find all but the *furiosus* to some extent both legally responsible and worthy of the law's protections of their rights. Against opinions like those of Stephen Morse and others who have written precisely in behalf of these rights, Scull offers counterexamples.

> Doubtless, the inalienable right to liberty must have been a great comfort to the severely impaired 89-year-old woman . . . slowly starving to death in her home. . . . Or to a Mrs. Simmons, of whom counsel testified: 'She was found on the floor of her apartment, where she had not gotten up for three months. She was malnourished. Maggots had eaten away part of her leg. She cannot be moved from the hospital until her leg is healed and she gains some weight. A neighbor had fed her on the floor for three months. She was lying in her own feces for three months.' In the future, if such persons 'really' disliked their situations, why then, they could always exercise the 'autonomy' Professor Morse had so sedulously and kindly preserved for them when he blocked their involuntary commitment.[59]

But of course the state is neither powerless nor at war with its own principles of liberty when it is a question of coming to the aid of malnourished citizens, even before maggots begin to attack their limbs. Nor does it seem probable that, under such circumstances, it is progress in psychiatry that allows the courts to reach the conclusion that intervention is in order. Serious versions of libertarianism are neither heartless nor headless. A principled opposition to state paternalism simply means being against the use of police power to impose standards of conduct on persons whose behavior is otherwise lawful, if odd. Yet even this is largely beside the point. The main point is, what counts as evidence when liberty interests (as in tests of civic competence), property interests (as in tests of testamentary competence), and the state's duty to the laws (as in tests of fitness to stand trial) are at stake. None of this is addressed by pointing an accusatory finger at those who would restrain the state's expression of solicitude toward unwilling beneficiaries. Nor is the point addressed by overlooking vexing problems that arise when liberty interests are abrogated on the grounds of insanity in ways that would be impermissible had the liberty been threatened through prosecution.

The Abuse of Solicitude

The issue is not the state's role as *parens patriae* where a citizen's death or severe degradation is involved, but its role in cases such as *Jones v. United States* (463 U.S. 354; 1983) arising in the wake of *Hinckley*. Jones, arrested for a minor theft, was found not guilty by reason of insanity and proceeded to spend eight years in confinement in St. Elizabeth's Hospital in Washington, D.C. Eight years being far longer than the time he would have served had he been convicted of the crime rather than acquitted, Jones's lawyers argued that Jones had a right to a commitment hearing. The linchpin of the argument was that the state should not derive greater powers of incarceration through acquittals than it enjoys as a result of successful convictions. By a narrow margin (one vote) the Supreme Court upheld the decision of the Appeals Court.

Those concerned with the preservation of defendants' rights are generally not unaware of the complexities of such cases from the court's perspective. Clearly, the manner in which the rights of the insane are safeguarded cannot perfectly mirror the protections available to competent defendants. There is, then, some sort of difference between a Jones who has logged eight years in a hospital and a prisoner who was convicted of theft. One difference is obvious: when a defendant is acquitted the grounds of punishment are removed. Accordingly—and in light of the indisputable fact that incarceration is punishment—committing acquitted people (as opposed to convicted felons) to places of confinement must be predicated on nonpunitive rationales. If the rationale is continued dangerousness, this has to be reconciled with the release of criminals who have served (determinate) sentences and are highly likely in the collective to be repeat offenders. If the rationale is the provision of needed and continuing treatment, this must be reconciled with the immunity enjoyed by citizens against unwanted assistance from the state. It may be assumed that any citizen is like Jones, who disliked his situation, and what he disliked about it was his inability to use that very autonomy that Morse and others would so sedulously and kindly preserve.

Over the past century, in cases involving both civil commitment and criminal responsibility, there has evolved a broad and controlling perspective arising from the belief that jurists and mental health professionals are engaged in common cause. The belief is not implausible, and properly framed it can operate in the cause of justice. In actual practice, however, it has generated what Michael Perlin has aptly dubbed "pretextuality." "By 'pretextual,' I mean simply that courts accept (either implicitly or explicitly) testimonial dishonesty and engage similarly in dishonest (frequently meretricious) decisionmaking."[60] He goes on to advance his "simple" and unsettling thesis that the entire relationship between the legal process and mentally disabled litigants is often pretextual. This pretextuality is poisonous. It infects all players, breeds cynicism and disrespect for the law, demeans participants, reinforces shoddy lawyering, invites blase judging, and, at times, promotes perjurious and corrupt testifying. The reality is well known to frequent consumers of judicial services in this area: to mental health advocates and other public defender/legal aid/legal service lawyers assigned to represent patients and mentally disabled criminal defendants, to prosecutors and state attorneys assigned to represent hospitals, to judges who regularly hear such cases, to expert and lay witnesses, and, most importantly, to the mentally disabled person involved in the litigation in question.[61]

What is behind Perlin's stern appraisal is the recognition that overburdened courts, lawyers eager to have cases settled, and a public increasingly impatient with the sea of incivilities it faces daily will combine to generate just those "pretexts" sufficient unto the purpose. There are no ideal solutions here or in all the kindred areas spawned by the special nature of mental defects, both real and hypothesized. The imperfect solution is to adopt legal criteria of insanity that do not depend upon psychological or psychiatric theories or experts as to the nature or true sign or invariable element of "mental disease," for all such promised *stigmata* have by now proved chimerical. The judging community itself, if not misled or confused by presumed experts and their conflicting texts, must finally be counted on to recognize those who can be justly held to the same standards the community has adopted for itself. The punishments of law typically include a period of exile from this same community; in this way members not only protect themselves but lay down the conditions under which they are prepared to have their own liberties constrained. If ordinary citizens are forced to accept the authority of expert judgment in such matters, this does not mean that they abandon confidence in their own competence to make such judgments. Instead, they end up with lower regard for the jural and moral precepts that seem to be at the bottom of the confusion. In the circumstance, the real danger is that, as public impatience mounts and various ad hoc remedies are applied in response to popular enthusiasms, an important provision of the law will be muted.

Lest the proposal here—to establish legal criteria of insanity independent of expertise—seem eccentric, it is worth noting that some jurists have reached a similar position in recent years. The Criminal Division of the British Court of Appeal offered reasoning in this area quite close to that advocated here, in *Regina v. Weightman* (92 Cr. App. Rep 291; [1991] Crim LR 204). The case involved a previous verdict of a child's accidental death, later retracted when the mother declared that she had actually suffocated her daughter. The central question at her trial was whether, in light of her histrionic tendencies, her confession should be taken as true. The trial judge of the Leicester Crown Court denied the defendant's request to call in psychiatric experts, expressing concern that the jury's functions would be usurped. He was also of the opinion that psychiatrists in a matter of this sort had no deeper insight into the personality and motivations of the defendant than would jurors of normal perception equipped with the relevant facts. Considering the earlier case of *Turner* (60 Cr. App. R. 80 [1975] QB 834), presented in behalf of this defendant's request, the judge repeated the opinion of Justice Lawton in that case in the matter of expert testimony:

> The foundation of these rules was laid by Lord Mansfield in *Folkes v Chadd* (1782) 3 Doug KB 157, and was well laid: the opinion of scientific men upon proved facts may be given by men of science within their own science. An expert's opinion

is admissible to furnish the court with scientific information which is likely to be outside the experience and knowledge of a judge or jury. If on the proven facts a judge or jury can form their own conclusions without help, then the opinion of an expert is unnecessary. In such a case if it is given dressed up in scientific jargon it may make judgment more difficult. The fact that an expert witness has impressive scientific qualifications does not by that fact alone make his opinion on matters of human nature and behaviour within the limits of normality any more helpful than that of the jurors themselves; but there is a danger that they may think it does.

The Appeals Court in *Weightman* upheld the conviction and supported the rationale advanced by the judge in that case and by Lawton in *Turner*. The judgment of the Appeals Court was given by Justice McCowan. The part of that judgment most relevant here is this:

It seems to us that the principle to be learnt from the cases, notably the case of Turner (supra), is that a psychiatrist's evidence is inadmissible where its purpose is in effect to tell a jury how a person who is not suffering from mental illness is likely to react to the stresses and strains in life. The point taken here is that the appellant has an abnormal personality. . . . What does that abnormal personality amount to however? It seems to us that it is not something which is beyond the experience of normal non-medical people.

The point is that the psychological defects and eccentricities that would clearly raise questions of competence and intent are either drawn from the domain in which jurors can enter empathically or are drawn from a domain so foreign as to require a guide or expert if the relevant signs are to be read right. But the need for expert guidance does not create it. Where the mental health professionals are on firmest footing is in diagnosing conditions so severe as to leave no doubt in any observer's mind: the legendary "wild beast."

There is no reason to fear that the rejection of expertise in these areas will result in a cruel or barbarous disregard of the mentally disturbed. If history is a guide, the mentally wayward have suffered more at the hands of experts armed with theories than when entrusted to that tireless rider on the Clapham omnibus. Left to his own judgment and experience, and despite confusions and misapprehensions, he is likely to remain open to the possibility that witches sometimes cry.

Notes

Index

Notes

1. *Furiosi*

1. *The Iliad of Homer,* Richmond Lattimore, trans. (Chicago: University of Chicago Press, 1951). All references to the *Iliad* rely on the Lattimore translation. The earliest recorded version of the epics probably appears around 700 B.C., while the events described occurred half a millennium earlier.

2. Plutarch, *Solon,* 17.2–4.

3. Walter Burkert, *Greek Religion* (Cambridge, Mass.: Harvard University Press, 1985), pp. 109–111.

4. Ibid.

5. Hesiod, Fr. 37.14; 133. The Hippocratic treatise *On the Sacred Disease* dismisses "quacks" and "purificationists"; see 1.42 (vol. VI, p. 362, ed. Littré, as cited by Burkert).

6. The procedural and public criteria are discussed and defended by Michael Gagarin, *Early Greek Law* (Berkeley: University of California Press, 1986). As Douglas MacDowell notes, Homer's epic poems and Hesiod's *Works and Days* are not legal or sociological treatises, but they do provide evidence of the sorts of disputes that arose in those times and the means by which they were settled. Douglas M. MacDowell, *The Law in Classical Athens* (New York: Cornell University Press, 1978), p. 11.

7. Aristotle, *The Constitution of Athens,* III, 4. In this passage Aristotle declares that the function of the elected legislators *(Thesmothetai)* is to record judgments *(anagraphantes ta thesmia)* for the benefit of later lit-

igants. As he notes in XVI, 10, the customary *nomoi* (Aristotle's word here, rather than *thesmia*) were in place before the written laws of Draco. Where customs are recognized as having binding force—the force of "law"—they are called *nomoi* or *thesmia* interchangeably. All references to Aristotle unless otherwise noted are taken from Aristotle, *The Complete Works* (2 vols.), Jonathan Barnes, ed. (Princeton: Princeton University Press, 1984). Here and elsewhere I identify *The Athenian Constitution* as one of Aristotle's works, though controversy about its authorship continues. Perhaps the most defensible position on this matter is Martin Ostwald's. Given the general agreement that the work arose within Aristotle's school, and the current fashion of denying authorship directly to Aristotle, Ostwald prefers "to ascribe the work to the author to whom tradition assigns it. Further, since its authenticity is not in question, it is immaterial for historical purposes whether or not Aristotle was himself its author"; see *From Popular Sovereignty to the Sovereignty of Law: Law, Society, and Politics in Fifth-Century Athens* (Berkeley: University of California Press, 1986); pp. xx–xxi. For another opinion, consult P. J. Rhodes, *A Commentary on the Aristotelian Athenaion Politeia* (Oxford: Oxford University Press, 1981).

8. See MacDowell, *The Law in Classical Athens*, pp. 21–22 on the part taken by public opinion.

9. Hesiod, *Works and Days*, 225–248. In fragment 7 he notes that it is Zeus who "straightens the crooked." Human law *(dike)* thus participates in and seeks to reflect the divine law. The straighter the judgment, the more faithful it is to the godly model. One need only consider the wages of injustice as envisaged by Hesiod to see that he is not offering a merely prudential view on how to make the *polis* successful. All it takes is one bad man to have the gods visit plague upon the city and barrenness upon the land and the women. Armies are defeated, houses razed, and fleets destroyed at sea; *Works and Days*, 238–247. Homer, too, connects the success of the *polis* to the adoption of formal procedures. As Michael Gagarin says, "The shield of Achilles thus contains the implicit message that judicial procedure is central to the life of the polis"; *Early Greek Law*, p. 46.

10. Eric Havelock, *The Greek Concept of Justice* (Cambridge: Harvard University Press, 1978); p. 12.

11. Ibid., chaps. 2 and 3. Havelock makes much of this difference and argues persuasively that the transition from method to principle is effected by Hesiod, now able to read (rather than merely hear) the epic, and thus able to conceptualize "justice" apart from specific (epic) activities and events. But as James H. Oliver noted, the archaic and ancestral law of the Greeks operated side by side with the later law of the *polis,* which gradually came to absorb the old moral laws and laws of Zeus and distill them into written constitutions. James H. Oliver, *The Athenian Expounders of the Sacred and Ancestral Law* (Baltimore: Johns Hopkins University Press, 1950), p. 47.

12. On the distinction between the legal and the moral as regards procedure in ancient Greek law, consider the discussion by Gagarin, *Early Greek Law,* ch. 1. For critical assessments of the general proposition that moral and legal systems are linguistically and socially "constructed," consult *Social Discourse and Moral Judgment,* Daniel N. Robinson, ed. (San Diego: Academic Press, 1992).

13. *Rhetoric* 1375a 30.

14. Eric Havelock, for example, argues that "an oral culture is incapable of conceptualizing justice apart from its pragmatic application in day-to-day procedure"; *The Greek Concept of Justice,* p. 217. Gagarin distinguishes a "proto-legal" from a genuinely legal stage of development, "a step that almost always requires the knowledge of writing"; *Early Greek Law,* p. 9. The deep tradition behind this line of thinking extends to Aristotle; he, however, tied moral and jural reasoning to speech but not specifically to *written* language. Illustrative of his position are passages in his *Politics* (1253a 10–19) in which he distinguishes between the merely gregarious tendencies of the bee and the principled social tendencies displayed by the one animal with speech. It is worth noting that the seventh and sixth centuries B.C. hosted a fairly widespread effort, in Egypt and throughout Western Asia, to compile age-old religious teachings in written form. The Greeks may well have followed this example and, in any case, approached Homer initially as "the great ethical, mythological and religious teacher who molded and educated his hearers by praise of the heroic example." James H. Oliver, *Athenian Expounders,* p. 4.

15. *Works and Days,* 275–280.

16. Ibid., 285–295.

17. Bruno Snell, *The Discovery of the Mind,* T. G. Rosenmeyer, trans. (New York: Harper and Row, 1960), p. 31; Julian Jaynes, *The Origin of Consciousness in the Breakdown of the Bicameral Mind* (Boston: Houghton Mifflin, 1977).

18. Jaynes, *Origin of Consciousness,* pp. 103–104.

19. On this important but somewhat tangential point, consult Joseph Fontenrose, *The Delphic Oracle.* (Berkeley: University of California Press, 1981), especially the pages devoted to "The Pythia's Ecstasy" (pp. 204ff). A sympathetic review of "possession" theories and the like is offered by Robert Eisner, *The Road to Daulis* (New York: Syracuse University Press, 1987), pp. 87–93. That Greek law in its earliest stages was fully indebted to such understandings is discussed in chap. 1 of J. H. Oliver, *Athenian Expounders.* Although the *chresmologi* did not have constitutional or official legal authority, the interpretations of sacred texts by *exegetes* were influential in guiding policy at least into the fifth century.

20. Martin Ostwald, *Popular Sovereignty,* p. 87.

21. Hesiod, *Works and Days,* 288–292.

22. Aristotle, *Politics* 1253a, 30–36, here echoing the Athenian Stranger of Plato's *Laws,* book VI, 766.

23. Plato, *Statesman,* 295.

24. Ibid., 294. For an enlightening discussion of how this fits into Plato's more general theory of the place of reason, passion, and desire in the good life, see Martha Nussbaum, *The Fragility of Goodness,* especially chap. 7 (Cambridge: Cambridge University Press, 1986).

25. Plato, *Laws,* 864 (Jowett translation). See also Trevor Saunders's careful examination of Plato's analysis of insanity, its medical and conceptual dimensions, and the bearing this has on law. Trevor Saunders, *Plato's Penal Code* (Oxford: Oxford University Press, 1991).

26. A thorough discussion of this, not likely to be improved on, is found in Martha Nussbaum, *Fragility of Goodness,* chaps. 5 and 7.

27. *Laws,* book XI, 934.

28. W. J. Jones, *The Law and Legal Theory of the Greeks* (Oxford: Clarendon Press, 1956), pp. 261–262. On Draco's homicide law, consult Michael Gagarin, *Drakon and the Early Athenian Homicide Law* (New Haven: Yale University Press, 1981), pp. 30–37, 140. On Aristotle's theory of agency and blameworthiness, a most instructive discussion is provided

by Richard Sorabji, *Necessity, Cause and Blame: Perspectives on Aristotle's Theory* (London: Duckworth, 1980), pp. 264–271.

29. Jones, *Law and Legal Theory of the Greeks,* pp. 17–18.

30. The extent to which the Roman *Twelve Tables* were indebted to Greek (and specifically Solonic) sources remains debatable. Nonetheless, developed ancient Greek law clearly anticipates laws in the *Twelve Tables,* and Greek moral philosophy pervasively animates the major legal treatises of the Roman Principate.

31. Martin Ostwald, *Popular Sovereignty,* p. 130.

32. Jan Bremmer, *The Early Greek Concept of the Soul* (Princeton: Princeton University Press, 1983), pp. 95ff.

33. A. M. Prichard, *Leage's Roman Private Law,* 3rd ed. (London: Macmillan, 1961), pp. 142–143.

34. Michael Gagarin, *Early Greek Law,* p. 87.

35. Cited by Douglas M. MacDowell, *Law in Classical Athens,* p. 101. MacDowell reviews the law as applied in the case summarized by Isaeus ("On the Estate of Hagnias") and shows the complexity of Greek inheritance laws in mid-fourth century B.C. In this particular case the dispute was about kinship, not madness, but the law referred to by Isaeus covered wills written by allegedly senile testators. For the actual cases, see *Isaeus,* E. S. Forster, trans. (Cambridge, Mass.: Harvard University Press, 1927). Further discussion of the complexities of testation is provided by A. R. W. Harrison, *The Law of Athens* (Oxford: Clarendon Press, 1968), vol. 1, pp. 138ff. See also the discussion of Greek law as it applied to the elderly in Robert Garland, *The Greek Way of Life* (Ithaca: Cornell University Press, 1990), pp. 261ff.

36. This is Law VII from Table V, in vol. I, *The Civil Law,* ed. and trans. by S. P. Scott (17 vols) (Cincinnati: Central Trust, 1973).

37. I exclude from consideration here such devices as the Lex Furia Testamentaria, which sought only to deny probate where testators had flagrantly ignored duties to next of kin. The law here assumes "madness" solely on the grounds that expected beneficiaries have been unmentioned, but there is no reason to think that praetors actually considered such testators as madmen. Indeed, nothing had to be affirmed or denied about the testator at all, according to this law, once the fact of disinheritance was established. See S. P. Scott's brief discussion in vol. I, *The Civil Law,* p. 66, n1.

38. MacDowell, *Law in Classical Athens,* p. 92.

39. *The Institutes of Justinian,* book I, tit. XXIII. Thomas Collett Sandars, trans. (1922; rpt. Connecticut: Greenwood Press, 1970), p. 75.

40. A thorough study of these practices is Stanley F. Bonner, *Education in Ancient Rome* (Berkeley: University of California Press, 1977). His discussions of the Stoic influence (pp. 109ff.) and classroom discipline (chap. 11) make evident how central citizenship status was to the entire educational industry, from cradle to grave. Much of the content, of course, was by way of Greece, the children of patrician families generally being bilingual. Hence Juvenal's claim that Rome was a Greek city!

41. Prichard, *Leage's Roman Private Law,* p. 143.

42. Ibid.

43. "No Greek speaking people has ever felt itself seriously perplexed by the great question of Free Will and Necessity." Henry Sumner Maine, *Ancient Law* (1861; rpt. New York: Dorset Press, 1986), pp. 294–295.

44. Hippocrates, *On the Sacred Disease,* in *Hippocrates,* Vol. II, vi–xx, W. H. S. Jones, trans. (Cambridge, Mass.: Harvard University Press, 1952). The treatise itself was probably composed between the fourth and third centuries B.C. and is fully consistent with the teachings of the Hippocratic school.

45. Hippocrates, *Airs, Waters, Places,* in *Hippocrates,* Vol. I, xxiii, W. H. S. Jones, trans. (Cambridge, Mass.: Harvard University Press, 1939).

46. Celsus, *De Medicina,* W. G. Spenser, trans. (Cambridge, Mass.: Harvard University Press, 1935), vol. 1, pp. 289ff.

47. Cited by Douglas MacDowell, *Law in Classical Athens,* pp. 129ff. Aristotle defines the offense by illustration: "If one hits, one does not in all cases commit *hybris,* but only if it is for a purpose, such as dishonouring the man or enjoying oneself." *Rhetoric,* 1374a 13–15.

48. MacDowell, *Law in Classical Athens,* p. 130. See also N. R. E. Fisher, *HYBRIS: A Study in the Values of Honour and Shame in Ancient Greece* (Warminster, Eng.: Aris and Phillips, 1992).

49. Plato's *Laws,* book I, 648ff. Aristotle addresses the issue in several places, notably the *Nicomachean Ethics,* 1113a 32–1114b 25, in which he criticizes those who would exonerate offenders on the grounds that they might be in a state that alters their judgments and perceptions. He says that "if each man is somehow responsible for the state

he is in, he will also be somehow responsible for how things appear . . . for we are ourselves somehow part-causes of our states of character." *The Complete Works of Aristotle,* Jonathan Barnes, ed. (Princeton: Princeton University Press, 1984).

50. *Infantes* were, in remote Roman antiquity, children too young to speak. In the *Institutes,* they are children below the age of seven. Between seven and fourteen, children could contract where they were not disadvantaged by the terms. They could, for example, accept donations. In these regards, even the *infantes* had somewhat greater legal latitude than the *furiosi.* See R. W. Lee, *The Elements of Roman Law,* 2nd ed. (London: Sweet & Maxwell, 1949), p. 343.

51. Table V, Law 1 states categorically, "No matter in what way the head of a household *(paterfamilias)* may dispose of his estate, and appoint heirs to the same or guardians; it shall have the effect of law." S. P. Scott, *The Civil Law,* vol. 1, p. 57.

52. Sir Henry Maine, *Ancient Law,* pp. 167ff. As plebeians were excluded from the Comitia Curiata—the assembly that settled testamentary disputes—the accommodation of the *Twelve Tables* was necessary for the orderly transfer of property within the growing and increasingly powerful middle class. When the Comitia Curiata was summoned *(calata)* for the purpose of private matters, it was referred to as the Comitia Calata.

53. The irrevocability of the transaction gave rise to the legal fiction of the *familiae emptor.* A father would not be inclined to transfer the *familia* irrevocably to offspring, thereby losing one source of his authority within the family. As the laws of testation developed, the *familiae emptor* was invented: it was a third-party to whom the *familia* was "sold" (by *mancipatio*), the transaction sealed before witnesses and by the symbolic striking of the balance-scale with copper *(per aes et libram).* The transaction permitted the testator (seller) to specify how the *familia* was to be disposed of on the occasion of his death, just as if the transaction had been a contract of sale. In this way the desired succession of the *familia* could be achieved without creating an irrevocable bequest within the family during the prime of life of the *paterfamilias.* Later on, the institution allowed the testator to grant legacies virtually equal to the value of the *familia,* thus passing on to an heir obligations that left him with nothing. Though the ritual *per aes*

et libram survived in the West even into the medieval period, the *familiae emptor* was removed by the time of Gaius, the laws of testation now involving testator and *heres* solely. See Justinian, *Institutes,* book II, tit. X. Unless otherwise specified, the edition used here is *The Institutes of Justinian,* Thomas Collett Sandars, trans. (1922; rpt. Westport, Conn.: Greenwood Press, 1970).

54. *Plebs gentem non habet* is a misleading maxim if it is intended to suggest any difference in familial structure and succession. The class of plebeians was outside the aristocratic circle of "first families," but they were born free and were Roman by birth, breeding, and outlook. Terminology at law then, as now, was cumbersome in the quest for precision. Thus the *familia* might also be called *hereditas* or *bona defuncti* or even *universum ius defuncti.* As noted above, the total inheritance (by any of these names) might well include obligations a beneficiary *(heres)* would seek to avoid. This is certainly one of the factors inclining an heir to challenge the testament by challenging the mental status of the testator.

55. Henry Maine, *Ancient Law,* p. 173.

56. Jerome Hannan, *The Canon Law of Wills* (Philadelphia: The Dolphin Press, 1935), p. 13.

57. Homer, *Iliad,* book IX, 63. In his *Politics* (1253a 9–10), Aristotle regards such a being as falling either at the bottom of the scale of humanity or rising above it.

58. Herodotus, *The Persian Wars,* book I, ch. 31, George Rawlinson, trans. In *The Greek Historians,* vol. 1, Frances Godolphin, ed. (New York: Random House, 1942).

59. James Hadley, *Introduction to Roman Law* (New York: D. Appleton, 1894), p. 121.

60. Harold Mattingly, *The Man in the Roman Street* (1947; rpt. New York: Norton, 1966), p. 104.

61. For a fuller discussion of this dynamic, see Peter Brown, *The Body and Society* (New York: Columbia University Press, 1988), chap. 1. This important study presents in vivid detail the transformation from the essentially classical to the early Christian perspective, and how it affected states, institutions, families, and communities.

62. Artemidorus, *The Interpretation of Dreams,* R. White, trans. (New Jersey: Noyes Press, 1975), p. 217.

63. Justinian, *Institutes,* book I, tit. II. The *Institutes* form part of Justinian's elaborate and successful attempt to codify legal teachings for scholars and for more general consumption alike. Earlier attempts (for example, the Lex Romana Visigothorum, A.D. 506) were defective in one way or another. The first Code was commissioned by Justinian in A.D. 528 and completed a year later by his ten appointees. To this large collection of laws Justinian ordered the addition of a vast supplemental work for scholars that would summarize the judgments and reasonings of the most celebrated of the older Roman jurists. This undertaking, directed by Tribonian, was published as the *Digest* in A.D. 533. Supplementing this and published in the same year were the *Institutes,* intended to be far more accessible, far less dependent on a sophisticated and trained readership. Of the various (and fragmentary) sources of Roman law that were available between the seventh and twelfth centuries, the *Institutes* or portions thereof probably head the list.

64. Peter Brown, *Body and Society,* pp. 10–11.

65. *Codex Theodosianus,* 9.7.1

66. Brown, *Body and Society,* 28.

67. For the requirements and liabilities of curatorship, see Book I, Tit. XXIII of the *Institutes.* On the protection of feeble-minded children, consult the *Corpus juris civilis,* 1.4, 21 (1). Curatorships of three sorts were recognized: (1) a person named in a will *(curator testamentarius),* (2) a dead or incompetent father's nearest relation *(curator legitimus),* and a person appointed by the court *(curator dativus).* The last of these could take precedence over the rest under various circumstances.

68. "Bits of terminology continued to be handed down. . . . But because the terminology was now cut loose from its moorings in a well-articulated intellectual structure, it tended to be tested against concrete circumstances rather than other legal possibilities." Charles Radding, *Medieval Jurisprudence,* pp. 18ff. The Visigoths of France and Spain probably adhered more closely than others to established Roman law; the Lombards and other Teutonic peoples, far less so.

69. Tony Honoré, *Emperors and Lawyers* (London: Duckworth, 1981). In chapter 1 of this exceptional study the author examines the legal responsibilities assumed by emperors, chiefly via the system of rescripts. These responsibilities, and the special part played by lawyers, survived into the age of Diocletian; see chapter 4 of *Emperors and Lawyers.*

70. Rutilius Namatianus, *The Homecoming,* George Savage Armstrong, trans. (1907); cited in Carolly Erickson, ed., *The Records of Medieval Europe* (Landover Hills, Md.: Anchor, 1971), p. 112.

71. Paul Vinogradoff, *Roman Law in Medieval Europe,* p. 25.

72. Ibid., pp. 25–26.

2. Immortal Souls, Mortal Cities

1. Hermann Fitting made a strong case for continuity a century ago. This issue is dealt with briefly by Charles M. Radding, *The Origins of Medieval Jurisprudence* (New Haven: Yale University Press, 1988), pp. 7ff.

2. Paul Vinogradoff, *Roman Law in Medieval Europe* (1909; rpt. Oxford: Oxford University Press, 1961), p. 24.

3. All quoted material in this section is from Katherine F. Drew, *The Lombard Laws* (Philadelphia: University of Pennsylvania Press, 1973), whose book and the Foreword by Edward Peters inform my discussion.

4. Ibid., p. 83.

5. Ibid., pp. 84–85.

6. Ibid., p. 115.

7. Ibid., p. 90.

8. Ibid., pp. 126–127.

9. Ibid., p. 144.

10. Ibid., p. 182.

11. For a summary of the Salic laws pertaining to these issues, see Emilie Amt, ed., *Women's Lives in Medieval Europe: A Sourcebook* (London: Routledge, 1993).

12. The records were kept at St-Bertin and were composed apparently by a number of chroniclers. Janet L. Nelson, trans., *The Annals of St-Bertin* (Manchester: University of Manchester Press, 1991).

13. Augustine, *Concerning the Truth of Religion,* book XIV, ch. 27.

14. Proteus, quoted in Gerard O'Daly, *Augustine's Philosophy of Mind* (Berkeley: University of California Press, 1987), p. 204.

15. Simon Kemp, *Medieval Psychology* (Westport, Conn.: Greenwood Press, 1990); p. 116.

16. Ibid., p. 119, where reference is made to the early Anglo-Saxon *Leech-*

book of Bald. This work can be found in vol. 2 of Oswald Cockayne, ed., *Leechdoms, Wortcunning, and Starcraft of Early England* (London: Longman, 1864).

17. Augustine, *Questions Concerning the Old and New Testament,* quest. 2, cited by R. Colin Pickett, *Mental Affliction and Church Law* (Ottawa: University of Ottawa Press, 1952), p. 44.

18. R. C. Pickett, *Mental Affliction,* p. 45, with reference to the seventh century *Penitential of Theodore.*

19. Ibid., p. 46.

20. Ibid., p. 39.

21. Ibid., p. 42. On Cassian, see Owen Chadwick, *John Cassian,* 2nd ed. (Cambridge: Cambridge University Press, 1968), pp. 96–97. Cassian was one of the founders of monasticism and wrote on the various psychological maladies to which followers of the monastic life are especially prone. His life and works were of abiding interest to writers throughout the Middle Ages and Renaissance. His thoughts on psychological disorders were included in Weyer's *De praestigiis daemonum* discussed in the following two chapters.

22. Peregrine Horden, "Possession without Exorcism: The Response to Demons and Insanity in the Earlier Byzantine Middle East." Paper delivered in a colloquium at the Wellcome Unit for the History of Medicine, Oxford, October 24, 1991. The discussion in the text is fully indebted to this address. Forthcoming in a special issue of *Studi Medievali* devoted to Byzantine medicine; page references here are to the unpublished ms.

23. Ibid., p. 1.

24. Ibid., p. 5.

25. Ibid., p. 5. Horden cites in this connection the *Historia Religiosa* of Theodoret, in which a dispute arises as to whether possession or a form of bulimia is involved.

26. Ibid., pp. 9–10.

27. Owsei Temkin, *The Falling Sickness: A History of Epilepsy from the Greeks to the Beginnings of Modern Neurology,* 2nd ed. (Baltimore: Johns Hopkins University Press, 1971), p. 51.

28. Ibid., p. 13.

29. Cited by Temkin, p. 92. Origen and other apologists of the period were fighting for the cause on two fronts. On the one hand, they had

to reconcile dogma to the widespread practices and beliefs of various sects; on the other, they had to convince the intellectual community that the new faith was not just another congeries of superstition. In his *Contra Celsum* Origen conducts a polemic against Celsus, who directs common sense, logic, and a scientific skepticism at the teachings of the Church. See *Origen: Contra Celsum*, Henry Chadwick, trans. (Cambridge: Cambridge University Press, 1953).

30. Galen, *On the Usefulness of the Parts of the Body*, Margaret Tallmadge May, trans. (Ithaca: Cornell University Press, 1968), vol. 1, p. 432.

31. Cited and discussed by Peter Brown, *The Body and Society*, pp. 334–335.

32. Midelfort, *Witch Hunting*, pp. 16ff.; Carlo Ginzburg, *Ecstasies: Deciphering the Witches' Sabbath*, Raymond Rosenthal, trans. (New York: Pantheon, 1991), pp. 90ff. The *Canon episcopi*, compiled by Regino of Prum in about 906 A.D., was regularly reproduced thereafter. It was incorporated into Gratian's *Decretum*, giving it continuing binding authority.

33. Theodore Wedel, *The Medieval Attitude toward Astrology* (1920; rpt. New Haven: Yale University Press, 1968). The discussion of the position of Albertus Magnus is provided on pp. 66–67.

34. Cited by Wedel, *Medieval Attitude*, p. 69.

35. Midelfort, *Witch Hunting*, p. 17. It was not only witchcraft that was absorbed into the ever-widening scheme of heresies. Between the tenth and thirteenth centuries leprosy, too, was treated as analogous to heresy, as the characteristics of lepers were not unlike those of heretics. See R. I. Moore, *The Formation of a Persecuting Society* (Oxford: Basil Blackwell, 1987).

36. Midelfort, *Witch Hunting*, pp. 17–18.

37. R. C. Pickett, *Mental Affliction*, p. 34.

38. Ibid., p. 30.

39. Ibid., pp. 49–50.

40. Ibid., pp. 49ff.

41. In the matter of psychological and psychiatric concepts adopted or taking root in this period, see Simon Kemp, *Medieval Psychology*; Jerome Kroll, "A Reappraisal of Psychiatry in the Middle Ages," *Archives of General Psychiatry*, 29 (1973), pp. 276–283; Richard Neugebauer, "Medieval and Early Modern Theories of Mental Illness,"

Archives of General Psychiatry, 36 (1979), pp. 477–483; Basil Clarke, *Mental Disorder in Earlier Britain* (Cardiff: University of Wales, 1973).

42. Naomi Hurnard, *The King's Pardon for Homicide before* A.D. 1307 (Oxford: Clarendon Press, 1969), p. 160.

43. Kroll, "Reappraisal of Psychiatry," p. 281.

44. Lynn Thorndike, *University Records and Life in the Middle Ages* (New York: Columbia University Press, 1944), p. 263.

45. Ibid., p. 265.

46. Ibid., p. 266.

47. On the recovery of the naturalistic perspective, see Kroll, "Reappraisal of Psychiatry," p. 281. Regarding mastery of Roman jurisprudence by Lombard lawyers of the twelfth century, see Radding, *Medieval Jurisprudence,* pp. 139ff.

48. At Bologna, with the active support of those (such as the Marchioness Matilda) eager to supply the papacy with experts in Roman jurisprudence. Paul Vinogradoff, *Roman Law in Medieval Europe* (Oxford: Clarendon Press, 1929), pp. 54ff.

49. Ibid., pp. 56–57.

50. See Norman Cohn, *Europe's Inner Demons: An Enquiry Inspired by the Great Witch-Hunts* (New York: Basic Books, 1975), pp. 126ff., in which the author makes clear that the long-believed hunts and prosecutions of the fourteenth century were not historical facts but the product of forged documents. Richard Kieckhefer was not able to discover enough trials before 1300 to identify patterns or historically informing principles; see his *European Witch Trials* (Berkeley: University of California Press, 1976), pp. 16ff.

51. George Rosen, *Madness in Society* (Chicago: University of Chicago Press, 1968), ch. 7.

52. R. C. Pickett, *Mental Affliction,* p. 63. It should be noted that a jurisprudential context for Thomas's own efforts was already in place at least as early as the middle of the twelfth century. In his chapter on "The Age of Mixed Jurisprudence," Charles Radding discusses the remarkable *Expositio* of this period as evidence of the revival of jurisprudence. The work "situates the study of law into the tradition of the liberal arts" (p. 129), as the expositor proceeds to list and interpret Lombard law. Radding, *Medieval Jurisprudence.*

53. R. C. Pickett, *Mental Affliction.*

54. Hannan, *Cannon Law,* p. 127.

55. Hurnard, *The King's Pardon,* p. 160.

56. Cited in Gene Brucker, ed., *The Society of Renaissance Florence* (New York: Harper & Row, 1971), pp. 170–172.

57. Henry de Bracton, *De legibus et consuetudinibus Angliae* (New Haven: Yale University Press, 1915). ("quia crimen non contrahitur nisi voluntas nocendi intercedat.")

58. Hurnard, *The King's Pardon,* p. 170.

59. Frederick Pollock and Frederic W. Maitland, *The History of English Law before the Time of Edward I* 2nd ed. (Cambridge: Cambridge University Press, 1968), vol. 2, p. 476.

60. Maurice Keen observes, "Chivalry's most profound influence lay in just this, in setting the seal of approbation on norms of conduct, recognised as noble when reproduced in individual act and style— and in dictating, in many respects, the mode of this approbation." *Chivalry* (New Haven: Yale University Press, 1984), p. 249. Further, "Magnanimity, and so *largesse,* were regarded as annexed to fortitude. Justice came next in order of importance with those who followed the formal categorisation of the cardinal virtues, since it defined the duty of the noble, as of the knight, to defend the poor and oppressed" (p. 158).

3. Possession and Witchcraft

1. This and other accounts are from H. C. Midelfort, *Witch Hunting in Southwestern Germany 1562–1684* (Stanford: Stanford University Press, 1972), pp. 101ff.

2. *The Civil Law,* S. P. Scott, trans. and ed. (Cincinnati: The Central Trust, 1973), vol. 1., p. 69.

3. Bennett Simon, *Mind and Madness in Ancient Greece* (Ithaca: Cornell University Press, 1978), p. 105.

4. Wedel, *Medieval Attitude,* p. 75

5. Christina Larner, *Witchcraft and Religion: The Politics of Popular Belief* (London: Basil Blackwell, 1984), p. 4.

6. Brian P. Levack, *The Witch-Hunt in Early Modern Europe* (London: Longman, 1987), p. 33.

7. C. L'Estrange Ewen, *Witch Hunting and Witch Trials* (London: Kegan

Paul, 1929), p. 6. The author has selectively reviewed the *Ancient Laws and Institutes of England* and provided the summary from which these examples were chosen. On the Catharist movement and persecution, see Emmanuel Le Roy Ladurie, *Montaillou: Cathars and Catholics in a French Village 1294–1324*, Barbara Bray, trans. (London: Scolar, 1978). On the medieval Inquisition, consult Bernard Hamilton, *The Medieval Inquisition* (New York: Holmes and Meier, 1981). In the matter of secular versus ecclesiastical enthusiasms, Edward Peters offers a concise summary: "A good deal of inquisition history has been written as if the papal inquisitors were the only ardent pursuers of alleged wrong-doers in thirteenth century Europe. In fact, they were always less numerous, and often less ardent than the judicial servants of secular powers" (p. 57); *Inquisition* (Berkeley: University of California Press, 1989).

8. Carlo Ginzburg, *Ecstasies: Deciphering the Witches' Sabbath*. Raymond Rosenthal, trans. (New York: Pantheon, 1991), pp. 90ff. For Eymeric's position, see Ruth Martin, *Witchcraft and the Inquisition in Venice 1550–1650* (Oxford: Basil Blackwell, 1989), pp. 42ff. D. P. Walker, *Unclean Spirits* (Philadelphia: University of Pennsylvania Press, 1981), p. 10. Walker cites Robert Mandrou's *Magistrats et Sorciers en France au XVIIe Siècle* (Paris, 1968) to support the claim that on some rare occasions insanity was pleaded in the witches defense, but here the exception points to the rule.

9. Under the laws of Henry I (1100–1135) and Henry II (1154–1189) the ruling maxim seems to have been, *Insanos et eiusmodi maleficos debent parentes sui misericorditer custodire*. See Nigel Walker, *Crime and Insanity in England* (Edinburgh: University of Edinburgh Press, 1968), p. 32. As Nigel Walker points out, *misericorditer* ("leniently") refers to the King's mercy. From the sixth century on, the Church had been consistently hostile to any form of magic or sorcery, whether "black" or "white," but, as noted, this hostility did not yield far-reaching, systematic, and persecutory measures of control before the fourteenth century. See N. Cohn, *Europe's Inner Demons*, pp. 147–163. Over a long course of years indictments for sorcery were brought against herbalists and other teachers and practitioners of folk medicine. Richard Kiekhefer, *European Witch Trials*, p. 97.

10. Henry Kramer and Jacob Sprenger, *Malleus maleficarum* (1486), Rev.

Montague Summers, trans. (1928; rpt. New York: Benjamin Blom, 1970), p. 277.

11. Levack, *The Witch Hunt,* pp. 8off.

12. Thomas Aquinas, *Summa Theologica,* q. 91. art. 6.

13. Levack, *The Witch Hunt,* pp. 72–74.

14. Midelfort, studying Southwest Germany, calculates about twice as many trials and 3.6 times as many executions in Catholic as in Protestant regions between 1561 and 1670. From 1560 to 1600 the rates were just about the same, but the Catholic rate began to climb again after 1600 (*Witch Hunting,* pp. 31ff). As Keith Thomas has observed, the blurring of religion and magic by the medieval Church provided grist for the ultra-Protestant wing of the Reformation. As early as the "Twelve Conclusions" of the Lollards (1395), exorcisms, enchantments, and the like are condemned as devil-worship and false belief. "Lollardy," notes Thomas, thereupon became generic for any denial of the Church's power to preside over miracles or to alter God's creation. Keith Thomas, *Religion and the Decline of Magic* (London: Weidenfeld and Nicolson, 1971), pp. 52ff.

15. D. P. Walker, *Crime and Insanity in England,* p. 34.

16. Martin Luther, "The Gospel for the Festival of the Epiphany, Matthew 2 [:1–12]," S. P. Hebart, trans. In *Luther's Works,* vol. 52, Hans J. Hillerbrand, ed. (Philadelphia: Fortress Press, 1973), pp. 160ff.

17. Ruth Martin, *Witchcraft and the Inquisition,* 218ff. Martin's study of Venice is important in a number of respects going beyond the aims of the present chapter. One point worth noting here is that the Venetian Inquisition tribunal, in taking firm control of matters and staying scrupulously within the bounds of prevailing law, precluded the appearance of "a particularly dynamic individual or group of individuals who created the momentum and enthusiasm for the hunt" (p. 256), as it would manifest itself in Germany, France, and elsewhere.

18. The King's titles are duly noted in the "Official Document of Approbation of the treatise *Malleus maleficarum,* and the subscription of the Doctors of the most honourable University of Cologne, duly set forth and recorded as a public document and disposition." In Henry Kramer and Jacob Sprenger, *Malleus maleficarum,* p. 277.

19. *Malleus maleficarum,* p. 7.

20. Ibid., p. 11.

21. Ibid., p. 234.

22. Ibid., p. 240.

23. C. L'Estrange Ewen, *Witch Hunting*, p. 53.

24. Kramer and Sprenger, *Malleus maleficarum*, p. 218.

25. Ibid., p. 266.

26. Ibid., pp. 216–219.

27. Ewen's careful study of English assizes over a period of nearly two centuries turns up only a handful of male defendants; less than a dozen in the list of some 300 given on pp. 102–108. Ewen notes further that even when pregnant women enjoyed a reprieve owing to pregnancy, the practice was to hang them a month after the birth of offspring (p. 33). On the limited benefit of doubt, see Kramer and Sprenger, *Malleus maleficarum*, p. 218. For the background consideration of the very nature of "woman," consult Ian Maclean's *The Renaissance Notion of Woman* (Cambridge: Cambridge University Press, 1980). This work documents the pervasive influences of Aristotle's and Galen's theories of gender differences, combined with scriptural and ecclesiastical teachings on the same subject. Given this perspective, the witch theory enjoyed even greater credibility.

28. Kramer and Sprenger, *Malleus maleficarum*, p. 227.

29. Ibid., p. 228.

30. George Rosen, *Madness in Society*, p. 148.

31. Kramer and Sprenger, *Malleus maleficarum*, pp. 122–123.

32. See Henry Chadwick's introduction to *Origen: Contra Celsum* (Cambridge: Cambridge University Press, 1953).

33. Origen, *Contra Celsum*, p. 354.

34. Ibid., p. 357.

35. Ibid., p. 440.

36. Frances Yates, *Giordano Bruno and the Hermetic Tradition* (New York: Vintage Books, 1969). Her brief discussion of the cycle of paintings in the palace of Duke Borso d'Este identifies the major figures depicted in "their charmingly modernised costumes . . . [as] really the Egyptian gods of time, the demons banned by Augustine" (p. 57). Yates's interpretation has been seriously challenged and variously supported by Renaissance scholars. For telling criticism, consult Brian Vickers, "Francis Yates and the Writing of History," *Journal of Modern History*, 51 (1979), pp. 237–316; also his edited volume, *Occult and*

Scientific Mentalities in the Renaissance (Cambridge: Cambridge University Press, 1984). On the side of Yates is Brian Copenhaver, *Annals of Science,* 35 (1978), pp. 527–531. I thank Ian Maclean for bringing these critical works to my attention and also beg his pardon for still retaining more than a little confidence in Yates's reading of Bruno on Copernicanism.

37. The quoted passage is taken from Yates, *Giordano Bruno,* p. 154.

38. Ibid., p. 155.

39. Lynn Thorndike, *University Records and Life in the Middle Ages* (New York: Columbia University Press, 1944), p. 352.

40. Walter Scott, ed. and trans., *Hermetica: The Ancient Greek and Latin Writings Which Contain Religious or Philosophic Teachings Ascribed to Hermes Trismegistus* (Boston: Shamabala, 1985), Vol. 1, p. 358–359.

41. Ibid., p. 361.

42. Marsilio Ficino, "The Soul of Man," in "Platonic Theology," J. L. Burroughs, trans. *Journal of the History of Ideas,* April 1944.

43. Marsilio Ficino, "Apology," in *Three Books on Life,* Carol Kaske and John Stark, trans. and eds. (Binghamton, N.Y.: Renaissance Society of America, 1989), p. 399.

44. In M. F. Jerrold, *Vittoria Colonna with Some Account of Her Friends and Her Times* (London: Dent and Sons, 1906).

45. Cited by E. T. Withington, "Dr. John Weyer and the Witch Mania" (p. 198) in Charles Singer, ed., *Studies in the History and Method of Science* (London: Dawson & Sons, 1955). The summary of Weyer's text is indebted to E. T. Withington's careful scholarship. Weyer is the object of Binsfeld's diatribe. Binsfeld's celebrity arises less from his *Tractatus de confessionibus maleficorum* than from his personal responsibility for the execution of more than 6,000 in his diocese, such that "in many villages round Trèves there was scarcely a woman left." Withington, "Dr. John Weyer," p. 197. For Weyer's classic, see "Johann Weyer," *De praestigiis daemonum,* John Shea, trans. In *Witches, Devils and Doctors in the Renaissance,* George Mora, ed. (Binghamton, N.Y.: Medieval and Renaissance Texts and Studies, 1991). On the skeptical endeavors of the Huguenot consult D. P. Walker, *Crime and Insanity in England,* p. 33.

46. Chap. II. *An Act against Witchcraft and Sorcerie.* A.D. 1586, I Ja. l.12.Eng.

47. Hurnard, *The King's Pardon,* pp. 159ff.

48. Rosen, *Madness in Society,* pp. 141–143. Even the possessed could count on subsidized exorcisms in some jurisdictions (p. 142).

49. Frederick Pollock and Frederic Maitland, *The History of English Law before the Time of Edward I* (Cambridge: Cambridge University Press, 1968), vol. II, p. 480.

50. Frederick Pollock and. F. W. Maitland, ed., *Select Pleas of the Crown,* vol. I: *A.D. 1200–1225* (London: Selden Society, 1888), p. 119 (#187).

51. Henry de Bracton, *On the Laws and Customs of England,* 4 vols. Samuel E. Thorne, trans. (Cambridge, Mass.: Harvard University Press, 1968), vol. 2, p. 28.

52. Ibid., p. 286. On this conflation of madness and infancy, Nigel Walker has identified a corruption in Bracton's use of ancient sources. Modestinus speaks of the *infelicitas fati* of the *furiosus,* whereas Bracton writes of the *infelicitas facti.* Walker notes that Roman law contained a waiver of liability for the madman whose illness was punishment enough, whereas children lacked the requisite intentionality. Nigel Walker, *Crime and Insanity in England,* p. 27. But Roman law did not confer comparable dispensations on others on whom the fates had visited the misfortunes of grave illness. It is safe to say that the infant and the *furiosus* were taken to have one relevant attribute in common, namely, insufficient rational power *(compos mentis)* to be responsible to the law.

53. As reported by Richard Cosin, *Conspiracie, for Pretended Reformation: viz. Presbyteriall Discipline* (1592), pp. 73–81, excerpted in Richard Hunter and Ida Macalpine, eds., *Three Hundred Years of Psychiatry* (London: Oxford University Press, 1963), pp. 42–45.

54. Francis Bacon, *The Judicial Charge upon the Commission of Oyer and Terminer Held for the Verge of the Court.* In *The Works of Francis Bacon,* Vol. II, Basil Montagu, ed. (Philadelphia: Louis Godey, 1841), p. 291.

55. Francis Bacon, *Sylva sylvarum or A Natural History.* In ibid., p. 131 (#950).

56. Ibid., p. 123 (#894).

57. Ibid.

58. Theophrastus von Hohenheim (Paracelsus). *The Writings of Theophrastus Paracelsus on Diseases That Deprive Man of Health and Reason,* Gregory Zilboorg, trans. In *Four Treatises of Theophrastus von Hohenheim Called Paracelsus* vol. 1, Henry Sigerist, ed. (Baltimore: Johns Hopkins University Press, 1941).

59. Paracelsus, *Diseases,* p. 167.

60. Ibid., p. 179.

61. "Psychiatry" here refers to the perspective on insanity rather than to the medical specialty itself, which would not come into being for another four centuries.

62. Paracelsus, *Diseases,* book VI, p. 357

63. Ibid., pp. 357; 362.

64. Ibid., p. 564.

65. Rosen, *Madness in Society,* p. 147. For a thorough and informing study of the trial of Elizabeth Jackson, together with Edward Jorden's *Discourse* in which a decidedly psychiatric interpretation of the victim's vexations is offered, see Michael MacDonald, ed., *Witchcraft and Hysteria in Elizabethan London: Edward Jorden and the Mary Glover Case* (London: Tavistock/Routledge, 1991). Although Jorden reflects the growing inclination to understand such matters medically, it remains the case that when Elizabeth Jackson's defense did avail itself of Jorden's medical testimony, Chief Justice Anderson was nearly peevish in his skepticism.

66. James I. *Minor Prose Works of James VI and I: Daemonologie, The True Lawe of Free Monarchies, A Counterblaste to Tobacco, A Declaration of Sports,* James Craigie, ed. (Edinburgh: Scottish Text Society, 1982), p. 56. I have changed the passages only to provide modern spelling. The King would oscillate in his commitment to the witch theory, being for a time ardent in his desire to have witches prosecuted, and then eager to develop methods for unearthing frauds and pretenders.

67. MacDonald, *Witchcraft and Hysteria,* pp. lii ff.

68. Martin, *Witchcraft and the Inquisition,* 28–29; p. 199.

69. Alan Macfarlane, *Witchcraft in Tudor and Stuart England* (London: Routledge & Kegan Paul, 1970), p. 129.

70. Henry Charles Lea's *Superstition and Force* appeared in 1866 and remains one of the most complete studies of the history of ordeal and torture in the English language. Edward Peters has edited and returned to print the final two parts of Lea's work, *The Ordeal* and *Torture,* both published in paperback by the University of Pennsylvania Press (1973). Lea's thesis attempts to explain the relative infrequency of torture in Northern countries. England's common law prohibits it from the time of Henry I. Confessions arising out of intimidation were invalid. At

the same time *ordeal* remained one of the chief methods of settling disputes. By the seventeenth century, however, all this was abandoned as the witch panic claimed, in Lea's phrase, "England and the Northern races." Henry Charles Lea, *Torture,* Edward Peters, ed. (Philadelphia: University of Pennsylvania Press, 1973), ch. 9.

71. Robert Burton, *The Anatomy of Melancholy,* Floyd Dell and Paul Jordan-Smith, eds. (New York: Tudor Publishing, 1951).

72. Thanks to the prodigious output of Renaissance printers, some of whom were leading scholars in their own right, Burton and his contemporaries could easily compile personal libraries containing the medical and scientific treatises of the Hippocratics, Theophrastus, Galen, Avicenna, Vesalius, and a legion of lesser figures. Travel and study in Italy had equipped English scholars with first-hand knowledge of the leading medical methods and findings of the age. Thomas Linacre, first president of the Royal College of Physicians (1518) and leading proponent of medical science, was but one of Burton's countrymen to have established teaching on an international basis. By the time of Burton's years at Oxford, there was no major obstacle to the study of the best thinking on virtually any medical topic. Still complete and authoritative on this is George Sarton, *The Appreciation of Ancient and Medieval Science during the Renaissance (1450–1600)* (Philadelphia: University of Pennsylvania Press, 1955); lect. 1, Medicine. But it would be wrong to assume that the principal cause of witch-accusations were illnesses that could not be explained in medical or scientific terms. At least in Tudor and Stuart England, Alan Macfarlane was not able to find evidence linking the incidence of outbreaks of illness to outbreaks of witch-accusations. Nor was one illness more likely to elicit such accusations than others. Even insanity was not attributed to witchery in any of the more than twenty cases turned up by Macfarlane. See *Witchcraft in Tudor and Stuart England,* chap. 13.

73. Burton, *Anatomy of Melancholy,* part I, sec. I, subsection 3.

74. Ibid., part I, sec. I, member 3, subsection 2.

75. Ibid., part I, sec. 2, member 1, subsection 2. The tradition had the witch as the *cause,* not the victim of insanity. Anthropological studies identify this as a general tendency. The witch is known through acts of social rather than mental deviancy. It is the element of willfulness, as Macfarlane says (p. 226), that is central in most of the cultures studied.

76. This point is developed in the Epilogue and elsewhere in Carol Karlsen's important study, *The Devil in the Shape of a Woman* (New York: Random House, 1987). Chapter 3 of this work outlines the economic motives behind five different trials, which had in common only the fact that the female defendants "stood in the way of the orderly transmission of property from one generation of males to another" (p. 116). In the New World, from the time an Irish washerwoman had been tried and hanged in Boston (1688) for bewitching the Glover child until 1692, the powers of accusers grew as did the social standing and political power of many of the accused. The latter would come to include Lady Phipps, wife of Sir William Phipps, recently appointed Governor of the Massachusetts colony. Cotton Mather had been involved in all of this, ardently believing that the devil was striving to thwart the progress of Christianity in America. Indeed, before his own wife was implicated, Phipps looked to Cotton Mather to establish the validity of the prosecutions on religious grounds.

77. On this point Keith Thomas has written, "Essentially the witch and her victim were two persons who ought to have been friendly towards each other, but were not. They existed in a state of concealed hostility for which society provided no legitimate outlet. . . . The great bulk of witchcraft accusations thus reflected an unresolved conflict between the neighbourly conduct required by the ethical code of the old village community, and the increasingly individualistic forms of behavior which accompanied the economic changes of the sixteenth and seventeenth centuries." Keith Thomas, *Religion and the Decline of Magic,* pp. 560–561.

78. A still fully informing discussion of this appears in Charles Lea, *The Inquisition of the Middle Ages* (1887; rpt. New York: Barnes and Noble, 1993).

79. John A. F. Thomson, *The Early Tudor Church and Society: 1485–1529* (London: Longman, 1993), pp. 356ff.

4. "Wild Beasts" and "Idle Humours"

1. Raymond Crawford, "The Blessing of Cramp-Rings." In Charles Singer, ed., *Studies in the History and Method of Science* (London: Dawson and Sons, 1955), p. 177. Examples abound. Consider that

John Locke urged that the Countess of Shaftesbury's urine should be buried as part of the treatment for her nephritis. Keith Thomas, *Religion and the Decline of Magic* (London: Weidenfeld and Nicolson, 1971), p. 544.

2. William Cullen, *First Lines in the Practice of Physic* (Edinburgh, 1784), vol. 4, pp. 151–155. This work was published in Edinburgh in 1772 in a Latin edition. Later volumes were added and the complete English version published in 1784 in four volumes.

3. Thomas, *Religion and the Decline of Magic*; pp. 54–75.

4. Edward Coke, *The First Part of the Institutes of the Laws of England,* first published in 1628. The edition used here is the 14th, dated 1789. Coke would vie successfully with Bacon both for the position of attorney general (1594) and for the hand of Lady Elizabeth Hatton (1598). And Bacon was the gray eminence behind the Privy Council's charges against Coke (1616) for disrespecting James I's commands against holding multiple livings *(commendams).* Coke persisted in proclaiming the authority of common law over both ecclesiastical and royal pronouncements. He played a main role in the evolution of the common law's supremacy in England.

5. Coke, *Institutes,* Book I, Chap. 1, Sect. 1, p. 2b; Ibid., *Liber* 3, Chap. 6, Sect. 405, pp. 246b–247a. The extent to which Coke's principles were actually applied varies. For example, "Every deed of feoffment or grant, which any man *non compos mentis* makes, is avoidable" was probably invariably applied, but that said deed "shall not be avoided by himself, because it is a maxim in law, that no man of full age shall . . . stultify himself, and disable his own person" may not ever have been accepted as law. On this, see Sir William Holdsworth, *A History of English Law,* Vol. VIII, p. 53.

6. There is a sharper distinction in modern times between and among the various mental faculties and powers, thanks chiefly to the "faculty" psychologies of the eighteenth century. From the medieval period onward and throughout the Renaissance, it was *memory* that was most often taken to be the mark of mental prowess. A large and culturally rich tradition stands behind this understanding. See Mary Carruthers, *The Book of Memory: A Study of Memory in Medieval Culture* (Cambridge: Cambridge University Press, 1990).

7. Temporary insanity as a legal concept is not indebted to modern psy-

chiatry, nor were medieval jurists at all reluctant to consider it. In a trespass case of 1378, for example, counsel for the defendant, Ralph Paranter, contends that "every month between lucid intervals he was stricken with a serious sickness and thus became virtually insane during those times." *Select Cases of Trespass from the King's Courts 1307–1399,* Morris Arnold, ed. (London: The Selden Society, 1987), vol. II, 34.23, p. 390.

8. Matthew Hale, *The History of the Pleas of the Crown,* 1778 ed. published from the original manuscripts by Sollom Emlyn. The first publication of Hale's papers was ordered by the House of Commons on November 29, 1680. There were many reprintings. The one used here was the new edition of 1778, corrected and annotated by George Wilson.

9. A number of these were published posthumously, such as *A Collection of Modern Relations of Matter of Fact Concerning Witches and Witchcraft upon the Persons of the People* (London, 1693).

10. Thomas Hobbes, *Leviathan* (1651), pt. IV, ch. 45. Hobbes observes here, "That there were many Daemoniaques in the Primitive Church, and few Mad-men, and other such singular diseases; whereas in these times we hear of, and see many Mad-men, and few Daemoniaques, proceeds not from the change of Nature; but of Names." Thomas Hobbes, *Leviathan.* C. B. Macpherson, ed. (Baltimore: Penguin Books, 1968), p. 664.

11. The trial of Rose Cullender and Amy Drury was reported in Cobbett's *State Trials,* vol. VI, 687–702. For Mather's indebtedness, see Cotton Mather, *A Discourse on The Wonders of the Invisible World* (1692) in *Cotton Mather on Witchcraft* (New York: Dorset Press, 1991). Mather's own thesis is given with directness thus: "PROPOSITION I. That there is a *Devil,* is a thing Doubted by none but such as are under the Influences of the *Devil"* (p. 37). He goes on to note that the great "humiliations" recently endured by the *"Turkish power"*, as well as the earthquakes in Europe are warnings; and that the *"Empire* of God" must overcome that *"Conscience* of man" celebrated in the late King James's *Liberty of Conscience* (pp. 60–61).

12. Hale in his student days, once he turned away from Oxford's several amusements, steeped himself in books on Roman law, philosophy, and medicine. At this impressionable point in life he read a biography

of Pomponius Atticus, scholar, *literatus*, and friend of Cicero, and thereupon took him as a figure worthy of emulation. For an informing and most admiring biography, consult J. B. Williams, *Memoirs of the Life, Character, and Writings of Sir Matthew Hale* (London, 1835).

13. Matthew Hale, *The History of the Pleas of the Crown*, ch. 4, p. 29.

14. Ibid., p. 30.

15. Ibid.

16. Ibid., p. 31.

17. Ibid.

18. Ibid., pp. 31–32.

19. Ibid., p. 32

20. Ibid., p. 33

21. Ibid., p. 36

22. Ibid., pp. 34–35.

23. Ibid., p. 37

24. 33 Henrici VIII, Cap. XX. The act seeks "to avoid all sinister, counterfeit and false practices and imaginations that may be used for excuse of punishment of high treasons." As for the defendant whose insanity occurs after the fact, "they shall have and suffer execution [their madness or lunacy notwithstanding]."

25. Joseph Klaits, *Servants of Satan: The Age of the Witch Hunts* (Bloomington: University of Indiana Press, 1985), pp. 164–165. I thank Mr. David Smith for bringing this book to my attention.

26. A most informing chapter on Willis, his Oxford context, and the influence of his research and writing is Robert Frank's "Thomas Willis and His Circle: Brain and Mind in Seventeenth-Century Medicine," in *The Languages of Psyche: Mind and Body in Enlightenment Thought*, G. S. Rousseau, ed. (Berkeley: University of California Press, 1990).

27. The "hecatombs" of animals killed by Willis and his close collaborator, R. Lower, were but the early victims of that expanding *abattoir* innocently called "the dissecting table." One cannot write about the scientific accomplishments of such industrious persons as Willis and Lower, not to mention the veritable legion of their greater and lesser successors, without noting their stubborn unwillingness to face the ethical challenges attendant upon their activities.

28. Frank, "Thomas Willis," p. 131. Michel Foucault relates the proposal of Morritz Hoffman in 1662 to replace the melancholic's "over-

charged, thick blood, encumbered with bitter humours," with a lighter weight. Such transfusions were attempted years later with favorable results. Michel Foucault, *Madness and Civilization: A History of Insanity in the Age of Reason,* Richard Howard, trans. (London: Routledge, 1989), pp. 162–163.

29. Quoted by Antonie Luyendijk-Elshout, "Of Masks and Mills: The Enlightenment Doctor and His Frightened Patient." In *The Languages of Psyche,* p. 223.

30. Ibid.

31. Robert Whytt attended Boerhaave's lectures in Leiden after studying medicine under the elder Alexander Munro at Edinburgh. He worked with the famous Cheselden in 1734 and then took his continental journey to Leiden and Rheims. A recent edition of his posthumously published *Works* is available in Series E, vol. 1, of D. N. Robinson, ed., *Significant Contributions to the History of Psychology* (Westport, Conn.: Greenwood, 1978).

32. David Hartley, *Observations on Man: His Frame, His Duty, and His Expectations* (1749; rpt. Gainesville, Fla.: Scholar's Facsimiles & Reprints, 1966). The sections pertaining to madness are Vol. 1, Pt. 1, Sec. 1, Prop. 7; Pt. 2, Prop. 43; Ch. 3, Sec. 6, Prop. 92. Quoted material is taken from this last, pp. 400ff.

33. These works and authors are the subject of part of that still illuminating study of eighteenth-century naturalism, Basil Willey's *The Eighteenth Century Background: Studies on the Idea of Nature in the Thought of the Period* (1940; rpt. New York: Columbia University Press, 1950).

34. Quoted in Richard Hunter and Ida Macalpine, eds., *Three Hundred Years of Psychiatry: 1535–1860* (London: Oxford University Press, 1963), p. 479. Pinel's translation of Cullen's *First Lines in the Practice of Physic* appeared in 1785 as *Institutions de médécine pratique, traduites sur la quatrième et dernière edition de l'ouvrage anglais de M. Cullen, etc.*

35. Julien La Mettrie, *Man: A Machine* (1748), Mary W. Calkins, trans. (New York: Open Court, 1912). This came on the heels of his *Histoire naturelle de l'ame* (1745), which was controversial enough to cause self-exile under the protection of Frederick the Great.

36. Panegyrics abounded, of course. These are taken from D'Alembert. Jean le Rond D'Alembert, *Preliminary Discourse to the Encyclopedia of*

Diderot (1751), Richard Schwab, trans. (Indianapolis: Bobbs-Merrill, 1963), pp. 74, 81. One might add Voltaire's contention that "nobody before Chancellor Bacon had understood experimental philosophy; and of all the physical experiments that have been made since his time, hardly one was not suggested in his book." Voltaire, *Philosophical Letters* (1732), Ernest Dilworth, trans. (Indianapolis: Bobbs-Merrill, 1962), p. 49.

37. Willey, *The Eighteenth Century Background*, p. 16.

38. Shaftesbury (Third Earl of), *Characteristics of Men, Manners, Opinions, and Times.* Vol. II, Book II, Pt. 2, Sec. 1 (1711). First published in 1699. The quoted passage is taken from *British Moralists*, L. A. Selby-Bigge, ed., originally published in 1897 by Oxford University Press (New York: Dover Publications, 1965), vol. 1, p. 46.

39. Francis Hutcheson, *An Inquiry Concerning the Original of Our Ideas of Virtue or Moral Good* (1725), Sec. III. The passage is taken from *British Moralists*, p. 110.

40. *Rex v. Arnold*, 16 *Howell's State Trials* 695 (10 George I. A.D. 1724). This case is important partly because of the standing of the judge. Robert Tracy (1655–1735) was fifth son of Robert Tracy, second viscount Tracy of Rathcoole. He studied at Oriel and the Middle Temple. He was an important jurist and served on the King's Bench in Ireland as a Baron of the Exchequer and as Commissioner of the Great Seal during the eight years (1710–1718) when the office of Lord Chancellor was unoccupied.

41. Nigel Walker has produced a letter from Lord Onslow intimating that the attack against him was part of wider plot, "for my life was not the only one to be taken away," and that the King had personal cause for concern. Walker suggests that the refusal to supply Arnold with counsel and Tracy's "plainly unfavourable" charge to the jury might both have been based partly on Onslow's theory. But, as Walker notes, the judge assisted Arnold throughout in the calling of witnesses, the procedure called for at the time. And it seems doubtful that Onslow would later seek clemency for Arnold if he really believed George II had been a potential victim of the defendant's wrath. It was Onslow's concern that prompted him to arrange for a full transcript of the trial proceedings, thus making *Rex v. Arnold* among the earliest insanity cases for which an accurate and thorough account is available. Nigel Walker, *Crime and Insanity in England*, pp. 53–54.

42. *Rex v. Arnold,* p. 700.

43. Ibid., p. 701.

44. Ibid., p. 703.

45. Ibid.

46. Ibid., p. 707.

47. Ibid., p. 710.

48. Ibid., p. 715.

49. Ibid., p. 721.

50. Ibid., p. 725.

51. Ibid., p. 754–765.

52. *Rex v. Ferrers* (1760), 19 Howell's *State Trials,* 886. Nigel Walker, who discusses this case at length, refers to it as "the earliest recorded example of psychiatric testimony in a criminal trial," *Crime and Insanity in England,* p. 58. It was not, however, the earliest recorded case in which medical testimony was solicited for the purpose of determining whether mental derangement was the result of natural or unnatural causes. In this connection I referred to the trial of Elizabeth Jackson (1602) in the previous chapter.

53. The second of four famous Monros who would serve as superintendents of Bethlem for over a hundred years.

54. *Rex v. Ferrers,* pp. 942–944.

55. Ibid., pp. 946–956.

56. *Cartwright v. Cartwright,* 1 *Phillimore Ecc.* 90.

57. Ibid., 91.

58. Ibid., 94.

59. Ibid., 121.

60. Ibid., 119.

61. Ibid., 122.

62. Cited and discussed in Ida Macalpine and Richard Hunter, *George III and the Mad Business* (1969, rpt. London: Pimlico, 1991), pp. 103ff.

63. Ibid., p. 277.

5. The Rise of Medical Jurisprudence

1. Cited in Henry May, *The Enlightenment in America* (New York: Oxford University Press, 1976), p. 208.

2. Ibid.

3. On aspects of the Scottish Enlightenment germane here, the following should be consulted: Manfred Kuehn, *Scottish Common Sense in Germany: 1768–1800* (Montreal: McGill, Queen's University Press, 1987), D. N. Robinson, "Common Sense at the 'Wise Club': Thomas Reid and the Aberdeen Years," *Journal of the History of the Behavioral Sciences*, 25 (1989), pp. 154–162; D. N. Robinson, "The Scottish Enlightenment and Its Mixed Bequest," *Journal of the History of the Behavioral Sciences* (1986); and Henry May, *The Enlightenment in America*.

4. *Rex v. Hadfield*. 40 George III. A.D. 1800. In Howell's *State Trials*, Vol. XXVII, 1820; 1281–1356.

5. Erskine's career had high peaks and deep valleys. For all his success as an advocate, his tenure as Lord Chancellor was lacking in distinction. His defense of Paine lost him his position as counsel to the Duke of Edinburgh, though he was restored to favor a few years later.

6. Alexander Crichton, *An Inquiry into the Nature and Origins of Mental Derangement, Comprehending a Concise System of Physiology and Pathology of the Human Mind, and History of the Passions and Their Effects* (London: Cadell and Davies, 1798).

7. Though he was impressed, it is with obvious irony that Pinel exclaims, "I cannot help admiring the courage of Dr. Crichton, who has lately published two volumes upon maniacal and melancholic affections, merely upon the basis of some ingenious elucidations of the doctrines of modern physiology, which he has extracted from a German journal" (p. 51). Philippe Pinel, *A Treatise on Insanity*, D. D. Davis, trans. (London: Cadell and Davies, 1806). (First published in France in 1800.) This translation is reproduced in Series C, Vol. 3 of D. N. Robinson, ed., *Significant Contributions to the History of Psychology*. The jointly influential contributions by Pinel, Crichton, and Esquirol toward establishing the modern psychiatric perspective are clearly and illuminatingly developed by Dora Weiner, "Mind and Body in the Clinic: Philippe Pinel, Alexander Crichton, Dominique Esquirol, and the Birth of Psychiatry." In, G. S. Rousseau, *The Languages of Psyche* (Berkeley: University of California Press, 1990). Weiner points out that Davies's translation of Pinel's *Treatise* omits the preface, in which Pinel expresses great praise of Crichton's work.

8. On this point see D. N. Robinson, "Thomas Reid's Critique of Dugald Stewart," *Journal of the History of Philosophy*, 27 (1989), pp. 405–422.

9. This passage from Pinel is illustrative: "The loss of a friend, who became insane through excessive love of glory, in 1783, and the inaptitude of pharmaceutic preparations to a mind elated . . . enhanced my admiration of the judicious precepts of the ancients." Pinel, *Treatise*, p. 52.

10. *Rex v. Hadfield*, p. 1308.

11. Ibid., p. 1309.

12. Ibid.

13. Ibid., p. 1310.

14. Ibid.

15. Ibid., p. 1312.

16. Ibid.

17. Ibid., p. 1313

18. Ibid.

19. Ibid., p. 1314. The entire shape of Erskine's analysis had been prefigured in John Locke's famous discussion of madness in that veritable handbook of Enlightenment psychology, *An Essay Concerning Human Understanding* (1690). The madman reasons rightly from wrong premises, Locke insisted. "Thus shall you find a distracted man fancying himself a king, with a right inference, requires suitable attendance, respect, and obedience." (Book II, Ch. XI, Sec. 13).

20. *Rex v. Hadfield*, p. 1314.

21. Ibid., p. 1320.

22. Ibid., pp. 1320-1321

23. Ibid., p. 1334.

24. 40 George III, Chaps. 93, 94.

25. The edition cited here is the new edition of 1798. John Gregory, *A Comparative View of the State and Faculties of Man with Those of the Animal World* (London: Cadell and Davies, 1798), pp. 270-271. Benjamin Rush could still look forward to a coherent system of health and disease while fully respecting Gregory's call for that knowledge drawn from life itself.

26. Nigel Walker, *Crime and Insanity in England*, pp. 12ff.

27. Henry Maudsley, *Responsibility in Mental Disease* (New York: D. Appleton, 1876), p. 91.

28. Ibid., pp. 275-277

29. *Rex v. Hadfield*, p. 1326.

30. Ibid., p. 1318
31. Ibid., p. 1328.
32. Ibid.
33. Ibid.
34. *Rex v. Bellingham*, 1 Collinson on Lunacy, 636–674. Nigel Walker reproduced the text of Mansfield's charge as it appeared in the *Old Bailey Sessions Papers* (1812) at p. 272. Nigel Walker, *Crime and Insanity in England*, pp. 270–272.
35. Maudsley, *Responsibility in Mental Disease*, p. 92.
36. Walker, *Crime and Insanity in England*, p. 270.
37. *Dew v. Clark and Clark*. 162 English Reports, 410–596. The passage quoted appear on p. 414.
38. Ibid., p. 455.
39. Foucault, *Madness and Civilization*, p. 269.
40. David Rothman, *The Discovery of the Asylum: Social Order and Disorder in the New Republic* (Boston: Little, Brown, 1971), p. 111. I thank Francine Robinson for bringing this book to my attention. For the statistics from the York Retreat, consult Anne Digby, *Madness, Morality and Medicine: A Study of the York Retreat, 1796–1914* (Cambridge: Cambridge University Press, 1985).
41. Pinel cites such predisposing conditions as disappointed ambition, religious fanaticism, profound chagrin, and unfortunate love. He is also somewhat skeptical of exclusively neurological theories of the "craniological" stripe. Philippe Pinel, *Treatise*, pp. 41ff. The statement by Dorothea Dix is cited by David Rothman, *Discovery of the Asylum*, p. 112. On the causes of insanity based on the overworked brain, see Hubbard Winslow, *Elements of Intellectual Philosophy*, 2nd ed. (Boston: Hickling, Swan and Brewer, 1858), p. 344.
42. Prichard's influential writing on moral insanity is in his *A Treatise on Insanity* (1835), the quoted passage from p. 4. Anne Digby, *Madness, Morality and Medicine*, p. 93.
43. W. Charles Hood, *Suggestions for the Future Provision of Criminal Lunatics*, p. 20.
44. Ibid., pp. 144–145.
45. Ibid., pp. 66 ff.
46. Ibid., p. 76.
47. Ibid., p. 127.

48. Ibid., pp. 161–162.

49. W. Charles Hood, *Statistics of Insanity*, p. 44.

50. James C. Prichard, *A Treatise on Insanity and Other Disorders of the Mind* (Philadelphia: Haswell, Barrington and Haswell, 1837); and *On the Different Forms of Insanity in Relation to Jurisprudence* (1842). Prichard's first development of his theory of moral insanity was in his *Treatise on Insanity and Other Disorders Affecting the Mind,* published in 1835. As he had previously and authoritatively written on diseases of the nervous system, his attention to *moral insanity* could not be dismissed as a scientifically naive work. His interests in physical anthropology and ethnology appear as early as 1813 and would culminate in the five-volume *Physical History of Man* in 1847, the year before he died.

51. Prichard, *On the Different Forms of Insanity,* p. 17.

52. Ibid., p. 19.

53. Ibid., p. 87.

54. Ibid., pp. 125ff.

55. Franz Joseph Gall, *On the Functions of the Brain and Each of Its Parts. With observations on the possibility of determining instincts, propensities, and talents, or the moral and intellectual dispositions of men and animals, by the configuration of the brain and head* (1825), 6 vols., Winslow Lewis, trans. (Boston: Marsh, Capen and Lyon, 1835). A redaction of Gall's work in English was Johann G. Spurzheim, *The Physiognomical System of Drs. Gall and Spurzheim* (London: Baldwin, Cradock and Joy, 1815). Phrenology would fill the pages of a score of specialty journals by mid-century. Strollers in leading American and European cities would occasionally be found palpating each other's heads. But behind the "bumpology" lay a neuropsychological theory of cognition and affect which inspired entire programs of research.

56. George Combe, *The Constitution of Man Considered in Relation to External Objects,* 11th ed. (Boston: Marsh, Capen, Lyon and Webb, 1841), p. 377.

57. William Battie, *A Treatise of Madness* (London, 1758), p. 41. Nigel Walker regards him as perhaps "the first English physician of status to make psychiatry his business." He would become president of the Royal College of Physicians in 1764.

58. This spelling will be used throughout when referring to the defendant, Daniel McNaughtan, following Richard Moran, *Knowing Right*

from Wrong: The Insanity Defense of Daniel McNaughtan (New York: Free Press, 1981). Moran's research (pp. xi–xiii) establishes "McNaughtan" as the correct spelling, though this was rarely used in the vast McNaughtan literature.

59. The great value of Richard Moran's work is that it traces in a most systematic fashion the social and political conditions that forged McNaughtan's plan and that inclined a Tory government insensibly toward the conclusion that only a "madman" would act so precipitously.

60. *Rex v. Oxford,* W. C. Townsend, *Modern State Trials,* 2 vols. (London: Longman, Brown, 1850), vol. I, pp. 102–150.

61. *Blackwood's,* November 1850.

62. A. C. Benson, *The Letters of Queen Victoria* (London, 1907), p. 581.

63. Cited by Moran, *Knowing Right from Wrong,* p. 70.

64. The summary here is taken chiefly from chapter 3 of ibid.

65. *Queen v. M'Naughten* (1843), 4 *State Trials* 847–934, including *Answers of the judges in the House of Lords to five questions propounded by the House.*

66. Ibid., p. 855.

67. Ibid.

68. Ibid., p. 873.

69. Ibid., p. 874.

70. Ibid., p. 877.

71. Ibid., pp. 876–877. Isaac Ray, *A Treatise on the Medical Jurisprudence of Insanity* (Boston: Little, Brown, 1838). This work became a classic almost from the moment of its appearance, and would draw the medical world's attention to America. Ray (1838–1881), a relatively inexperienced 31-year-old physician when his book was published, would become a tireless contributor to the *American Journal of Insanity* and other periodicals, and an ardent and capable defender of the special standing of the experienced clinician in adjudicative settings in which questions of mental health were at issue. More than a century after its publication, Ray's *Treatise* would be cited in another famous case, this time by David Bazelon in developing the opinion in *Durham v. United States.* 214F. 2d 862 (1954).

72. Isaac Ray, "Objections to Moral Insanity Considered," *American Journal of Insanity* (October 1861). Reprinted in Isaac Ray, *Contributions to Mental Pathology* (Boston: Little, Brown, 1873), p. 108–110.

73. *Queen v. M'Naughten*, p. 887.
74. Ibid., 893–894.
75. Ibid., p. 923.
76. Ibid., p. 924.
77. Ibid., pp. 926–934. These pages were appended to the trial record and contain the questions advanced by the House of Lords and the replies of Tindal and Maule.
78. *State v. Jones.* 50 New Hampshire 369. Judge Ladd's remarks are at 388.
79. The complete account of this trial is found in G. T. Bigelow and G. Bemis, *The Trial of Abner Rogers* (Boston: Little, Brown, 1844). Isaac Ray discussed this trial in an article in the *Law Reporter* in 1845, reprinted in his anthology, *Contributions to Mental Pathology*. He said of this case that "No criminal trial in this country, in which insanity was pleaded in defence, has become more widely known and been oftener cited than that of Abner Rogers" (p. 210).
80. Ray, *Contributions to Mental Pathology*, p. 213.
81. Prichard, *On the Different Forms of Insanity in Relation to Jurisprudence*, pp. 16–17.
82. Maudsley, *Responsibility in Mental Disease*, p. 100ff.
83. *Boardman v. Woodman.* 47 New Hampshire 120 (1869); *State v. Jones.* 50 New Hampshire 369 (1872); *State v. Pike.* 49 New Hampshire 399 (1872)
84. *Boardman v. Woodman*, p. 139. In his dissenting opinion, Justice Doe insisted that insanity, which is a disease of the brain, is a matter of fact to be determined by the jury, and not a matter of law to be determined by the courts. He also rejected the proposition that laymen are not competent to supply relevant information regarding the state of mind of those whom they know well.
85. Ibid., p. 148.
86. *State v. Pike*, p. 150.
87. *State v. Bartlett.* 43 New Hampshire 224.
88. *State v. Pike*, p. 444.
89. Ibid., p. 437.
90. Ibid., p. 441.
91. Ibid.
92. *State v. Jones*, pp. 393–400.
93. The phrase is repeated as the title of Roger Smith's excellent study,

Trial by Medicine: Insanity and Responsibility in Victorian Trials (Edinburgh: Edinburgh University Press, 1981).

94. Isaac Ray, "Medical Experts," in *Contributions to Mental Pathology,* p. 432.

95. In *State v. Kraemer* (1897), for example, the defense was that Kraemer suffered from *delerium tremens,* and that he killed Mary Cooney while under the influence of alcohol. Judge Miller instructed the jury that, for Kraemer's defense to succeed, it would be necessary to show that it was the mental disease that caused the alcoholism, such that both the homicide and the *delerium tremens* were due to factors beyond the defendant's control. If, instead, Kraemer seeks exculpation on the grounds of drunkenness, he must then prove that the *delerium* "antedated the fit of drunkenness" and was the cause of it (at 774).

96. "Medicine and law alike set out to make decisions on the basis of facts. As specific trials have shown, they had very different ideas of what qualified as a fact." Roger Smith, *Trial by Medicine,* p. 173.

97. David Rothman, *The Discovery of the Asylum.*

6. Jural Science and Social Science

1. W. Griesinger, *Mental Pathology and Therapeutics,* C. Robertson and J. Rutherford, trans. (New York: William Wood, 1882). The work first appeared in German in 1845 and was immediately accepted as authoritative.

2. Ibid., p. 1.

3. *Schmidt v. New York,* 1915; p. 339.

4. See, for example, Kenneth K. Fukunaga et al., "Insanity Plea: Interexaminer Agreement and Concordance of Psychiatric Opinion and Court Verdict." 5 *Law & Human Behavior,* 325, 328 (1981); Henry J. Steadman et al., "Factors Associated with a Successful Insanity Plea," *American Journal of Psychiatry,* 140 (1983), pp. 401, 404–05. For an excellent critical appraisal of relevant research see Norman J. Finkel, *Insanity on Trial.*

5. George Harrison, *Legislation on Insanity: A Collection of All the Lunacy Laws of the States and Territories of the United States to the Year 1883, Inclusive. Also the Laws of England on Insanity, Legislation in Canada on Private Houses, and Important Portions of the Lunacy Laws of Germany,*

France, etc. (Philadelphia: 1884), vol. 1, p. 14. George Harrison had been appointed by the Governor of Pennsylvania to compile a comparative study of statutes covering insanity throughout the United States and in select foreign jurisdictions. The result of the research appeared in the two volumes cited.

6. *Holloway v. United States,* 326 U.S. 687 (1945).

7. In his first book B. F. Skinner made clear that a scientific psychology was not to be hostage to the uncertain progress of the biological disciplines; psychology could develop as a science of behavior while remaining neutral and even indifferent to such events, occurring "under the skin," as might excite the interests of a physiologist. B. F. Skinner, *The Behavior of Organisms* (New York: Appleton, Century, 1938). Freud's famous "Project," an abandoned scheme for absorbing psychoanalytic concepts into a developed brain science, won few adherent in the psychoanalytic community and was never pressed by Freud himself.

8. *Durham v. United States.* 214 F. 2d 862 (1954).

9. Ibid.

10. Sheldon Glueck, "Psychiatry and Criminal Law," *Mental Hygiene,* 12 (1928), pp. 575, 580.

11. *Royal Commission on Capital Punishment Report,* (Cmd. 8932), 1953; p. 113.

12. *Durham v. United States.*

13. *Leach v. Overholser.* 257 F. 2d 667 (1957). In this connection, the testimony of Dr. Duval, then assistant superintendent of the hospital, revealed that hospital staff had adopted this strategy and applied it with the express purpose of avoiding the consequences of the *Durham* rule.

14. *Blocker v. United States.* 274 F. 2d 572 (1959); 288 F. 2d 853 (1961). An informative discussion of these cases and the problems of diagnosis is provided by Jonas Robitscher, *The Powers of Psychiatry* (Boston: Houghton Mifflin, 1980), chap. 11.

15. As cited in *United States v. Brawner.* 471 F. 2d 969 (1972).

16. *Washington v. United States.* 390 F.2d 444 (1967).

17. *United States v. Brawner.*

18. Ibid. For a discussion of the abolition of the defense consult Norval Morris, *Madness and the Criminal Law* (Chicago: University of Chicago Press, 1982). Morris would replace the defense with other pro-

cedures in which psychiatric considerations may have mitigating effects; for example, downgrading a charge of murder to that of manslaughter.

19. Griesinger, *Mental Pathology,* pp. 83–84.

20. H. L. A. Hart, *Punishment and Responsibility* (Oxford: Oxford University Press, 1968), p. 230.

21. John Austin, *The Province of Jurisprudence Determined* (1832; rpt. London: Library of Ideas, 1954). The thin record of Austin's publications obscures the immense impact they had on his distant successors. In the 1909 Preface to his own classic, John Chipman Gray owned that he had read Austin's *Province* fifty years earlier, "then little read in England, and all but unknown in this country" (p. vii), and had been influenced by it ever since. John Chipman Gray, *The Nature and Sources of the Law* (New York: Columbia University Press, 1920). For the authoritative statement of legal positivism at the present time, see H. L. A. Hart, *The Concept of Law* (Oxford: Clarendon University Press, 1961).

22. For Holmes's position, see O. W. Holmes, "The Path of the Law," *10 Harvard L. Rev. 457* (1897).

23. Austin, *Province of Jurisprudence,* p. 369.

24. There is a vast literature on the Vienna Circle and those who formed it. For a perceptive cultural history of the background of the movement see Allan Janik and Stephen Toulmin, *Wittgenstein's Vienna* (New York: Simon and Schuster, 1973). For a strong version of the position, see Rudolf Carnap, *Philosophy and Logical Syntax* (London: Kegan Paul, 1935). The pages devoted to "The rejection of metaphysics" are especially illuminating.

25. Janik and Toulmin, *Wittgenstein's Vienna,* p. 133. Kelsen's realist philosophy of law is set forth in Hans Kelsen, *Pure Theory of Law,* Max Knight, trans. (Berkeley: University of California Press, 1967). The initial conference organized to publicize the ideas of the leading members of the Circle on the map was dubbed by them Verein Ernst Mach.

26. Ernst Mach, *The Analysis of Sensations and the Relation of the Physical to the Psychical,* C. M. Williams, trans. (New York: Dover, 1959).

27. For one influential statement of this position see Carl Hempel, *Aspects of Scientific Explanation,* (New York: Free Press, 1963), especially the chapter of the same title.

28. A. I. Melden regards the causal accounts as "wholly irrelevant." A. I. Melden, *Free Action* (London, 1961), p. 184. The quoted passage is by Stephen J. Morse, "Acts, Choices and Coercion: Culpability and Control," *142 U. Pa. L. Rev. 1587* (1994). Daniel Dennett, too, has defended what he calls the "intentional stance" in attempts to explain behavior, this stance being kindred to the teleological explanations discussed here; see his "True Believers: The Intentional Strategy and Why It Works." In A. F. Heath, ed., *Scientific Explanation* (Oxford: Oxford University Press, 1981). In the cited work Dennett's teleological orientation is most discernible in his tendency to account for the success of intentionalist accounts of human behavior in terms of adaptive processes that are part of the course of evolution.

29. Donald Davidson, "Actions, Reasons and Causes," *Journal of Philosophy,* 60 (1963), pp. 685–700.

30. An especially clear exposition and defense of teleological alternatives to the Davidsonian approach is Arthur Collins, *The Nature of Mental Things* (Notre Dame, Ind.: Notre Dame University Press, 1987), chap. 6.

31. The example and summary argument borrow *mutatis mutandis* from Collins.

32. Collins, *The Nature of Mental Things,* p. 150.

33. *United States v. Hinckley.* 672 F.2d 115 (1982).

34. Barbara Wootton, *Social Science and Social Pathology* (London: George Allen and Unwin, 1959), pp. 234–235.

35. K. W. M. Fulford, *Moral Theory and Medical Practice* (Cambridge: Cambridge University Press, 1989), pp. 198ff.

36. *Graham v. Darnell,* 538 S.W. 2d 690.

37. Ibid., p. 204.

38. H. L. A. Hart, *Punishment and Responsibility,* p. 230.

39. One need cite only H. L. A. Hart and A. M. Honoré, *Causation and the Law* (Oxford: Oxford University Press, 1959).

40. H. L. A. Hart, *Punishment and Responsibility.* pp. 200 ff.

41. The example, with minor modifications, is taken from Michael Moore, "Intentions and *Mens Rea.*" In *Issues in Contemporary Legal Philosophy: The Influence of H. L. A. Hart,* Ruth Gavison, ed. (Oxford: Clarendon Press, 1987), pp. 245–333. Moore's important contributions to the debate include a strong defense of "mental-cause" expla-

nations, and this defense informs the conclusions reached in this chapter. The term "mental state" as used here refers to a wide range of conscious deliberations dispositions, and feelings sufficiently available to actors to be judged by them as supporting and directing their actions. No firm position is taken here, however, on the interesting literature in philosophy of mind as to the ontological standing of things mental.

42. Deborah Denno, "Human Biology and Criminal Responsibility: Free Will or Free Ride?" *137 U. Pa. L. Rev. 615* (1988).

43. Stephen Morse, "Acts, Choices and Coercion."

44. For an interesting discussion of such cases see Michael Slodov, "Criminal Responsibility and the Noncompliant Psychiatric Offender: Risking Madness." *40 Case W. Res. 271* (1990).

45. Stephen Morse, "Acts, Choices and Coercion."

46. Ludwig Wittgenstein, *Philosophical Investigations,* 3rd ed. (Oxford: Basil Blackwell, 1958), sect. 621.

47. Robert Audi, "Metaphysics of Action: Volition, Intention, and Responsibility," *142 U. Pa. L. Rev. 1675* (1994).

48. Norval Morris, "The Planter's Dream," *49 U. Chi. L. Rev. 609* (1982).

49. Michael L. Perlin, "Unpacking The Myths: The Symbolism and Mythology of the Insanity Defense," *40 Case W. Res. 599* (1990).

50. Richard Bonnie, "The Moral Basis of the Insanity Defense," *69 A.B.A. L. Journal 194* (1983).

51. David Bazelon, "Psychiatrists and the Adversary Process," *Scientific American* (1973), 230.

52. The classical study here is that of Bruce J. Ennis and Thomas R. Litwack, "Psychiatry and the Presumption of Expertise: Flipping Coins in the Courtroom," *62 Cal. L. Rev. 693* (1974). Comparable data and arguments have been developed by Henry Steadman, "The Failure of Psychiatric Predictions of Dangerousness: Clear and Convincing Evidence," *29 Rutgers L. Rev. 1084* (1976). More recently, however, methodological deficiencies in the earlier research have suggested that the record may be better than reported. For a review of the newer findings and methods see R. Otto, "On the Ability of Mental Health Professionals to 'Predict Dangerousness': Commentary on Interpretations of the 'Dangerousness' Literature,". *Law and Psychology Review,* 18 (1994).

53. The NIH data are cited by R. Otto, "Dangerousness." On the periods of confinement suffered by defendants acquitted because of insanity see E. Silver, "Punishment or Treatment? Comparing the Length of Confinement of Successful and Unsuccessful Insanity Defendants," *Law and Human Behavior,* 19 (1995) pp. 375–388.

54. Andrew Scull, "1984 Survey of Books Relating to the Law: III. Law and Society," *82 Mich. L. Rev. 793* (1985).

55. Samuel Walker, "1983 *Survey of Books Relating to the Law:* V. Legal History." *81 Mich. L. Rev. 946* (1983), p. 948.

56. Scull, "Law and Society."

57. Carol Warren, *The Court of Last Resort: Mental Illness and the Law;* p. 195.

58. Scull, *Museums of Madness,* p. 202.

59. Scull, "Law and Society," p. 802.

60. M. Perlin, "Pretexts and Mental Disability: The Case of Competency," *47 U. Miami L. Rev. 625* (1993).

61. Ibid.

Index